JURISPRUDENCE

TITLES IN THE SERIES

Administrative Law

Business Law

Child Law

Civil Liberties

Commercial Law

Company Law

Conflict of Law

Constitutional & Administrative Law

Contract Law

Criminal Law

Criminal Litigation and Sentencing

Criminology

Employment Law

English Legal System

Equity & Trusts

European Community Law

Evidence

Family Law

International Trade Law

Jurisprudence

Land Law

Law of Torts

Public International Law

Revenue Law

Succession, Wills & Probate

'A' Level Law - Paper I

'A' Level Law - Paper II

JURISPRUDENCE

L B Curzon
Barrister

First published in Great Britain 1993 by Cavendish Publishing Limited, The Glass House, Wharton Street, London WC1X 9PX.
Telephone: 0171-278 8000 Facsimile: 0171-278 8080

First edition 1993
Second edition 1995

British Library Cataloguing in Publication Data

Curzon L B
Jurisprudence - (Lecture Notes Series)
I Title II Series
340

ISBN 1-85941-161-4
Cover photograph by Jerome Yeats
Printed and bound in Great Britain

Preface to the second edition

This text is made up of chapters designed for students who are approaching jurisprudence for the first time, and for those who are embarking on a scheme of revision prior to a first examination in the subject. The summaries at the end of each chapter are intended for those who wish to refer to the gist of the chapters. The text is intended to be read in conjunction with *Questions and Answers in Jurisprudence* (1995) (2nd edn) (Cavendish Publishing Limited).

The inclusion of subject matter has been determined largely by the contents of the London University LLB examination syllabus in Jurisprudence and Legal Theory; there is additional material which is based on the syllabus requirements of other universities.

One of the principal problems for students of jurisprudence has been, and remains, the covering of background reading. Jurisprudence has produced a vast range of literature which would require more than a lifetime for anything more than a mere perusal. But an acquaintance with a representative range of the classics of jurisprudence is essential, and rewarding. Valuable selections may be found in the texts by Freeman, and Davies and Holdcroft.

For this second edition, most of the original chapters have been extended; new material includes a section on the postscript to the second edition of Hart's *The Concept of Law* (1994). Additional chapters include material relating to rights, codification, and the principal features of feminist jurisprudence.

Professor Ervin Pollack, in his text, *Jurisprudence: Principles and Applications* (1979) (Ohio State University), writes:

> 'Philosophical thought plays a relevant role in the solution of legal problems. Stripped of its verbiage, the generative source of the law is in legal theory - in the nature of reality, in the elements of knowledge, in the requisites of morality, in the fulfilment of a good life, and in the objectives of social institutions.'

It is in the spirit of these observations that this book on jurisprudence has been compiled.

L B Curzon
1995

Outline of Table of Contents

Detailed Table of Contents

Table of Cases

Table of Statutes

Chapter 1

Introduction to Jurisprudence

1.1 The essence of definition in relation to jurisprudence

Controversy surrounds not only the *acceptability* of the many attempts made to define jurisprudence; the very *possibility* of producing a precise definition is challenged, as is the *validity* of the defining process. This chapter is predicated on the assumptions that any aspect of human knowledge, such as jurisprudence, is amenable to investigation and analysis; that these activities can result in the *delineation* of content, the *recognition* of the existence of sets of interrelated phenomena from which specific types of problem emerge; and that the essential *qualities* of content underlying patterns of recognition can be adumbrated in the form of a tentative definition.

1.2 The problems of definition

To define is to state with an acceptable degree of precision the sets of properties possessed by the phenomenon which is to be defined, ie, *to determine essential qualities*. Jurisprudence presents some difficulties: it seeks to range over law in its entirety; it embraces a large variety of peripheral matters (eg, psychological and economic interpretations of legal phenomena); it involves enquiries of a fundamental nature (What is a 'right'? What is a 'duty'?), which, in themselves, turn upon the definition of other terms and the essential nature of 'meaning'. Specifically, the following problems may arise in the process of seeking an appropriate definition:

- How, in the sense that we define a book, a pen, may we define the type of concept used in law? Terms such as 'agreement', 'possession', are, it is suggested, incapable of precise definition because of their subjective nature.
- Many legal terms change in 'meaning'. Consider, for example, the continuing argument on the meaning of 'appropriation' for the purposes of the Theft Act 1968, s 1 (see, eg, *R v Morris* (1984); *R v Gomez* (1991) or the meaning of 'dishonesty' after *R v Ghosh* (1982) (see *R v O'Connell* (1992)). Context is all. Thus, the meaning of the phrase 'natural law' has tended to be coloured by the general philosophical principles of the jurist who is using it. When the Scandinavian jurist, Ross (see Chapter 17), refers to the phrase as 'a harlot – at the disposal of everyone', he has in mind the endless variety of meanings which have been attached to it.

- Definition often involves comparisons with accepted norms. But it is the very lack of accepted norms which has characterised much argument among legal theoreticians. Consider, for example, the use of the term 'freedom' in the writings of Marx and John Stuart Mill.
- Note Bentham's basic objection: 'A definition *per genus et differentiam* when applied to [abstract legal terms] it is manifest can make no advance ... As well in short were it to define in this manner a preposition or a conjunction.' (Note: definition *per genus et differentiam* refers to the outlining of a general category to which a thing belongs and the stating of the particular species to which it belongs in that category.)
- The contemporary philosopher, Popper, suggests that the 'value' of definitions is generally low. The process involves little more than 'infinite regressions', reducing any discussion concerning definition to mere argument over the meaning of words. Thus, Popper would reject as 'meaningless' a definition of 'killing' as 'causing the death of another by some act or omission'. This would be viewed as mere tautology or as the presentation of a group of words (eg, 'causing', 'act', 'omission') which require precise elucidation.

1.3 The problems considered

The following comments illustrate the views of some jurists in response to the questions raised by those who query the value of definitions of jurisprudence.

The very wide range of phenomena covered in jurisprudence presents a difficult, but not insuperable, problem in the attempt to impose theoretical boundaries of subject matter. Thus, advances in our understanding of the chemistry of the brain might be considered as irrelevant to jurisprudence; but a general understanding of psychological processes of motivation could be considered as having a direct bearing upon problems of responsibility which are at the heart of an understanding of criminal liability. Boundaries must be drawn between subject areas, and the very awareness of this necessity can be the beginning of useful attempts to consider the essence of subject matter. In Chesterton's words: 'the frame can be as important as the picture'.

1.3.1 Boundaries

Allen warns against the 'megalomaniac jurisprudence' which suggests that jurisprudence should be all-embracing and know no boundaries. Jurisprudence, he declares, 'cannot hope to be the compendium of all the social sciences ... Knowledge of everything usually ends in wisdom in nothing.'

Immediately one begins to follow Allen's suggestion of placing some practical limits upon our conception and definition of law so as to avoid an 'unbounded jurisprudence', one is involved, effectively, in the preliminary processes of definition.

1.3.2 Subjectivity

The presence within one's area of study of purely subjective phenomena (such as concepts of 'justice') does not destroy the effectiveness of analysis and differentiation which can result in definition. 'Rational expectation', 'utility', and similar highly-subjective concepts within the field of economic investigation have not prevented valuable attempts at defining their context. Further, psychology, by its very nature, is replete with subjective material: this has not rendered impossible general agreement among psychologists as to the boundaries of their subject area.

1.3.3 Shifts in meaning

The undeniable fact that legal terms shift their meanings and that accepted jurisprudential norms are few does not make definition impossible. Physics, anthropology, linguistics, portray the same phenomenon but do not abandon definition as a tool in fashioning an account of the range of their activities.

1.3.4 Bentham and Popper

The comments of Bentham and Popper are extremely important. Bentham's objection seems to be aimed at the *mode* of defining legal terms and not necessarily at definition in itself. The call for precision in the very method of definition ought not to be disregarded. Popper's objection to definition as a process is accepted as valid by some jurists; others suggest that he ignores the advantages of attempts to know, as precisely as possible, the nature of that which is the object of study. Advocates of definition would argue that it provides a *tabula in naufragio*, enabling some aspects of reality to be grasped, and that it allows the emergence of a unified perception of reality.

1.4 Examples of definitions of jurisprudence

It is suggested that the following definitions be considered at this early stage of studies, then at repeated intervals and, finally, at the end of the course. Certain questions require immediate answers. Do the definitions embrace the essential features of jurisprudence? Do they call attention, explicitly or implicitly, to the boundaries of the subject area? Is it possible to use definitions of this nature as tools in the analytical tasks of the jurist?

- Ulpian

  'The knowledge of things divine and human, the knowledge of the just and unjust.'

- Allen

  'The scientific synthesis of the law's essential principles.'

- Fitzgerald

  'The name given to a certain type of investigation into law, an investigation of an abstract, general and theoretical nature, which seeks to lay bare the essential principles of law and legal systems.'

- Jolowicz

  'A general theoretical discussion about law and its principles, as opposed to the study of actual rules of law.'

- Stone

  'The lawyer's examination of the precepts, ideals and techniques of the law in the light derived from present knowledge in disciplines other than the law.'

- Schumpeter

  'The sum total of the techniques of legal reasoning and of the general principles to be applied to individual cases.'

- Holmes

  'Jurisprudence, as I look at it, is simply law in its most generalised part. Every effort to reduce a case to a rule is an effort of jurisprudence, although the name as used in English is confined to the broadest rules and most fundamental conceptions.'

- Cross

  'The study of a lawyer's fundamental assumptions.'

- Llewellyn

  'Jurisprudence means to me any careful and sustained thinking about any phase of things legal, if the thinking seeks to reach beyond the practical solution of an immediate problem in hand. Jurisprudence thus includes any type at all of honest and thoughtful generalisation in the field of the legal.'

1.5 Jurisprudence as a 'science'

Some definitions of jurisprudence (see, eg, that of Allen) suggest that it possesses some of the characteristics of a science. It may claim a place in the *social sciences*, ie, those 'inexact areas' of knowledge based on the study of aspects of social organisation and the interrelationships of individuals. The collection and systematisation of facts, the deduction of general principles from data concerning legal systems, may suggest that jurisprudence is a methodical study of an aspect of society and may be classed, therefore, as a social science. But the pretensions of some jurists, implying the right of jurisprudence to be classed as an *exact science* are difficult to support.

1.5.1 Problem of verifiability

The essence of the exact sciences rests in their formulation of universally-verifiable principles which may be used for purposes of prediction. 'If *X*, then *Y*; if not *X*, then not *Y*.' Few such universal principles may be discovered in jurisprudence.

1.5.2 Scientific method

Scientific method (the rigorous testing of data, for example) is to be found rarely in juristic investigation. Attempts to introduce a scientific vocabulary (see, eg, Hohfeld's categorisation of rights, in Chapter 23) have not met with universal approval among jurists. Experimentation, which is essential to scientific enquiry, is virtually impossible in jurisprudence.

Jurisprudence is concerned in large measure with the posing of types of question which cannot be answered within the modes of expression common to the scientific disciplines. Loevinger notes: 'The unanswerable questions of life belong to the realm of philosophy, and jurisprudence is the philosophy of law ...'

Many significant questions pertaining to the sciences are based on 'How ... ?' 'How may we test the relationship of energy to mass and the speed of light?' 'How may we create an embryo *in vitro*?' This is a total contrast to the essence of the type of question posed and considered by jurists. Loevinger reminds legal theorists that 'one cannot convert philosophy to science merely by adopting the vocabulary or imitating the methods of science'.

1.6 Jurisprudence as a 'philosophy'

The term 'philosophy' refers, in its overall sense, to man's attempts to understand the universe as a whole and to comprehend his place in it. This involves, in McMurrin's words, 'a reflective and reasoned attempt to infer the character and content of the universe, taken in its entirety and as a single whole, from observation and study of the data presented by all its aspects'. Curiosity, contemplation and attempted explanation are characteristics of the process of philosophical enquiry, placing the study of jurisprudence, according to some jurists, firmly within the realms of philosophy. Questions on the nature of law, the essence of good law, the nature of the obligation to obey the law, demand a rational, methodical and systematic consideration of the type which may be discerned in general philosophical speculation. Jurisprudence, it is argued, is related more to the tradition, style and methodology of philosophy than to the spirit, language and boundaries of science. Note the statement of Cicero in *De Legibus* (see 2.10) that the study of law should be derived from the depths of philosophy. Legal rules, he declared, have an importance which is relative only; they are insignificant except in their relationship to more fundamental principles.

1.6.1 Philosophy and 'the real world of the law'

Philosophy, in its application to the real world of the law, does not involve in any sense an escape from the rigours of that world. Holmes (see 18.3) observed that persons who are able to perceive the true nature of the forces behind details will grasp the differences 'between philosophy and gossip'. The consideration and deep study of the nature of law acquire their significance and, therefore, their worth, only when they emerge from a contemplation of action, controversy and conflict within society and its legal institutions. Jurisprudential philosophy appears to be at its most fruitful stage when rooted in the realities of everyday legal practice. In the words of an 18th century thinker: 'In the same way as many plants only bear fruit when they do not shoot too high, so in the practical arts the theoretical leaves and flowers must not be made to sprout too far, but kept near to experience, which is their proper soil.'

1.6.2 Philosophical divisions as reflected within jurisprudential theory

Many of the controversies of modern jurisprudence reflect arguments within the schools of general philosophy. Controversy on, say, the nature, significance and value of imprisonment as a legal sanction, is mirrored in conflicts of ideas concerning positivism, metaphysics, etc. Jurisprudence does not stand outside these arenas of debate.

1.7 The vocabulary of jurisprudence

The jurist has derived his terminology from a variety of sources – law, philosophy, sociology, for example. Additionally, he has fabricated a specialised, 'technical' vocabulary. Historical context is of much significance, so that it is important to note the exact era within which a jurist is writing. Thus, the term 'justice' is often used by sixteenth-century Catholic clerical jurists in a sense which is at variance with the use of the term by, say, Bentham, two centuries later. 'In interpreting words, one ought to look not only to the words but to the things and meaning behind them': *Jenk Cent 132*. Recent developments in linguistic philosophy, attempting to elucidate 'the meaning of meaning' and the structures upon which language rests, have a clear significance for jurisprudence.

1.7.1 Analytical and linguistic philosophy

Analytical and linguistic philosophy, derived from the work of Russell, Carnap and Wittgenstein, seeks to clarify the area of 'what we can know' and what we may speak of 'with meaning'. The very *structure* of language has been held to be the true object of linguistic analysis. The structures of linguistic expression adopted by jurists demand analysis.

A study of the meaning of words, say linguists, is without value unless it takes into account the *nature of the facts* described by words.

Words do not always possess unique, 'correct' meanings, and they may have an emotive rather than a descriptive purpose. Consider, for example, a description by 'the man in the street' of the government's taxation policy as 'a crime against the taxpayer'. The meaning here is clear although based upon the use of the term 'crime' in a sense with which no jurist would agree. Additionally, 'facts' are not always the same as 'verbal statements of fact'.

1.7.2 Hart's comments

Hart, in *Definition and Theory in Jurisprudence* (1953), seeks to stress the difficulties inherent in the search for satisfactory definitions of legal terms. He was influenced by the writings of Carnap and Ayer, who had insisted that 'enquiry into *the use of words* can equally be regarded as enquiry into the nature of the facts which they describe'.

Hart points out that questions such as 'What is a State?', 'What is a right?', are intrinsically highly ambiguous. The same form of words may be used to demand a definition or the origin, cause or purpose, of a legal institution. Hart would, therefore, rephrase the question, 'What is a corporation?' by asking, 'Under what types of condition does the law ascribe liabilities to corporations?' Words must be studied in context so that their functions become evident. Contextual explanations of legal terms are more valuable than mere definitions; indeed, preoccupations with definitions can distort the essential purpose of jurisprudence: see *HLA Hart (1907-92)*, by J Raz (*Utilitas*, November 1993). In relation to language, meaning *is* use, and legal language differs fundamentally from ordinary language.

1.7.3 Danet's analysis

Danet, in *Legal Discourse* (1980), analyses sections of the vocabulary of the law as aspects of the nature, functions and consequences of language used 'in the negotiation of social order'. The restricted capacity of legal language, reflecting its occasional inability to transfer messages at appropriate 'shared levels' (eg, between lawyer and client), has produced inefficient communication which characterises a large range of legal documents. (For effective communication involving legal vocabulary, the parties must have mutual knowledge and understanding of the relevant contextual background of the subject-matter of the communication.) Jackson, in *Semiotics and Legal Theory* (1985), shows how verbal utterances constitute one aspect only of the communication processes of the law.

1.8 Classification of jurisprudential thought

Attempts have been made to categorise the wide variety of theories of jurisprudence. Thus, Hall's text, *Readings in Jurisprudence* (1938), is arranged as follows: Natural Law; Historical Jurisprudence; Transcendental Idealism; Utilitarianism; Social Functionalism; Pragmatism. Bodenheimer's *Jurisprudence* (1974) arranges legal theories under the following headings: Greek and Roman theory; Legal Philosophy in the Middle Ages; Natural Law in the Classical Era; German Transcendental Idealism; Historical and Evolutionary theories; Utilitarianism; Analytical Positivism; Sociological Jurisprudence; the Revival of Natural Law.

1.8.1 Salmond

Early editions of Salmond's *Jurisprudence* (see, eg, the 10th edition by Glanville Williams, 1947) included an analysis of the content of jurisprudence ('the science of civil law').

Three types of jurisprudence were enumerated: 'legal exposition' (the purpose of which is 'to set forth the contents of an actual legal system'); 'legal history'(the purpose of which is to set forth 'the historical process whereby a legal system came to be what it was or is'); 'the science of legislation' (which sets out the law as it ought to be).

Jurisprudence could be divided into three fundamental branches: 'analytical' (essentially, an investigation of the law's first principles); 'historical' (involving the origin and development of the law and legal concepts); 'ethical' (concerning the theory of justice in relation to law).

1.8.2 Stone

Stone, in *Western Philosophy of Law* (1974), considers it convenient to organise jurisprudence into three principal branches: 'analytical' (involving the articulation of axioms and the definition of terms so as to 'maximise awareness' of the legal system, its self-consistency and logical structure); 'sociological' (concerned with the effect of law upon attitudes and behaviour involved in the maintenance of society, and the effects of social phenomena upon the legal order); 'theory of justice' (the evaluation of law in terms of the ideals or goals postulated for it).

1.8.3 Keeton

Keeton, in his *Elementary Principles of Jurisprudence* (1949), suggests the following structure.

- Classifications derived from the standpoint of the content of legal systems.

  These comprise: civil or municipal jurisprudence (an analysis of State law); international jurisprudence (an analysis of inter-State law).

- Classifications derived from the standpoint of time.

  These include: 'historical jurisprudence', based upon an analysis and interpretation of the development of legal systems; 'analytical jurisprudence', involving an examination of the basic propositions upon which a legal system is built; 'critical jurisprudence', comprising an estimation of the value of existing legal institutions and an examination of necessary changes in the law.

- Classifications based on the standpoint of the number of legal systems involved.

  These include: 'particular jurisprudence' (relating to any single legal system); 'comparative jurisprudence' (an examination of a variety of legal systems); 'general jurisprudence' (a study of rules found widely in developed systems).

- Classifications based on the standpoint of the areas of knowledge fundamental to an examination of law.

  These include: 'sociological, realist and functional jurisprudence' (the latter examining the true nature of legal concepts, rules and institutions); 'psychological jurisprudence' (including an analysis of the minds of those affected by the legal process); 'ethnological jurisprudence' (an analysis of the relationships and interactions of tribal organisations); 'ethical jurisprudence' (an examination of the ends which the law is intended to achieve).

1.9 Problems of classification

Classification in relation to jurisprudence is neither easy nor exact. The following problems have arisen.

'Arrangement is not classification, although classification is arrangement; the difference being that while arrangement may be empirical, classification must be in accordance with some principle': De Witt Andrews ('The Classification of Law' in *Readings in Jurisprudence*, ed Hall (1938)). It is not easy to discover an appropriate principle: classifications based upon historical context or methodology, for example, are rarely satisfactory and tend to be little more than arrangements of legal authors and their ideas.

1.9.1 Compartmentalisation

Some schools of thought overlap, and a rigid compartmentalisation of 'schools of jurisprudence' may perpetuate perceptions of sharp divisions where, in reality, none exists. Conversely, dissimilar types of jurisprudential speculation may be brought together under one heading, suggesting a unity of thought where none exists; thus, it is not easy to perceive similarities between the thoughts of Savigny and

Maine (see Chapter 13) beyond a common interest in the significance of a study of the past in jurisprudential thought.

It is virtually impossible to place some jurists in any of the 'standard schools' of jurisprudence. Thus, the contemporary American jurist, Dworkin, appears to be in a category of his own. How may we categorise Fuller, a self-declared proponent of natural law, who rejects many aspects of thought associated with that doctrine?

How does one classify the thought of jurists such as Radbruch (see Chapter 9) who embraced opposing principles during successive stages in his career?

Is there not a real danger in stressing some apparent differences in doctrine where they are nothing more than superficial, as where relatively minor aspects of interpretation produce those differences?

1.9.2 Purposes of convenience

It may be that a classification of jurisprudential thought can be little more than an arrangement *for purposes of convenience*. It would be wrong to consider any of the better-known classifications of jurisprudence as based upon the type of reality associated with, say, botanical classifications. Whether to place the work of Pashukanis in the 'Marxist school' because he was a Soviet jurist seeking to interpret history, or in the 'Natural Law school' because his writings appear to reflect a deep belief in 'a universal movement of history' and in 'the inevitability of the egalitarian society', must be, in the final analysis, a purely subjective judgment.

Summary of Chapter 1

Introduction to Jurisprudence

The problem of definition in jurisprudence

By definition we mean 'stating with an acceptable degree of precision what a thing is'. 'A molecule is ... ' 'A conditional fee simple is ...'

Specific problems associated with definitions in jurisprudence concern: the highly-subjective nature of many terms used by jurists; changes in the meaning attached to many legal terms, eg, 'dishonesty', following *R v Ghosh* (1982).

Popper warns of the danger of 'infinite regression' in defining terms.

Defining 'jurisprudence'

Difficulty in defining jurisprudence arises from the very broad nature of the subject-area. But boundaries *must* be drawn.

Attempts to define jurisprudence have been made repeatedly. Such attempts have a value in the fixing of a general perception of the subject and its content.

The following examples may be noted:

Allen: 'The scientific synthesis of the law's essential principles.'

Jolowicz: 'A general theoretical discussion about law and its principles, as opposed to the study of actual rules of law.'

Can jurisprudence be classified as a 'science'?

It is doubtful whether jurisprudence can be classified as a science: scientific method is rarely used in jurisprudential investigation; few universal, verifiable principles have emerged from jurisprudence.

Loevinger reminds us: 'The unanswerable questions of life belong to the realm of philosophy, and jurisprudence is the philosophy of law.'

The vocabulary of jurisprudence

The vocabulary of jurisprudence is eclectic, drawn from political science, economics, social theory and legal philosophy and procedure.

The nature of the facts described by words is to be taken into account by the jurist. The emotive nature of words must not be overlooked.

Hart stresses the need to study legal words in their context.

Danet suggests that the carefully restricted nature of legal language tends to vitiate communication.

Classifying 'movements' (or 'schools') in jurisprudence

Bodenheimer arranges jurisprudential thought under the following headings: Greek and Roman theory; Legal philosophy of the Middle Ages; Natural Law in the classical era; German Transcendental Idealism; Historical and Evolutionary theories; Utilitarianism; Analytical Positivism; Sociological Jurisprudence and Legal Realism; Natural Law revived.

Salmond subdivides jurisprudence thus: analytical; historical; ethical.

Stone finds it convenient to organise jurisprudence into three branches: analytical; sociological; theory of justice.

Difficulties in classification

'Arrangement is not classification, although classification is arrangement; the difference being that while arrangement may be empirical, classification must be in accordance with some principle': De Witt Andrews.

The problem of overlap is considerable.

Rigid divisions tend to perpetuate the initial problems arising from the compartmentalisation of thought.

It is not easy to place some jurists in appropriate 'pigeon holes'.

Classification may be a convenient method of overviewing a subject; but it is little more than that in jurisprudence.

Chapter 2

Founders of the Western Tradition (1): Plato, Aristotle, Cicero

2.1 Western jurisprudence

By 'Western jurisprudence', we have in mind the overall attitudes of jurists in the West to questions of justice and the law and the patterns of legal theory which have prevailed in Western Europe and the United States. The legal tradition of the West, as interpreted by its jurists, has been, in the words of JC Smith, 'to regard the Graeco-Roman synthesis as a superior form of law' which concentrates on 'the individual man with his attendant rights and obligations'. Some jurists find the rationale of Western jurisprudence in a general desire to move towards 'the securing of a social order not based on irrational dogma, and insuring stability without involving more restraints than are necessary for the preservation of the community' (Russell). We select for discussion in this chapter Plato, Aristotle and Cicero, and, in the next chapter, Hobbes, Locke and Rousseau.

2.2 Greek legal thought

It is important to understand that Greek political and legal thought was concerned essentially with concrete *problems of social and individual life*. Plato's aim was to furnish the analytical concepts with which man might build the perfect State. Aristotle was concerned, too, with the ideal State in which man might realise 'the good life', achieve the *summum bonum*, and dwell in justice. Law was perceived as a means to this noble end. It conferred a general benefit; in Plato's words, 'We deny that laws are true laws unless they are enacted in the interest of the common weal of the whole State' (*The Laws*). Justice was all: it constituted a 'general virtue', a 'harmony', in which man would flourish and achieve his fulfilment.

It is from this tradition of thought that there was spun the thread which was used to fabricate a significant portion of the vast tapestry of Western legal theory.

2.3 Plato's concept of the State

Plato (c 427 – c 347 BC) expounded his theories of justice and the State in *The Republic* (c 370 BC) and *The Laws* (c 340 BC). The starting point for his discussion on the nature of the State is the dialogue in *The Republic* between Socrates (Plato's mouthpiece in this work) and a group of friends who are asked to define 'justice'. Their attempts collapse under the weight of Socrates' superior dialectical skills, and the concept of the State emerges from the subsequent enquiry by Plato into its fundamental nature.

In order to understand the nature of justice it is better to examine it 'writ large' in the structure and functions of the State. Contemplation of 'the just State' will be more productive than concentration on 'the just individual'.

2.3.1 State and human nature

The State reflects human nature. No man is self-sufficing, and a division of labour is needed, allowing each member of society to perform the tasks for which he is, by nature, best-fitted. The result is the emergence of a variety of groups within society: *craftsmen* (farmers, artisans) will produce food, shelter, clothing, etc; inevitable wars will produce an army of warriors who, as *guardians*, will protect the community; the most highly-trained guardians will become an élite of *rulers*.

2.3.2 Groups in the State

Each of these groups epitomises one of the three parts of the human soul. The craftsmen symbolise the 'appetitive' aspect of the soul; their specific virtue is *temperance*. The guardians represent the 'spirited' part of the soul; their specific virtue is *courage*. The rulers exemplify the 'rational' part of the soul; their specific virtue is *wisdom*. Members of the community will be taught to believe that Nature demands a harmonious and stratified society, and, so that this end might be achieved, has mixed brass and iron in the composition of craftsmen, silver in the composition of the guardians, and gold in the composition of the rulers.

The ideal State is, in essence, *a balanced structure in which all groups work in harmony*. Its unity is an amalgam of diversities.

2.4 Plato's concept of justice

The State is a means to an end, namely, the attainment of justice. The general virtue of 'justice' arises when each class within the State is fulfilling its own special functions and thereby attaining its own virtues.

2.4.1 Social harmony

When every class within the State performs according to its destined function, then social harmony will result. When each individual is set free from all other occupations 'to do, at the right time, the one thing for which he is naturally fitted', then the possibility of true justice will emerge.

Harmony, involving the virtues of temperance, courage and wisdom, must be attained by the individuals who comprise the State. Knowing and accepting one's limitations and one's place, acknowledging the need to obey orders - here is the essence of what is necessary for the maintenance of social unity and justice.

Balanced uniformity is, then, the *sine qua non* of that degree of social perfection from which true justice will flow.

2.4.2 Types of State

Not all States are able to achieve the level of harmony appropriate to the creation and maintenance of justice. States have a tendency to degeneration. Plato classifies five types of State:

- The ideal State is the *aristocracy* controlled by philosopher-rulers, in which justice reigns.
- The *timocracy* epitomises irrational ambition and love of honour.
- A further degeneration is evident in the rise of the *plutocracy*, in which greed and the pursuit of wealth predominate.
- *Democracy* is characterised by a very low level of justice; it is an inadequate system and produces antagonisms.
- The final degeneration is *despotism*. Each type of State reflects human mental constitutions, and despotism reflects 'the enlargement of the unjust soul', enslaved by a master-passion, with justice totally absent.

2.5 Plato's Utopia

In *The Laws*, Plato produced detailed plans for his ideal State, in which justice emerges from the harmonious interaction of classes functioning within a structure of law designed for the 'moral salvation' of the community. The result is interpreted by many contemporary jurists as a bizarre, totalitarian society in which every aspect of life is controlled.

2.5.1 Morality and obedience

The ideal State (named 'Magnesia') will achieve 'the true good' through a minutely-detailed code of laws, enforced rigidly, and based upon absolute standards of morality and total obedience.

'Modest living standards' will be a goal; the 'excess' which can destroy social harmony is forbidden.

Each family within the community (which is limited to 5,040 persons) will own a farm; manual labour will be performed by slaves; trade will be in the hands of resident aliens.

Education will be aimed at fitting individuals for their destined occupations. All men and women will be taught to defend the State.

2.5.2 Guardians of the law

The 'guardians of the law' will impose standards and appropriate legal regulations. Persons who break the law will be punished by the imposition of penalties aimed at reform rather than vengeance. An offender is to be 'cured' because his true nature has been 'conquered against his wishes'.

Harmony, balance, virtue, are to be seen as the ends of the State and all its activities. The law assists those activities.

2.6 Aristotle's concept of law

Aristotle (384-312 BC) was educated at Plato's Academy in Athens. His fundamental concern, in his writings on politics, law and justice, was with the delineation of the path which had to be followed if man was to achieve 'the good'. Man, although a part of nature, could control nature through the exercise of his will: it is this which separates him from all other creatures. When man is perfected he is, indeed,' the best of animals', but, if removed from the ambit of law and justice, 'he is the worst of all' (*The Politics*).

Man's laws must be judged by the extent to which they assist him in developing his innate powers to the full.

2.6.1 Embracing nature of law

Laws that are rightly constituted are to be the community's guide in all matters pertaining to social life. The law must be concerned, therefore, with all issues related to the community.

'The law must rule.' Aristotle sees the difficulties inherent in personal rule by an autocrat. The rule of law involves rule 'by God and reason'; rule by one man becomes a perversion, based on 'appetite and high spirit'. Law must exemplify reason free from passion, and it must direct magistrates in the execution of their office and the punishment of offenders.

Law may be employed also as an instrument of education, habituating the citizen to understanding 'the good' and training him to contribute to the welfare of society through his good behaviour.

2.6.2 Equity

Rigidity in the law is to be eschewed. Aristotle built the foundations upon which contemporary concepts of equity rest.

In the *Ethics* Aristotle states:

> 'That which is equitable is just, not legally just, simply a correction of legal justice. This is so because law is universal, but it is not possible to make universal statements about some things. When the law makes a universal statement and a case arises out of it which is not embraced in that statement, it becomes right when the law-maker falls into error by over-simplifying, to correct the omission ... this is the nature of the equitable, to correct the law where, because of its universality, it is defective.'

In the *Rhetoric* Aristotle notes:

> 'It is equity to pardon the human failing, to look to the law-giver and not to the law, to the spirit and not to the action ... to prefer the arbitrator to the judge, for the arbitrator observes what is equitable whereas the judge sees only the law.'

In the *Nichomachean Ethics* Aristotle argues:

> 'When, therefore, the law lays down a general rule, and thereafter a case arises falling outside the general model,

it is then right, where the lawyer's words have turned out to be too simple to meet the case without doing wrong, to rectify the deficiency by deciding as the law-giver would himself decide if he were present on the occasion and would have enacted if he were aware of the case in question.'

2.7 Aristotle's concept of justice

Justice, for Aristotle, exists among those persons whose relationships are truly regulated by law. To administer the law is to distinguish the just from the unjust. Justice may be classified as follows.

2.7.1 Distributive justice

Distributive justice is, essentially, that which is exercised in the distribution of honour, wealth, 'and the other divisible assets of the community', and these may be allotted among its members in equal or unequal shares. Equals must be treated equally; unequals unequally. Justice, in the distributive sense, would aim at 'proportion', in contrast to the 'disproportion' which characterises injustice.

2.7.2 Corrective justice

Corrective justice stands in contrast to 'distributive' (or 'legislative') justice; it is concerned with the restoration of a disturbed equilibrium. The judge will treat parties as equals, will investigate the nature of the damage done, and will seek to equalise the situation by imposing penalties which will take away any ill-gotten gains and will take into account the suffering caused by the offence. Aristotle notes that corrective justice may be administered in the following situations:

- *Voluntary transactions*, such as selling, buying, hiring, lending, pledging.
- *Involuntary transactions* (of a furtive or violent nature) such as theft, assault, maiming.

2.8 Aristotle and the State

The aim of government is, according to Aristotle, to fit the individual for the good life and to satisfy his social instincts. He discusses 'monarchy', 'aristocracy' and 'polity', and their perverted forms.

> 'A constitution is the organisation of offices in a State, and determines what is to be the governing body, and what is the end of each community. But laws are not to be confounded with the principles of the constitution; they are the rules according to which magistrates should administer the State and proceed against offenders. We must know the varieties, and the number of varieties, of each form of government, if only with a view to making laws ... Having determined these points, we have next to consider how many forms of government there are, and

what they are; and in the first place what are the true forms, for when they are determined the perversions of them will become apparent ...' (*Politics*).

2.8.1 Monarchy

The desirability of a State governed by a monarch is rejected by Aristotle because it is generally obsolete and objectionable. Monarchy arose to meet the needs of a primitive type of society which is obsolete. It is objectionable because: it tends to become hereditary; it subjects equals to the rule of equals; an individual monarch may be misled by his passions; no one man can attend to all the functions of government. The only exception to this may be found where a whole family, or some individual, is so outstanding in virtue as to surpass all others; then it is just that they should be 'the royal family' or that the individual should be king.

2.8.2 Aristocracy

By 'aristocracy', Aristotle has in mind 'the best citizens', ie, those whose natural endowments and standards of educational attainment equip them to rule. (This form of government seems to be the one favoured by Aristotle.)

2.8.3 Polity

Polity is the type of State which rests upon a constitution allowing the rule of the masses under the law and a system of justice which is enshrined in that constitution.

2.8.4 Tyranny

Tyranny is the degenerate form of monarchy, and is characterised by the predominance of the ruler's selfish wishes over justice and law.

2.8.5 Oligarchy

Oligarchy is the corrupted form of aristocracy and is exemplified by rulers who reject the aim of the general good in favour of their individual advancement.

2.8.6 Democracy

Democracy is a degraded form of polity. A lack of moderation, an absence of justice, and the dominance of selfishness characterise this type of government.

2.9 Cicero and Roman law

It has been said of Rome that 'her mission was war and her vocation law'. The Romans' encounter with Greek civilisation and culture produced a deep impression on Roman jurists (but not on the *practical activities* associated with the law). The interpretation of laws, the collection and systematisation of data by Roman jurists so that principles might be elicited, owed much to the dialectical method and the rules of rhetoric favoured by the Greeks. Cicero (106 BC-43 BC), statesman, scholar, and, reputedly, Rome's greatest legal orator, is said to have given the West the basis of its philosophical vocabulary. His major contribution to jurisprudence rests upon his concept of Nature as providing a source of rules by which man ought to live.

2.10 Cicero and the 'natural law'

In *De Legibus* (begun in 52 BC, but published posthumously), Cicero examines the basis of law. To him, law is 'the highest reason', implanted in man, and commanding that which we ought to do and prohibiting the opposite.

The 'highest form of reason', which may be discovered in nature, becomes, when firmly rooted in the human mind and further developed, law.

Law is the standard by which justice and injustice may be measured.

2.10.1 True law

'True law' – the eternal law – came into existence simultaneously with the Divine Mind. It is, in essence, 'reason in agreement with nature'. It applies to all men, and is unchangeable and eternal.

To curtail the true law is 'unholy'; to attempt to amend it is illicit; to repeal it is impossible. We cannot be dispensed from it by any order of any institution; nor does it require clarification or interpretation.

2.10.2 Universality of law

The true law is universal. One of Cicero's celebrated theses proclaims:

> 'Nor will it be one law at home and a different one at Athens, nor otherwise tomorrow than it is today; but one and the same law, eternal and unchangeable, binding all peoples and all ages; and God, its designer, expounder and enactor, will be, as it were, the sole and universal ruler and governor of all things.'

There are those who will disobey the true law. By such acts they turn their backs on themselves and, indeed, on man's very nature. They will, therefore, pay the heaviest penalties by denying their nature, even though avoiding those other punishments considered appropriate to their conduct.

2.11 Cicero and the State

Cicero's view of the origins and functions of the State is to be found in his treatise *De Republica* (52 BC).

At the basis of the creation of the State is man's instinct to associate with others. He is, in Aristotle's phrase, a 'political animal' who can fulfil himself only within society: he who is unable or unwilling to live in society 'is a beast or a god'. In coming together, men give evidence of a deep instinctive desire to form communities, 'for the human race is not one of solitary wanderers'. This desire is, in Cicero's words, 'the origin of the city, indeed, the very seed-bed of the State'.

Men's coming together involves an act of partnership which can be weakened or destroyed by a tyrannical State. Where a tyrant rules, the State is, in reality, non-existent.

2.11.1 Obedience and freedom

Our privileges within the State are secured by the bonds established by law. A State without law is like a human body without a mind.

All members of a State, without exception, and including, therefore, those who administer it, are under the law. 'For as the laws govern the magistrate, so the magistrate governs the people, and it can truly be said that the magistrate is a speaking law, and the law a silent magistrate': *De Legibus. We obey the law so that we might be free.*

In a State which recognises the rule of law, any departure from its tenets is 'a matter of great shame'.

The State's responsibilities for the punishment of offenders must be guided by principle. Above all, the intention of the offender must be examined, lest punishment fall upon a person who is not really at fault.

2.11.2 Property

The State must not accept any argument which stands in opposition to the fundamental view that man's goods are his own property.

In the construction of a system of law, and by the arranging of social relationships upon which legal obligations can be founded, the State, its officials, magistrates and scholars, must remember that 'man is born for justice and law is not based on opinion but on man's very nature'.

2.12 The Graeco-Roman legacy

Friedmann suggests, in *Legal Theory* (1967), that it is difficult to overestimate the rich and enduring legacy of the legal thought associated with the Greeks and Romans.

Aristotle's work, argues Friedmann, seems to anticipate all the major themes and conflicts evident in modern Western jurisprudence. The nature and purpose of justice, the significance of Aristotle's distributive and corrective justice, the need for equitable principles to supplement the law - all exemplify the range of topics which constitute the agenda of much modern jurisprudence.

The Platonic concept of law as a means to an end, the recognition of the necessity for unity within the State, the interpretation of justice in terms of harmony, continue to exercise the minds of Western jurists.

Cicero's enunciation of the basic principles of a natural law which can provide guidance for those who have the responsibility for articulating a community's laws provided a foundation upon which the edifice of a natural law has rested for many centuries.

In sum, our contemporary jurisprudence cannot be comprehended fully without reference to its ancestry. Graeco-Roman patterns of legal thought remain interwoven, inextricably, with the thought of our own era, particularly in relation to justice. In the words of Stammler (see 5.3):

> 'This, in my opinion, is the universal significance of the classical Roman jurists; this, their permanent worth. They had the courage to raise their glance from the ordinary questions of the day to the whole. And in reflecting on the narrow status of the particular case, they directed their thoughts to the guiding star of all law, namely the realisation of justice in life.' (*The Theory of Justice*)

Summary of Chapter 2

Founders of the Western Tradition (1): Plato, Aristotle, Cicero

Greek legal thought

Greek legal thought is a fundamental contribution to the Western tradition in jurisprudence. It was concerned, essentially, with problems of daily existence. 'Justice' and 'the good life' featured prominently in Greek political and legal analysis.

Plato and the State

Plato (c 427-347 BC) approaches the idea of justice through an analysis of the State.

The ideal State reflects harmony among its classes of citizens, comprising craftsmen, guardians and the ruling elite. Balance, harmony are essential if justice within the community is to prevail. Justice is 'the end'; the State merely the means.

Knowing one's place, working at that for which one is naturally fitted, is a prerequisite for the social harmony from which justice will flow.

Plato categorises the types of State thus: Aristocracy (the 'philosopher-rulers'); Timocracy; Plutocracy; Democracy; Despotism (the final degeneration).

Plato's ideal State

Plato's theory of justice is set out in *The Republic*; the ideal State is outlined in *The Laws*.

The ideal State ('Magnesia') is intended to achieve 'the good', essentially through balance, morality, obedience and virtue. Conformity to the detail of the law is essential; obedience is to be absolute.

Law will assist the State in the achievement of its ends.

Aristotle's concept of the law

According to Aristotle, the function of law is to assist man in the full development of his powers. Law must embrace all activities within the community. Equitable principles must be developed so as to soften the rigours of the law.

Aristotle's classification of 'justice'

According to Aristotle, justice may be classified as follows:

- *Distributive justice* is that which aims at 'proportion' and is concerned with the correct allocation of wealth, honours and other divisible assets of the community among citizens.
- *Corrective justice* is concerned with the effective restoration of any disturbance of social equilibrium.

Aristotle and the State

The aim of government is the 'good life' for the individual.

The State exists so as to assist in the attainment of the ends of government. It may take the form of: Monarchy; Aristocracy; Polity; Tyranny; Oligarchy; Democracy.

Cicero and the 'natural law'

Cicero (106-43 BC) sees law as representing the 'mind' of the State. All must obey the law if freedom is to prevail. Law is the standard whereby justice and injustice are measured.

The 'true law' is universal and should reflect the 'eternal law' - 'reason in agreement with nature'.

Cicero and the State

Man's instinct to associate with others is at the basis of the desire to form communities. Men come together in the State in an act of partnership.

The State must be guided and protected by the principles of law.

The Graeco-Roman legacy

Aristotle and Plato seem to have anticipated many of the major themes which continue to preoccupy Western jurisprudence in our time.

Harmony within society and the balance necessary to achieve this end remain a concern for political scientists and jurists of our day.

Cicero's enunciation of the principles of a law related to nature and reason became a fundamental principle for jurists who sought standards beyond those of the positive law.

Chapter 3

Founders of the Western Tradition (2): Hobbes, Locke, Rousseau

3.1 Government, citizens and natural rights

In this chapter we select for comment two seventeenth-century English philosophers and jurists: Hobbes (1588-1679), Locke (1632-1704), and an 18th century Swiss-French philosopher, Rousseau (1712-78). They prepared the foundations of that important segment of Western jurisprudential thought concerned with problems arising from the relationship of citizens with their government. By what *right* does a government purport to exercise rule over its citizens? Has a citizen a *natural right* giving him an interest in the maintenance of good government? What are the *natural rights* of a citizen confronted by a monarch who proclaims his 'divine right' to rule? Is there a point at which a citizen may invoke a 'right' to rebel against a government which is seen to be depriving him of his 'basic, natural rights'? The answers given by Hobbes, Locke and Rousseau continue to hold the attention of democracy. Indeed, they may be considered as having developed concepts which have become fundamental in relation to topics such as man's basic rights, the essence of State authority, and the rule of law.

3.2 The jurist as a creature of his time

The jurist cannot step outside the events of his time, so that jurisprudential speculation rarely takes place to advantage *in vacuo*. Both Hobbes and Locke lived through periods of constitutional upheaval, precipitated by the conflicts between Parliament and a monarch who claimed that 'it is seditious in subjects to dispute what a king may do in the height of his power'. Both propounded unpopular views; both were obliged to flee from England. Their investigation of the legal basis of the bonds between ruler and ruled took place against a background of civil unrest, violence and its aftermath. The legal theories associated with Hobbes and Locke represent much more than scholarly ratiocination; they may be interpreted as deep personal reactions to social strife and as attempts to stress the significance of consensus in civil government so as to avoid conflict. Rousseau, too, spent a period of his life in exile and under police surveillance. His works were banned in Switzerland and France as they were considered to be subversive of religion and authorised government.

3.3 The 'Social Contract' myth

Theories suggesting a *compact* between rulers and ruled may be found in political and legal thought over the centuries. Hobbes, Locke and Rousseau were among those who developed the theory of a *Social Contract*. Its essential features are as follows:

- In 'primeval times', individuals were born into a 'state of nature' which was generally anarchic.
- Man's natural reason and his innate need to live within society led him to create a society by contracting with others.
- The essence of the Social Contract was the surrender of some rights and powers to a Sovereign in the expectation that he would safeguard individuals and protect them against oppression.
- The Sovereign to whom powers were transferred did not necessarily consider himself as a party to a contract.

3.4 Hobbes and the Social Contract

Basic to Hobbes' philosophy was his belief that man is dominated by the instinct of self-preservation. Persistence of this instinct is evidenced by his reactions to the primeval conditions of life which led to an intensification of his efforts to ensure survival.

Before the emergence of civil society man lived in a 'state of nature' in which all were equal and all had the right to act so as to ensure survival. But strife was rarely absent. 'The most frequent reason why men desire to hurt each other, ariseth hence, that many men at the same time have an appetite to the same thing; which yet very often they can neither enjoy in common, nor yet divide it; whence it follows that the strongest must have it, and who is strongest must be decided by the sword': *De Cive* (1642).

The continuous clash of wills produced a war 'of all against all'; events which assisted survival were 'good'; those which threatened survival were 'evil'. There could be no ordered community in these circumstances, because 'there was no society, continual fear and danger of violent death', and man's life was 'solitary, poor, nasty, brutish and short'.

It became obvious that individual survival might be more assured in peaceful conditions.

3.4.1 The compact

Eventually, men, wishing to end an intolerable state of affairs, were ready to make a compact among themselves. Each would surrender his right of governing himself to some person or assembly, on the vital understanding that others would surrender similar rights in the same manner.

The Sovereign authority would have an absolute power to govern; in no sense was the Sovereign a party to the contract, nor was he subject to those who had contracted among themselves.

3.4.2 The Common-Wealth

The essence of the 'Common-Wealth' thus created was, in Hobbes' words (*Leviathan* (1651)):

> 'One person, of whose acts a great multitude, by mutual covenants one with another, have made themselves everyone the author, to the end he may use the strength and means of them all, as he shall think expedient, for their peace and common defence. And he that carrieth this person is called Sovereign, and said to have Sovereign Power; and everyone besides, his subject.'

(Note that the name 'Leviathan' appears in Job, 12, where it is used to signify a monster.)

3.5 Legal implications of Hobbes' doctrine

Total obedience to an absolute Sovereign power is the essence of Hobbes' version of the Social Contract. Law is, in reality, the command of that Sovereign power and requires an unchallenged ability to enforce it. Remove that ability and a covenant becomes mere words.

'Good law' should not be seen as the equivalent of 'just law', because a law made by the Sovereign cannot be unjust. When the Sovereign enacts a law he does so as though all his subjects were making it collectively; to enact that upon which his subjects have agreed cannot be unjust.

To obey the Sovereign is a prerequisite of justice. Law is the Sovereign's command, and justice requires obedience to the law if the subjects' wishes are to be carried out. 'Unjust law' is, therefore, a contradiction in terms.

3.5.1 Bad law

'Bad law' can exist. Where, in making a law, the Sovereign fails to exercise the protective function on the basis of which the people have promised submission, that law may be considered 'bad', in that it is 'outside' the purposes of the covenant made by subjects with one another. The common peace and safety which were the objectives of the covenant are the touchstones of the laws made by the Sovereign; if they are placed in peril then the very purposes of the covenant are challenged.

3.6 Disobedience and rebellion

Hobbes is essentially an authoritarian and a supporter of absolute government. The fear of anarchy and the social violence which may follow on from sustained opposition to the central authority runs through his writings. He had witnessed the turmoil which attended the breaking of an obdurate monarch by a resolute Parliament; he was aware of the growing influence within the Parliamentary army of 'levelling' anti-authoritarian doctrines and he had heard powerful calls for an initiative to revive 'the Good Old Cause'. He was fearful of the likely consequences. Hence his attitude to disobedience and rebellion stemmed from the following principles:

- Even though a law be considered unsatisfactory, this is not a matter for the people to judge lightly. *It is not in itself a justification for general disobedience.*
- The Sovereign *alone* possesses the power to judge what needs to be done in the interests of his subjects; he must act on the basis of an exercise of that power.
- To question the judgment of the Sovereign is to revert to the anarchy of the 'state of nature' from which men had wished to be delivered. The duty not to question is part of the price to be paid for social peace.
- Unsatisfactory laws are a matter between the Sovereign and his God, not between him and his subjects. Hence, if Christians perceived the actions of their Sovereign as contrary to Divine injunctions, their obedience to the Sovereign must not falter. The church enjoyed the legal status of any other corporation, and its subordination to the State was a necessary consequence of the principle of total submission which was required from *all* within the Sovereign's realm. There was to be no special privilege accorded to the church and its members.

3.6.1 Ending the duty of obedience

Hobbes makes clear, however, that when it has become obvious that a Sovereign can no longer exert the power necessary to maintain the peace and to protect his subjects' safety, or when he has behaved in a manner which suggests unequivocally that his activities constitute a clear attempt to destroy his subjects' rights of self-preservation, then the duty of obedience ceases. 'The obligation of subjects to the Sovereign is understood to last as long, and no longer, than the power lasteth by which he is able to protect them': *Leviathan*. This is the sole condition relating to the Sovereign's deployment of absolute power; it constitutes a vital check upon the exercise of absolute authority by one who acts in opposition to the demands of the common good.

3.7 Locke and the Social Contract

Locke's life overlapped that of Hobbes. Whereas Hobbes had experienced the particular turmoil of the Civil War, and had propounded a theory based upon a model of absolutist rule, Locke was affected specifically by the events which culminated in the 'Glorious Revolution' of 1688, ending the

Stuart dynasty, and with it any lingering beliefs in that dynasty's claim to rule by Divine right. Locke articulated, in opposition to Hobbes, a theory based upon subjects' individual and inalienable rights. He developed an individualistic interpretation of the Social Contract based upon the following principles:

- 'To understand political power aright, and derive it from its original, we must consider what state all men are naturally in, and that is a state of perfect freedom to order their actions and dispose of their possessions and persons as they think fit, within the bounds of the law of nature, without asking leave, or depending upon the will of any other man. A state also of equality, wherein all the power and jurisdiction is reciprocal, no one having more than another; there being nothing more evident than that creatures of the same species and rank, promiscuously born to all the same advantages of nature, and the use of the same faculties, should also be equal one amongst another without subordination or subjection ...' (*Two Treatises on Government* (1690)).
- Dangers and inconveniences arose: enjoyment of the natural right to liberty was curtailed; disputes could not be settled equitably, and revenge, rather than appropriate punishment, prevailed.
- Men found it necessary to unite in one 'political society' so as to preserve their lives, liberties and estates. The unity thus created was built upon a *pactum unionis*. A further agreement, a *pactum subjectionis*, represented the giving of power to a government which would protect the individual.
- The governing body's powers should be limited to what was necessary for the good of society.

  'And so whoever has the legislative or supreme power of any Common Wealth is bound to govern by established standing laws, promulgated and known to the people, and not by extemporary decrees; by indifferent and upright judges who are to decide controversies by those laws, and to employ the force of the community at home, only in the execution of such laws, or abroad to prevent or redress foreign injuries, and secure the community from inroads and invasion. *And all this to be directed to no other end but the peace, safety, and public good of the people*' (*Treatise on Government* (1690)).
- The contract bestows no arbitrary powers upon the government, because 'Nobody can transfer to another more power than he has in himself, and nobody has an absolute, arbitrary power over himself or over any other.'

- The *fiduciary nature of government* resulting from the contract is important. *Two Treatises of Government* (1690):

  'Political power is that power which every man living in the state of Nature has given up into the hands of the society, and therein to the governors whom the society hath set over itself, with this *express or tacit trust*, that it shall be employed for their good and the preservation of their property.'

3.8 Legal implications of Locke's doctrine

Locke is perfectly clear as to the implications of his advocacy of *government with limited powers*. Government, for him, has no other end but preservation, 'and therefore can never have a right to destroy, enslave, or designedly to impoverish the subjects'. The legal implications of this doctrine are far-reaching.

It is the very right to enforce 'nature's laws' which is surrendered to the body politic - and nothing more. The enforcement of those laws demands from the government the activities of an 'umpire', that is, 'a judge on earth' with the appropriate powers to determine controversies and redress injuries.

3.8.1 Property

Because, according to Locke, the great and chief end of men's uniting and putting themselves under a government is the preservation of their property (and that term includes 'life, liberty and estates'), no part of a man's property may be taken from him by a government without his consent.

> 'Though the earth and all inferior creatures be common to all men, yet every man has a property in his own person; this nobody has any right to but himself. The labour of his body and the work of his hands are properly his' (*Treatise on Government* (1690)).

3.8.2 Equality

Since 'extemporary arbitrary decrees' are unacceptable modes of exercising governmental powers, the legislative authority 'is bound to dispense justice and decide the rights of citizens by promulgating laws'. These laws must be based upon the concept of equality; they may not be varied so as to have 'one rule for the rich and poor, for the favourite at Court, and the countryman at plough'.

3.9 Resisting abuses

Where law ends, there tyranny begins. Locke insists upon the ultimate right of the community to check unbridled power and to confine a government to areas of activities agreed with the people:

> 'The legislator being only a fiduciary power to act for certain ends, there remains still in the people a supreme power to remove or alter the legislative when they find the legislative act contrary to the trust reposed in them. For all

power given on trust for the attaining of an end being limited by that end, whenever that end is manifestly neglected or opposed, *the trust must necessarily be forfeited,* and the power devolve into the hands of those that gave it, who may place it anew where they shall think best for their safety and security.'

3.9.1 Resistance to government

Popular resistance to a government may be justified only where there has been a long series of abuses and where the very 'lives, liberties and estates' of citizens are imperilled.

Resistance does not necessitate acts of revenge. Its aim must be the restoration of the pattern of social order which has been disturbed or destroyed by an absolutist ruler.

Disobedience and rebellion are difficult to justify when a government observes its pledges faithfully.

3.9.2 Preservation of life

The preservation of life was to be considered as one of mankind's inalienable rights. Hence a government which failed in the particular task of preserving life, or which took away from men the means whereby they might claim and protect this basic right, was signally unfit to be obeyed.

3.10 Rousseau and the Social Contract

Rousseau (1712-1778), a Swiss-French social philosopher and political theorist, whose writings were to have a significant impact on the doctrines of the French Revolution, was concerned with the problem of discovering the type of association which would defend and protect the person and goods of each associate 'and in which each, while uniting himself with all, may still obey himself alone, and remain as free as before'. He emphasised the 'natural goodness' inherent in human nature: man is born good and innocent, free and equal, 'but he is everywhere in chains'. Civilisation is responsible for this state of affairs, and a return to the simplicity of nature is essential if man is to recover his freedom.

3.10.1 *Du contrat social* (1762)

'Each of us puts his person and all his power in common under the supreme direction of *the general will*, and, in our corporate capacity, we receive each member as an indivisible part of the whole'. (The social order is, according to Rousseau, 'a sacred right which is the basis of all other rights'.) Rousseau argues that in civil society no individual is subject to another individual; he is subject to 'the general will', ie, the will of the community. Sovereignty is, therefore, the exercise of society's 'general will'. Because 'the sovereign' is the resultant of those individuals who make up society, he cannot have an interest which is in opposition to the interests of individuals. As a result of the social contract which is the basis of the State, the 'general will' is manifest in the majority vote of all individual citizens. Because people are good, they will cast their votes for measures which are 'good'. 'The people are never corrupted, though they are often deceived, and it is only then that they apparently will what is evil.' Sovereign power should rest with the people because of the importance of their will – which is inalienable. Although the people may delegate power to their elected officials, they never *surrender* their right of sovereignty.

3.10.2 Respect for the law

Respect for the law, because it reflects the general will, is of much importance in Rousseau's scheme of government. Should a person disagree with a law emanating from the people's institutionalised general will, the State may insist on his obedience; such insistence (which may lead to the use of force) embodies freedom, but does not violate it. In an important sense, therefore, the individual is 'forced by the State to be free'. Freedom resides in forced obedience to the law which reflects the popular and sovereign general will.

3.11 The legacy of Hobbes, Locke, Rousseau

The writings of Hobbes and Locke exemplify what has been named 'a practical jurisprudence', in which the agenda for discussion is set by the everyday problems of society. Hobbes had in mind a definite purpose: to assist in the avoidance of civil strife by providing ideological support to the authority of the State as vested in an absolute Sovereign. Locke's purpose was also clear: to invest individual members of the community with fundamental and inalienable rights. The jurisprudence of the 18th-20th centuries reflected these concerns, and the conflict between the ideals of liberty and authority has produced a variety of legal theories, some seeking to demonstrate the incompatibility of these ideals, others attempting a reconciliation by synthesis.

Friedmann suggests that Hobbes effectively destroyed 'all that was left of medieval conceptions of law and authority ... He has shaken himself free from medieval society and medieval ideas' and has thus 'completed the revolution of the Renaissance'. Locke's achievement is characterised by Friedmann as having provided a theoretical framework for opposition to absolutism, which prepared the way for the planting of the seeds of parliamentary democracy. Both assisted in freeing Western jurisprudential thought from the fetters of those doctrines supporting the Divine right of kings, which implied a duty of subjects to obey *absolutely*. Rousseau proclaimed that as long as a people is forced to obey, and does obey, it does well, but as soon as it throws off its yoke it does still better. If complete freedom is impossible, and human behaviour is to be partially controlled by government, then the legitimation of such a government demands a firm acknowledgment of man's rights. Hobbes, Locke and Rousseau contributed to the growing concerns of legal theory with concepts of inalienable human rights, and corresponding duties of governments to assist in the preservation and intensification of those rights. Contemporary Western jurists have, perhaps, no need of the fictions of a Social Contract upon which Hobbes, Locke and Rousseau erected their theories of men's rights in relation to the State; but the need for a continuous assessment of the legal implications of government functions and practices remains, however, as important for us as it was during their day.

Summary of Chapter 3

Founders of the Western Tradition (2): Hobbes, Locke, Rousseau

The 'Social Contract' myth

In essence, the theory of the social contract suggests a compact between rulers and ruled.

Man discovers that if he is to be safe from oppression he and his fellows must contract with one another so as to surrender some rights and powers in exchange for a measure of protection from a Sovereign.

Hobbes and the Social Contract

Hobbes (1588-1679) believed that self-preservation was man's key basic instinct.

The continuous clash of wills in the early society in which man lived led to intolerable tensions. As a result men made compacts involving the surrender of individual rights of self-government to a Sovereign.

The Sovereign had an absolute power to govern and obedience was required from all as the prerequisite of justice.

Law was the Sovereign's command. 'Unjust law' was a contradiction in terms; the Sovereign was merely carrying out the wishes of those who had surrendered their rights of individual self-government.

But laws might be 'unsatisfactory', ie, they imperilled the very purpose of the surrender of powers.

The Sovereign alone possesses the overall power to judge what needs to be done in the interests of his subjects.

The absolute authority of the Sovereign may be justified only as long as he has the power to protect his subjects effectively. The duty of obedience to the Sovereign is brought into doubt if the Sovereign seeks to destroy his subjects' rights of self-preservation.

Locke and the Social Contract

Locke (1632-1704) believed that man's 'primeval state' was one of perfect freedom which degenerated when dangers threatened individual existence.

Men united and became a political society by contracting to give power to a governing body which would act so as to protect the individual. A *pactum unionis* and a *pactum subjectionis* assured the essence of the contract.

The governing body enjoyed the trust of the governed only so long as it carried out its basic duties - preservation of 'life, liberty and estates'.

'Tyranny begins where law ends.' Locke insisted that the trust enjoyed by the government would be forfeited where there was a failure to protect subjects.

Where man's inalienable right to the preservation of life is ignored by government, Locke suggests that such a government ought not to be obeyed.

Rousseau and the Social Contract

Rousseau (1712-1778) argued for the natural goodness of human nature. Man is born innocent and good, free and equal, but the corrupting powers of civilisation are responsible for the evil situation in which he finds himself.

The foundation of the State is a Social Contract made by citizens who enter into it on the basis of their inalienable rights to freedom and equality. Democracy thrives when the general will prevails. The people's right of sovereignty must never be surrendered.

The legacy of Hobbes, Locke and Rousseau

Both Hobbes and Locke were concerned with discovering the principles of the links which bound the rulers and the ruled. The duty of the ruler (the government) was to protect the fundamentals of social existence. The duties of the ruled involved obedience.

Hobbes stressed the absolute nature of the Sovereign's powers. Locke emphasised the rights of individuals, particularly when the Sovereign fails to carry out his duties.

Rousseau bequeathed a theory which continues to attract those who call for the people's inalienable rights to be respected and to be recognised in the political structure of the State.

The theory of the 'Social Contract' receives little support in modern political science or jurisprudence. It is of importance, however, in any consideration of the development of popular democratic government and of appropriate laws. Modern concepts of 'inalienable human rights' owe much to theories of Hobbes and Locke which explored the nature of such rights.

Chapter 4

Natural Law (1): Aquinas and Neo-Scholasticism

4.1 Normative jurisprudence and natural law

Normative jurisprudence is that branch of enquiry concerned with *the validity of the law*, rather than with, say, its structure or efficacy. It involves evaluations and judgments in relation to fundamental criteria. Theories of natural law, which seek to discover criteria and enunciate relevant value-statements, constitute an enduring aspect of Western jurisprudence. The following statements give an indication of some of the essential basic features of natural law.

4.1.1 Burlamqui, Kelsen and Radbruch

- Burlamqui, *Principles of Natural Law* (1751)

  'Natural law comprises rules which so necessarily agree with the nature and state of man, that, without observing their maxims, the peace and happiness of society can never be preserved ... They are called natural laws because a knowledge of them may be attained merely by the light of reason, from the fact of their essential agreeableness with the constitution of human nature: while, on the contrary, positive or revealed laws are not founded upon the general constitution of human nature but only upon the will of God: though in other respects such law is established upon very good reason and procures the advantage of those to whom it is sent.'

- Kelsen, *What is Justice*? (1957):

  'The natural law doctrine undertakes to supply a definitive solution to the eternal problem of justice, to answer the question as to what is right and wrong in the mutual relations of men. The answer is based on the assumption that it is possible to distinguish between human behaviour which is natural, that is to say which corresponds to nature because it is required by nature, and human behaviour which is unnatural, hence contrary to nature and forbidden by nature. This assumption implies that it is possible to deduce from nature ... certain rules which provide an altogether adequate prescription for human behaviour ... *Nature is conceived of as a legislator, the supreme legislator*.'

- Radbruch, *Five Minutes of Legal Philosophy* (1945):

  'There are principles of law that are stronger than any statute, so that a law conflicting with these principles is devoid of validity. One calls these principles the natural law or the law of reason ... the work of centuries has established a solid core of them.'

4.2 Essential principles of natural law

It is possible to discern the following principles among a variety of typical theories of natural law:

- There are absolute values, and ideals emerging from those values, which can be used as touchstones in a test of the validity of laws.
- There exists in nature an order which is rational and which can be known by man, so that the norms of human conduct may be considered as a 'law of nature'.
- Nature, if observed and understood correctly, will provide criteria allowing us to become aware of universal, eternal and comprehensible values from which we may derive appropriate value-statements.
- That which is good is in accordance with nature; that which is evil is contrary to nature.
- A law which lacks moral validity is wrong and unjust. Natural law invalidates certain manifestations of the positive law and provides an ideal towards which the positive law should strive.

4.3 Aquinas and his predecessors

St Thomas Aquinas (1225-1274) sought to advance the systematisation of Catholic doctrine in which law was viewed as *an aspect of God's plan for mankind*. Natural law did not begin with Aquinas: he built upon principles formulated by Greek and Roman scholars (who had written of 'the immutable unwritten laws of heaven'), including Aristotle, who had differentiated the 'naturally just' from the 'conventionally just', and Cicero, who had proclaimed 'the true and primal law ... the right reason of the high God'. Within the Catholic church, natural law doctrines had been shaped by scholars such as the following.

4.3.1 Augustine

Augustine (354-430), one of the early Fathers of the Church, taught that the absolute ideal of laws of nature had been evident in the 'golden age' of mankind, which had preceded the fall of man. That age had seen man in a state of innocence and justice; he had lived under the guidance of the rules of reason. After his fall, the 'absolute law of nature' could no longer be realised. As a result, human law, together with property and institutions had appeared. Positive (man-made) law must strive so as to assist man in fulfilling the command of God's eternal law: law of this type does not necessarily make men good. In its role of guardian of *lex aeterna* (God's eternal law), the church must exercise total sovereignty over the State. If worldly law conflicts with the eternal, natural law, the provisions of that worldly law should be ignored; worldly law which was unjust could not be 'law'.

4.3.2 Isidore

Isidore (560-636) reiterated Augustine's teachings on the law and taught that only those rulers who acted in a spirit of justice ought to command the respect of their subjects. He said of natural law:

> 'Natural law is common to all peoples in that it is possessed by an instinct of nature, not by any human agreement, as marriage, the begetting and rearing of children, the common possession of all things, the universal freedom of all ... the restoring of property contracted or lent ... For this or whatever is like this could never constitute an injustice but must be considered in accord with natural equity.'

4.3.3 Gratian

Gratian (fl 1140), a Benedictine, published a collection of texts (*Decretum Gratianum*) in which he noted that the law of nature was to be considered as the law of God. It was 'antecedent both in point of time and in point of rank to all things', was immutable, and prevailed unquestionably over man-made law. If a custom were to be recognised as valid law it would have to conform to the golden rule of the Gospel ('All things whatsoever ye would that men should do to you, do you even so to them'). Statutes, secular and ecclesiastical, were to be rejected totally if shown to be contrary to natural law.

4.4 Aquinas' concept of the law

The writings of Aquinas on law, recorded largely in the *Summa Theologica*, Part II (c 1266), have dominated the thinking of Catholic jurists for centuries. The contemporary emergence of the neo-Scholastic movement testifies to the enduring influence of the remarkable synthesis of law achieved by Aquinas. Fundamental to that synthesis is a set of precisely-enunciated beliefs.

God is the highest 'good' and from him all things emerge.

The order of nature which we can observe and analyse is God's creation, and, because order presupposes reason, there is some transcendent reason behind the creation.

4.4.1 Law and Divine Reason

Law in all its manifestations flows ultimately from Divine Reason.

Aquinas argued:

> 'Law is a rule and measure of acts, whereby man is induced to act or is restrained from acting ... Now the rule and measure of human acts is the reason, which is the first principle of human acts ... Consequently it follows that law is something pertaining to reason.'

Man's laws are ordinances 'of reason for the common good made by him who has the care of the community, and promulgated'.

> 'The natural law is nothing else than the rational creature's participation in the eternal law ... Human law falls short of the eternal law.'

4.5 Aquinas' four-fold classification of law

Law may be categorised according to the following scheme.

4.5.1 *Lex aeterna*

Lex aeterna (the eternal law). This is God's rational direction of all created things. All things are ruled, therefore, by this law; unreasoning things must obey it, but man, who has free will, has the capacity to disobey. The eternal law in its totality is known to God only, but some blessed persons may perceive it in its full truth. The broad, general principles that mirror God's intentions for mankind comprise the natural law.

4.5.2 *Lex divina*

Lex divina (the Divine law), as revealed in the Scriptures. Although not identical with natural law, it is not contrary to it. Divine revelation - God's law - overcomes the limitations of the law known through human reason, and provides a guide for man's reason, allowing his nature to be perfected by Divine grace.

4.5.3 *Lex humana*

Lex humana (the human law) involves particular uses of the natural law (as in legislation by States). Human law which conforms to the law of reason ('the reason of divine wisdom') must conform to the law of God.

4.5.4 *Lex naturalis*

Lex naturalis (the natural law). Because man possesses God-given reason he may share in Divine reason and derive from it a natural inclination to such actions and ends as are fitting. The natural law results from man's participation in the workings of the cosmic law.

Natural law teaches us that precepts which emerge from man's exercise of his reason should include 'seek good and avoid evil'.

Every thing seeks the preservation of its own being according to its nature. By reason of this inclination 'whatever is a means of preserving human life and warding off its obstacles, belongs to the natural law'. Gilson writes, in *The Philosophy of St Thomas Aquinas* (1929):

> 'Man is a being. On this ground he desires the preservation of his being, ie, he desires to preserve himself by securing the integrity of everything that belongs by right to his nature. What is usually called "the instinct of self-preservation" means simply what this law expresses: each strives with all his power, and must strive, towards whatever can preserve his life or protect his health. *The tendency to preserve in his being is consequently the first precept of the natural law imposed on man.*'

Man has an inclination to good according to the nature of his reason: thus he desires to know the truth. Whatever pertains to this inclination (eg, the desire to shun ignorance) belongs to the natural law. 'To the natural law belongs those things to which a man is inclined naturally, and among these it is proper for man to act according to reason.' Gilson writes:

> 'A precept of the natural law imposed on man as a rational being prescribes to him the pursuit of everything that is good according to the order of reason: to live in communities, in order to pool the efforts of all and help one another; search for truth in the order of natural sciences, or, better still, concerning the Supreme Intelligible which is God; correspondingly not to harm those with whom he is called upon to live; to avoid ignorance and to try to dispel it – *all these are imperative prescriptions of the natural law which in its turn is but one aspect of the eternal law willed by God*. The natural law is literally written upon the human heart and cannot be cancelled from it.'

The principles of natural law as expounded by Aquinas have been placed by commentators in three groups:

- *The supreme group*, which demands love for God and one's neighbours, the doing of good and the avoiding of evil.
- *The second group*, based on the first group and reiterating the principles of the Ten Commandments.
- *The third group*, which is constituted by the rules of justice resulting from the application of principles in the first and second groups to particular situations.

4.6 When is a law not 'law'?

Aquinas argued that, in the light of 'natural principles', laws framed by men are either just or unjust. A law is not law merely because it is decreed by a Sovereign.

Where a law has the appropriate moral dimension and is ordained 'to the common good', it is a 'just law'. Hence, where it conforms to natural law it is just.

4.6.1 Unjust laws

Laws may be unjust in two ways:

- A law which is contrary to human good, either in respect of its form or end, is no law at all: it cannot bind in conscience. It might be temporarily obeyed, however, 'in order to avoid scandal or disturbance, for which cause a man should even yield his right'.
- A law which is opposed to the Divine good, such as the law of a tyrant 'inducing to idolatry' (and, therefore, a

violation of the natural law), must be disregarded, because it is better to obey God than man.

4.7 Significance of Aquinas' view of natural law

Natural law is viewed by Aquinas as part of a wide system of phenomena revealed by the light of Catholic doctrine. It is a source of *general principles* rather than detailed, day-to-day rules. Essentially it demands 'the elevation of human reason': God's purposes may be discerned in part by reason. God's law is 'the reason of his wisdom', and human laws and institutions are best-founded when built upon reason. However, not all Catholic scholars in the time of Aquinas accepted his conclusions.

4.7.1 John Duns Scotus

John Duns Scotus (1265-1308), a Franciscan scholar, argued that, in relation to natural law, reason was not superior to will. Man's will, not his reason, guides his intellectual insight. The single principle of natural law is to love God; other principles of human behaviour are matters for decision within man-made law.

4.7.2 William of Occam

William of Occam (1290-1349), suggested that philosophical speculation be confined to the observable. It was possible to discover law from an exercise of the reason. The modification by man-made law of principles deduced from natural law was permissible and was not, as Aquinas seemed to suggest, contrary to reason and Divine law.

4.8 Neo-Scholasticism and the natural law

Today's neo-Scholastic movement in the field of natural law is concerned with the further development and adaptation of the teachings of Aquinas on law. It is important to note that not all members of this movement accept the theology of Aquinas: thus, Adler (b 1902), a prominent American advocate of 'a contemporary natural law', and a non-Catholic, notes six widely-held principles derived directly from Aquinas, which have unusual relevance for law today:

- Government-made laws do not constitute the sole directions of human conduct which ought to apply to persons within society.
- There can be discovered rules and principles with application to all persons in all types of society.
- General principles of conduct exist outside man-made rules of law.
- These principles will emerge through man's exercise of his reason.
- General principles, resulting from man's reason, should be the source of all particular rules of conduct.

- These general principles can provide an overall standard by which the rules of law may be judged.

4.8.1 Adler's critique

In his *Dialectic of Morals* (1941), Adler urged the creation of a barrier against the advance of legal positivism (see Chapter 8). Human conduct can and must be based on a knowledge of right and wrong; moral judgments are more than mere matters of opinion. In the absence of principles of natural law, concepts such as 'natural rights' are meaningless. If disputes are to be settled without prejudice and pressure, the ideals of the natural law must be kept in mind.

4.9 Dabin, Rommen, Le Fur

Three prominent members of the neo-Scholastic school are selected as exemplifying the principles of the movement within a Catholic context.

4.9.1 Dabin

Dabin (1889-1970), a Belgian jurist, considers that the legal order within society may be comprehended as the sum total of the rules of conduct enunciated by that society under the sanction of public compulsion, intended to realise social ends. Law is an effective vehicle in the movement towards those ends. In *The General View of the Law* (1929), Dabin insists that the natural law shall dominate the positive law. The precepts of the natural law, 'which allow neither doubt nor discussion', may be deduced from the very nature of man. Legislators must work for the public good, and anything perceived as contrary to natural morality, and, therefore, natural law, is to be condemned as *contrary to the public good.*

4.9.2 Rommen

Rommen (1897-1967) is one of the group of German jurists who were deeply affected by the perversions of the German legal system during the era of dictatorship. For him, the natural law points to the inviolability of the dignity of human personality. He emphasises two 'self-evident propositions' of the natural law. First: 'What is just is to be done, and injustice is to be avoided', and, second, 'Give to everyone his due'. Unjust laws are utterly devoid of obligation. *The true and the just are conterminous.* Man's freedom requires that he be bound firmly by a justice which will recognise the imperatives of natural law.

4.9.3 Le Fur

Le Fur (1870-1943), a French writer on natural law, outlined in *Problems of Law* (1947) a restatement of Thomist principles. The rules of law which govern a community should comprise *rights granted to citizens together with duties.* The will of the majority must prevail, provided that they act, in the words of Aquinas, with consciousness of 'the ultimate need of preserving the life of the community'. Modern legislators must be imbued with the spirit of the natural law and should seek to build the positive law upon a foundation of three principles: *first*, the sanctity of obligations (which necessitates the keeping of freely-concluded contractual agreements); *second*, respect for properly-constituted authority; *third*, the duty to compensate for, or repair fully, unlawfully-inflicted damage.

4.10 Lucey and Maritain

Lucey (b 1899), an American jurist and priest, and Maritain (1882-1973), a French philosopher and convert to Catholicism, call for attention to be paid to that aspect of natural law doctrine which demands that respect be shown to the dignity of man, who is created in the image of God.

4.10.1 Lucey

Lucey affirms the significance of *the duties and rights given to man by God*, 'which no one has a right to destroy'. Man is social by nature and requires for his self-fulfilment a civil society and a civil law which he must respect and which will respect him. The positive law which guides society must alter in accordance with perceptions of 'the common good' and its requirements; these perceptions should be guided by the principles of natural law.

4.10.2 Maritain

Maritain, in *Rights of Man and Natural Law* (1947), affirms the significance of the natural law as 'an expression of what is natural in the world'. Man is naturally inclined towards the moral law, and he must so use his reason as to implement that law. A knowledge of the moral and the natural law allows man to attune himself to humanity's ends and needs. Above all, says Maritain, with his experiences of the Second World War in mind, jurists must assert forcefully that *an unjust law is no law*. Maritain sums up in terms which are accepted widely within the contemporary natural-law movement: 'Natural law is the ensemble of things to do and not to do which follow in necessary fashion from the simple fact that man is man, nothing else being taken into account.'

Summary of Chapter 4

Natural Law (1): Aquinas and Neo-Scholasticism

Essence of natural law doctrine

The doctrine of natural law is based on a belief that there are principles of law stronger than any statute. 'Nature is conceived of as a legislator, the supreme legislator.'

Principles of natural law include the following:

- The validity of man-made laws should be tested by reference to 'absolute values' and these can be deduced by reason from the observation and comprehension of nature.
- Absolute values are universal and eternal. That which is in accordance with nature is 'good'; that which is contrary to nature is 'evil'.
- Laws lacking moral validity are 'wrong' and 'unjust'.

Aquinas and natural law

Aquinas (1225-74) attempted to interpret law as an aspect of God's plan for mankind. Law could be categorised thus:

- *Lex aeterna*. God's rational direction of all created things.
- *Lex divina*. God's law as revealed in the Scriptures.
- *Lex humana*. Human law must conform to reason and the law of God.
- *Lex naturalis*. This should emerge from man's exercise of his reason in the light of God's word.

Where a law is 'moral' and assists the 'common good', it is just. Unjust law, which is contrary to human good, cannot bind in conscience and must be disregarded where opposed to the Divine good.

Neo-Scholasticism and the natural law

The neo-Scholastic contemporary movement represents an attempt to rethink the essence of 'Scholasticism' (the term which indicates reasoning along lines set out in the works of Aquinas) in relation to 20th century life with particular reference to law within society.

Adler

Adler (b 1902), a contemporary American jurist, advocates that attention be paid to the following principles: that the positive (ie, man-made) law should not constitute the sole direction of human conduct; that universal rules of conduct can be discovered; that general principles of conduct emerging from man's exercise of his reason can provide touchstones in order to judge the validity and worth of the rules of the law.

Dabin

Dabin (1889-1970) urges the supremacy of natural law in relation to the positive law. Anything contrary to natural morality, ie, law which fails to assist in the realisation of social ends, is to be condemned as contrary to the public good.

Rommen

Rommen (1897-1967) argues that 'the true' and 'the just' should be considered as synonymous. Justice involves recognition of man's dignity, the implications of which can be deduced from natural law principles.

Le Fur

Le Fur (1870-1943) advocates legislation imbued with the spirit of the natural law. Such legislation will be based upon the sanctity of human obligations, respect for properly-constituted authority, and the payment of compensation for unlawfully-inflicted damage.

Lucey

Lucey (b 1899) affirms the importance of the 'common good', derived from principles of natural law, and reflecting the significance of God-given rights and duties.

Maritain

Maritain (1882-1973) seeks to persuade jurists and legislators that an unjust law is no law, and that natural law is 'the ensemble of things to do and not to do' which follow from the recognition of man's essential humanity.

Chapter 5

Natural Law (2): Stammler, Radbruch, Finnis

5.1 A changing doctrine

The 20th century has witnessed a general revival of interest in the concept of natural law, as evidenced by the neo-Scholastic movement, perhaps because of disenchantment with perceived inadequacies of 'value-free' legal relativism. Calls for a return to 'just law' based upon immutable values intensified after each of the two world wars. Demands for a recognition by jurists and legislators of a need to preserve human dignity in *all* circumstances were linked to movements calling for a restatement of human values and a recognition of the responsibility of the legal system for their protection. Some important twentieth-century international conventions enunciating human rights include prologues referring to 'inalienable rights'.

5.1.1 Essence of the classical natural law

The natural-law jurists discussed in this chapter are far-removed in their approaches to the essence of law from their predecessors. It is useful to be reminded of the certainties which characterised the classical natural law, by referring to Blackstone's *Commentaries on the Laws of England* (1765):

> 'Natural law being coeval with mankind and dictated by God himself, is of course superior in obligation to any other. It is binding all over the globe in all countries and at all times: no human laws are of any validity if contrary to this; and such of them as are valid derive all their force and all their authority, mediately or immediately, from this original.'

Stammler, Radbruch and Finnis, whose legal theories are mentioned in this chapter, are attracted to the overall philosophy and the principal tenets of the early natural law doctrine, but each calls for a modification of that doctrine so as to meet the exigencies of circumstances which could not have been envisaged in earlier days.

5.2 Stammler: natural law with a variable content

Stammler (1856-1938), a German jurist, was concerned with the formulation of 'a right law' based upon justice. In his *Theory of Justice* (1902), which was later revised, he argues that each era requires its own 'right law' which should co-exist with its positive law. The rules of the community's positive law should be evaluated, so as to justify their use, by reference to standards derived from the prevalent ethical and philosophical doctrines, and a law found to be deficient would be corrected by the courts or the legislature. Stammler set out his views as follows:

- The jurist's task is to assist in the function of providing the law with a quality of objective justice through the frequent appraisal of empirically-conditioned legal rules.
- Law is a vital aspect of man's social existence, embodying, in an important sense, the 'collective will' of the community and binding citizens in a 'unity of purpose'.
- Man must be treated as an end in himself, not as the mere object of an arbitrary will.
- The exercise of reason is essential for the understanding and acceptance of one's responsibilities to other members of society.
- A society in flux requires no modification of the essential 'idea of law'; what is needed is a modification of rules in accordance with the realities of that society - essentially, a 'natural law with a variable content'.

5.3 Stammler's principles of respect and participation

Freedom under the law and the effective expression of the community's collective will necessitate the observance of two principles.

First, no act of an individual is to be subjected to the mere whim of another. Respect for human dignity (a key principle of the natural law) requires that where a juristic claim is made by an individual, he shall be allowed to retain his 'self-respecting personality'.

Second, no individual may be excluded from the community in an arbitrary fashion. A man's dignity demands recognition of his right to participate in the affairs of society; to interfere in the exercise of that right is to take from him the essence of that dignity.

5.4 The essence of Stammler's jurisprudential thought

It is not the law of nature but the nature of law which is common to mankind everywhere. Rules within a community must be 'right' for that community, given its unique features. Those rules require testing, but the test must not be a reflection of mere relativism. The aim of the natural law - harmony within society enabling man to live in dignity, justice and according to truth - is Stammler's fundamental concern. Law related to the specific needs of society at a given stage of development will assist man in realising the purpose of the natural law.

5.5 Radbruch: a return to transcendent law

Radbruch (1878-1949), a German jurist, was Minister of Justice under the Weimar Republic and, in his final years, following the defeat of the Nazi regime, assisted in the drafting of the constitution of the German Federal Republic. He had been a powerful advocate of legal relativism: 'absolutes' relating to justice and law could not be discovered, and in the event of a dispute between legal certainty, justice and expediency, legal certainty ought to prevail. Law was little more than 'the sum of the general arrangements for human coexistence'. Radbruch's experience of Nazi laws in the service of a tyranny led to his dramatic conversion to a philosophy based upon the need for a law 'above statute'.

5.5.1 Radbruch's theses

In *Five Minutes of Legal Philosophy* (1945), a succinct account of his beliefs, he indicates a move in the direction of natural law. His views are set out in that work in the form of five theses:

- The teachings of positivistic theory, equating the law with power, render the jurist and other members of the community defenceless against laws 'however arbitrary, cruel or criminal they may be'. In the end, the positivistic theory equates the law with power; there is law only where there is power.
- It has been said that law is what benefits the people. This means, practically speaking, that 'every whim and caprice of the despot', punishing persons without laws or judgment, killing the sick lawlessly – 'whatever the State authorities deem to be of benefit to the people' – is law. This is wrong. *'Only what is law benefits the people.'*
- If laws consciously deny the will to justice (and justice involves judging without regard to the person and treating all according to the same standard), then they lack validity. 'The people owe them no obedience, and even the jurists must find the courage to deny their legal character.'
- There can be laws that are so unjust, so 'socially detrimental', that their very character as laws must be denied. This must be 'indelibly impressed on the consciousness of the people and the jurists.'
- There are principles of law stronger than any statute. A law which is in conflict with these principles has no validity. We may refer to these principles as 'the natural law' or 'the law of reason'. Details of these principles remain somewhat doubtful, but over the centuries a solid core of such principles has been established; indeed, they now enjoy such a wide consensus in declarations embodying civil and human rights, 'that only a deliberate sceptic can still entertain doubts about some of them'.

5.6 Finnis: the universality of basic values

Finnis, a British lawyer and philosopher (b 1929), is a Catholic scholar who seeks to investigate the relevance of natural law to contemporary society. In his *Natural Law and Human Rights*

(1980) he restates aspects of natural law doctrine in novel form. Morality and law are given a 'rational basis' which rests upon two principles. *First*, there are certain basic values of human existence ('human goods') which are self-evident. They may be secured only through the law and its institutions. *Secondly*, 'practical reasonableness' is required in order to achieve human goods and this necessitates the existence of an appropriate system of law.

5.6.1 Natural law and the legal system

Finnis keeps in mind the nature, purposes and ultimate significance of society: its appropriate system of law a matter of concern for jurists. What makes a law important from a practical point of view is always of interest; jurists must keep in mind the need to bring definition, clarity and predictability into the reactions of members of society, and this requires organised rules and institutions.

Human well-being and the flourishing of the individual require a legal system which will exemplify the 'rule of law', as derived from the natural law. The rules of such a system would ensure clear, coherent and stable regulations, accountability of those who administer the law, and administration carried out in a manner which is seen to be consistent with promulgated principles.

5.6.2 The concept of 'human goods'

Finnis sets out a catalogue of 'forms of human flourishing', that is, the requirements of individuals who are to attain their potential. Seven such 'irreducibly basic goods' are enumerated. Finnis emphasises that there are many forms of 'human goods' outside his enumeration, but they are no more than methods of attaining those he has listed.

- Life

  'Life' is – in accordance with traditional principles of natural law – a basic value which corresponds to the human being's drive for self-preservation. 'Life' is used by Finnis as signifying 'every aspect of the vitality ... which puts a human being in good shape for self-determination'. The realisation of such a basic human purpose involves the existence of a functioning system of law. Finnis notes that all human societies appear to show a significant measure of concern for the value of life; none allows killing without a fairly definite justification.

- Knowledge

  'Speculative knowledge', with which Finnis is concerned, comprises knowledge sought *for its own sake* rather than in pursuit of some other objective. It will embody 'the drive of curiosity' and range from scientific enquiry to mundane questioning. Truth as the end of knowledge is worth pursuing. The principle that knowledge is a good to be pursued is, according to Finnis, 'self-evident'; its value as a guide to action requires no further principle to support it.

- Play

  'A large and irreducible element in human culture', involving 'engaging in performances which have no point beyond the performance itself, enjoyed for its own sake.'

- Aesthetic experience

  This need not involve an action of one's own; it may be the inner experience of, say, an appreciation of beauty.

- Sociability

  In its strongest forms, this involves friendship. 'To be in a relationship of friendship with at least one other person is a fundamental form of good ...'

- Practical reasonableness

  This basic good involves bringing one's intelligence to bear effectively on problems related to the choosing of one's actions and life-style and moulding one's character.

- Religion

  Finnis gives this term a wide meaning - recognition (however residual) of, and concern about, an order of things 'beyond each and every man'.

5.6.3 Justice and liberty

Justice and liberty will clearly pervade the institutional framework intended to protect the 'human goods' Finnis has enumerated. In the words of Grisez, who shares the stance of Finnis on the natural law in relation to human goods (see *Life and Death with Liberty and Justice* (1979)): 'Justice requires due respect for liberty which, while itself not one of the basic human goods, is a necessary condition for the active, human realisation of any of those goods'.

5.6.4 Pleasure as a human good?

'Pleasure' is not listed by Finnis as a basic human good. Grisez (*op cit*) states: 'Pleasure is an experience, and experiences are not actions, whereas human flourishing is constituted of acts. The human goods are not products of human acts or ideals at which actions aim. They are realised within human acts by the very doing of these acts – realised not exhaustively, but participated to a greater or lesser degree'.

5.6.5 The concept of 'practical reasonableness'

Finnis classifies under ten headings the essential features of 'practical reasonableness' (which features also as a 'human good'). These headings encapsulate principles which seem to be in the spirit of the classical natural law.

- If the individual is to distinguish morally-right actions from wrong actions, he must have a rational life-plan, 'a harmonious set of orientations, purposes and commitments'.
- He must pay equal regard to each of the basic human goods.
- He must not leave out of account the necessity for others to participate in these goods.
- He must not attribute to any project the overriding significance of a basic human good.
- He must pursue his general commitments with creativity and must not abandon them lightly.
- He must not waste his opportunities by acting inefficiently.
- He must not choose directly against any human good.
- He must foster the common good of his community.
- He must not act contrary to his conscience.
- He must not choose 'apparent goods' which he knows to be merely 'the simulations' of real goods.

5.7 Unjust laws

Finnis stands within the tradition of the natural law in his consideration of 'just' and 'unjust' laws. For purposes of assessing one's legal obligations 'in the moral sense', the individual may exercise his right to discount those laws which are unjust. Laws of this type do not possess the moral authority which ought to stem from their origin or formal source. But an unjust law is *not* a nullity. Finnis interprets the aphorism *lex injusta non est lex* as suggesting merely that unjust laws, although formally valid, do not meet the demands of the natural law.

5.8 Finnis and natural rights

Finnis refers in his text to certain 'exceptionless or absolute human claim-rights'. They include: the right of an individual not to have his life taken directly 'as a means to any further end'; the right 'not to be positively lied to' in situations in which one expects reasonable factual information; the right not to be condemned on charges which are known to be false; the right not to be deprived of procreative capacities; the right to be considered in any assessment of what is required in the name of 'the common good' of society.

5.9 Criticisms of Finnis

Criticisms of Finnis have drawn attention to the very wide nature of the categories of 'human goods', rendering analysis of 'knowledge', 'sociability', extremely difficult. His classification of 'religion' as a human good gives rise to unusual problems of interpretation. Some jurists see in the list of human goods yet another highly-subjective catalogue of principles which most religions have advocated as constituting paths to virtue. Others note the real difficulty – perhaps insuperable – of obtaining a significant measure of agreement among the many groups which make up a modern community on the true nature of human goods such as 'aesthetic experience' or 'knowledge'.

Weinreb notes, in his *Natural Law and Justice* (1987), that although the neo-Thomist outlook accepted by Finnis is not free from difficulty of interpretation, Finnis has nevertheless assisted jurisprudential enquiry in the task of recognising the level of agreement about human ends and how they might be attained. 'He has provided a shelter from the winds of moral relativism' – an achievement of some significance.

5.10 Criticism of natural law by positivists

Criticism of the doctrines of natural law has been continuous and intense, particularly from the philosophers, jurists and linguists who reject any doctrine based on metaphysical speculation.

5.10.1 Hume

Hume (1711-1776) exemplifies in his writings the doctrine of philosophical positivism. He holds that our knowledge of matters of fact can be derived solely from the data of experience. So-called 'transcendental knowledge' which is not based upon experience has no value; the metaphysical basis of natural law invalidates its methodology and conclusions. Natural law is 'real' only in the sense that some individuals entertain a feeling that it exists. Its 'truths' cannot be asserted meaningfully, nor can they be demonstrated in acceptable fashion. Its attempts to derive 'ought' from 'is' are meaningless.

5.10.2 Bentham

Bentham (1748-1831) (see Chapter 6) attacked natural law, in the name of his doctrine of 'utilitarianism', as nothing but a phrase - 'nonsense upon stilts'. The metaphysical basis of natural law was anathema to him. Additionally, the spread of the doctrine of natural law would undermine the fabric of sovereignty within a community. Bentham argued:

> 'If there be scarce any law whatever but what those who have not liked it have found, on some account or other, to be repugnant to some text of scripture, I see no remedy but that the natural tendency of such doctrine is to impel a man, by the force of conscience, to rise up in arms against any law whatever that he happens not to like.'

5.10.3 Carnap and Ayer

The logical positivists, and the jurists who accepted the teachings of Carnap (1891-1970) and Ayer (1910-89) (see 8.5), urged a total rejection of any statements not based upon tested and verified experience of the senses. Carnap dismissed all metaphysical assertion as meaningless. Ayer argues that a proposition is understandable only when one knows what facts would verify it. Genuine propositions (ie, those that are capable of being true or false) cannot be derived from any metaphysical argument. Hence, he would have argued, the entire edifice of natural law doctrine is insubstantial, incapable of proof and, ultimately, worthless.

5.11 Ross' critique of natural law

The Danish jurist, Ross (1899-1979), (see Chapter 17) delivers a sustained attack on the entire conceptual basis of natural law in his *On Law and Justice* (1958).

- The metaphysical speculation underlying natural law is totally beyond the reach of verification; such speculation belongs to 'the childhood of civilisation'.
- The doctrines of natural law are neither eternal nor immutable. They have not existed for ever and they have been used to defend or fight for 'every conceivable kind of demand'.
- Natural law has been used to defend slavery and fraternity. How may one make a valid choice between these absolutes 'except by an absolute assertion elevated above all rational argumentation'?
- The ultimate basis for every so-called 'natural right' is the individual's private and direct insight, ie, intuition. It cannot be otherwise. But one person's intuition is as good as that of another.
- The metaphysical postulates of natural law are no more than 'constructions to buttress emotional attitudes and the fulfilment of certain needs'. There are psychological reasons for the attraction of certain doctrines of natural law: the desire for 'safe' absolutes, for unassailable truths built upon a rock-like faith, may explain illusions of 'eternal validity' and 'absolute rightness'. Illusions of 'moral consciousness' have a mystical significance which 'is like manna from Heaven to the metaphysically hungry'.

5.12 All things to all men

Ross notes that many disparate political doctrines have assembled under the banner of the natural law. Friedmann observes that 'natural law has at different times been used to support almost any ideology'. Support for the suppression of liberties (in the name of 'the natural unity of State and People'), as well as for campaigns for the expansion of free political institutions (seen as 'an extension of man's rights') has been canvassed under the wide heading of the claims of the natural law. Totalitarians have found support in the natural law writings of Del Vecchio and Duguit ('the only right which any man can possess is the right always to do his duty'); advocates of greater social freedom have turned recently to the interpretation of natural law favoured by Maritain.

Some jurists see in the eclecticism of natural law doctrine, however, and its ability to synthesise a variety of apparently different points of view, its abiding strength. Others see this as its essential weakness, depriving its doctrine of credibility and authority. The attacks of the legal positivists (see Chapter 8) have contributed to a further weakening of its power. It constitutes, however, in its essentials, a compelling appeal to those who perceive the need for something standing higher than the positive law.

Summary of Chapter 5

Natural Law (2): Stammler, Radbruch, Finnis

Natural law and change

Natural law jurists of the twentieth century include some who call for a modification of early doctrines so as to take into account problems which could not have been envisaged in earlier centuries. The modifications would allow the development of a 'natural law with a changing content'.

Stammler's natural law with a variable content

Stammler (1856-1938) suggests that each era requires its own 'right law' based upon justice. The task of the jurist is to assist in the appraisal of the positive law in relation to the demands of objective justice.

Man is to be treated as an end in himself, and the law must ensure that he does not become the object of an arbitrary exercise of will.

Freedom, and the expression of the community's collective will, should be based on natural law with a variable content. Two principles will result from investigation of the application of natural law:

- The principle of respect. No act of an individual should be subjected to another's whim.
- The principle of participation. No one may be excluded from the community in arbitrary fashion.

Radbruch: back to transcendent law

Radbruch (1878-1949) abandoned his belief in legal relativism following his experiences during the era of the German dictatorship and embraced the concept of a law 'above statute'.

His views may be summarised as follows:

- To equate law and power is to render the community defenceless against a tyranny.
- Only what is law benefits the people.
- Unjust laws ought not to be obeyed.
- Some laws are so socially detrimental that their very character as laws ought to be denied.
- There are principles of law stronger than any statute - these are the principles of natural law or 'the law of reason'.

Finnis: 'human goods'

Finnis calls for a rationally-based law which will recognise the basic values of human existence ('human goods'). These goods can be secured only through appropriate laws and legal procedures.

'Human goods' are 'the forms of human flourishing' necessary for the full development of individuals. They are as follows: life, knowledge, play, aesthetic experience, sociability, practical reasonableness, religion.

Finnis: 'practical reasonableness'

The concept of 'practical reasonableness' involves principles which stem from classical natural law doctrine. Thus: the individual must follow a 'rational life plan'; he must pay equal regard to each basic human good; he must recognise that others will participate in attaining these goods; he ought not to waste his opportunities by inefficient action; he must not act contrary to his conscience.

Natural law criticised

Philosophers, such as Hume, criticised the unreal basis of natural law and drew attention to its confusion of 'ought' and 'is'. Bentham attacked natural law as metaphysical nonsense.

Logical positivists, such as Carnap, argued that the very propositions of the natural law are incapable of verification and are, therefore, worthless.

Ross, the Danish jurist, argued that the speculation upon which natural law is built is of no value. The term 'natural law' has been used as an umbrella for many different doctrines, so that it is difficult to attach a meaning to it. Natural law seems to depend upon intuition and that is not an adequate basis for a theoretical construct.

Chapter 6

Utilitarianism (1): Bentham

6.1 Antecedents of Bentham's utilitarianism

Bentham (1748-1832), jurist, economist and social reformer, was the leader of the group of 'Philosophical Radicals' who espoused the doctrine of utilitarianism, which defined virtue in terms of utility. 'The greatest happiness of the greatest number' was accepted as the true goal of society. This philosophy had roots in early Greek thought and had been developed in the writings of some of Bentham's contemporaries.

6.1.1 Epicureans

The Greek Epicureans believed that pleasure was the highest, the only intrinsic, good. The moral quality of an action depended upon the amount of pleasure to be derived from it: an action which produced the greatest pleasure was 'morally right'; an action which produced pain was 'wrong'. But the most desirable life was one of simple pleasures controlled by 'rational prudence', the best of all 'goods'.

6.1.2 Helvetius

Helvetius (1715-1771), a French philosopher, argued that all of man's faculties could be reduced to physical sensation; self-interest, founded on the love of pleasure and fear of pain is, he argued, the basic guiding principle of man's actions.

Bentham claimed to have discovered the utilitarian doctrine as a result of his reading Joseph Priestley's *Essay on the First Principles of Government* (1769).

6.2 Essence of Bentham's utilitarianism

Bentham's *Introduction to the Principles of Morals and Legislation* (1789, 1832) sets out the doctrines from which he derived his jurisprudential thought. The key doctrine is stated thus:

> 'Nature has placed mankind under the governance of two sovereign masters, pain and pleasure. It is for them alone to point out what we ought to do, as well as to determine what we shall do. On the one hand the standard of right and wrong, on the other the chain of causes and effects are fastened to their throne. They govern us in all we do, in all we say, in all we think.'

6.2.1 Principle of utility

The 'principle of utility' subjects us to the 'sovereign masters'.

Bentham outlines the concept of 'utility' in the following words:

> 'By utility is meant that property in any object, whereby it tends to produce benefit, advantage, pleasure, good or happiness (all this in the present case comes to the same thing) or (what comes again to the same thing) to prevent

> the happening of mischief, pain, evil or unhappiness to the party whose interest is considered: if that party be the community in general, then the happiness of the community; if a particular individual, then the happiness of that individual.'

The principle allows man to approve or disapprove of an action according to its tendency to promote or oppose his happiness.

6.2.2 Pleasure and pain

'Pleasure' is to be equated with 'good', and 'pain' with evil.

> 'A thing is said to promote the interest, or to be for interest, of an individual, when it tends to add to the sum total of his pleasure: or, what comes to the same thing, to diminish the sum total of his pains.'

Pleasures and pains may be enumerated as pleasures of the senses (riches, knowledge, etc) and pains of senses (privation, fear, etc).

The distinguishable sources from which pleasure and pain flow (the 'sanctions') are physical, political, moral and religious.

In relation to the 'proofs' of utilitarianism, Bentham writes:

> 'Is it susceptible to any direct proof? It should seem not; for that which is used to prove everything cannot itself be proved; a chain of proofs must have their commencement elsewhere ... To give such proofs is as impossible as it is needless.'

6.3 The 'Hedonistic' or 'Felicific' Calculus

Bentham argued that it was possible to make a quantitative comparison of the pleasure and pain likely to occur as the consequences of courses of action. This necessitated taking an account of each 'distinguishable pleasure' produced in a person by a given act, and of each pain similarly produced. The appropriate evaluation would take into account: intensity of the pleasure, its duration, certainty, extent (ie, how many persons may share the pleasure). Pleasures and pains would be summed so as to arrive at the good or bad tendency of an act. Individual happiness would then be summed (algebraically) into a 'social total', each component being weighed equally ('everyone to count for one, nobody to count for more than one'). The resulting 'social total' would be identified with 'the common good' of society, which was pursuit of the greatest happiness of the greatest number:

> 'It is not to be expected that this process should be strictly pursued previously to every moral judgment, or to every legislative or judicial operation. It may, however, be always kept in view; and as near as the process actually pursued on these occasions approaches to it, so near will such process approach to the character of an exact one.'

6.4 The nature of a 'law'

Bentham defined law, thus:

> 'An assemblage of signs declarative of a volition conceived or adopted by the Sovereign in a State, concerning the conduct to be observed in a certain case by a certain person or class of persons, who in the case in question are or are supposed to be subject to his power.'
>
> 'Sovereign' is defined further as:
>
> 'any person or assemblage of persons to whose will a whole political community are (no matter on what account) supposed to be in a disposition to pay obedience: and that in preference to the will of any other person.'

6.4.1 Law as command

Essentially, this is a statement of the 'command theory' of law. This theory views law as the command of a Sovereign (a person or body), or supreme governor. His authority is not infinite, but it must be accepted as indefinite ('unless we are limited by express convention').

6.4.2 Sanctions

The sanction of the law rests upon 'the expectation of certain events ... the prospect of which it is intended should act as a motive upon those whose conduct is in question'.

Bentham suggests that his definition of 'law' allows consideration of a law in relation to its *source* (the person or persons of whose will it is the expression); its *subjects* (persons to whom it is to apply); its *objects* (the circumstances to which it may apply); its *extent*; its *aspects*; its *force* (the motives upon which it relies for effectiveness); its *expression* (the nature of the signs by which it becomes known).

6.5 The fundamentals of legislation

The *science* of legislation is, according to Bentham, knowledge of 'the good'; the *art* of legislation is the discovery of the means to realise the good. The foundation of a legislator's reasoning must be the principle of utility, which involves his taking into account the knowledge that the acts he wishes to prevent are 'evils' and that they are greater evils than the laws (which are, fundamentally, infractions of citizens' liberties) to be used to prevent them. Legislation intended to produce happiness for the community must reflect a desire to attain these goals:

- To provide subsistence and, where possible, abundance.
- To provide security. This was the most important goal for the legislator, and involves the protection of a man's honour, status and property. Bentham defined property as 'a basis of expectation, of deriving certain advantages from a thing which we are said to possess, in consequence of the relation in which we stand towards it'. Liberty - which, for Bentham, was not a goal of the legislator - might have to give way to the wider considerations of security.

- To diminish inequalities. The pursuit of perfect equality was a chimera. Equality of opportunity should not be pursued, save where it did not interfere with security.

6.6 Natural law and natural rights

Bentham rejected natural law as 'nothing but a phrase': its claims to authority based on its transcendent nature were meaningless. In similar vein, the concept of 'natural rights' was discarded. The *Declaration of the Rights of Man*, published by the French revolutionaries in 1789, was dismissed as 'the *ne plus ultra of* metaphysics'. The so-called 'rights of man' could not be justified philosophically or, indeed, in any other way. The promulgation of 'rights' of this nature ought not to be allowed to place any limits on the concept of political sovereignty and its practices:

> 'How stands the truth of things? That there are no such things as natural rights anterior to the establishment of government – no such things as rights opposed to, in contradistinction to, legal: that the expression is merely figurative; that when used, in the moment you attempt to give it a literal meaning it leads to error, and to that sort of error that leads to mischief ... to the extremity of mischief ... This rhetorical nonsense ends in the old strain of mischievous nonsense; for immediately a list of these pretended natural rights is given, and those are so expressed as to present to view legal rights. And of these rights, whatever they are, there is not, it seems, any one of which any government can, upon any occasion whatever, abrogate the smallest particle.'

6.7 Bentham and the criminal law

Bentham devoted much of his time to an application of utilitarian principles to the criminal law, the punishment of offenders and the reform of conditions in which prisoners were held. The principle of utility was the basis of his articulation of the elements of a 'censorial jurisprudence' (a critical study of law intended to effect improvements in its mode of operation). The following general principles emerge from his consideration of the criminal law:

- The mischief of an act (ie, the pain or evil produced by the act) must be taken into account. The law must discourage those acts which tend to produce evil . Evil may be considered under the following headings: *primary evil*, as where X robs Y; and *secondary evil*, as where X's act weakens general respect for the safety of persons and their property. It may be that secondary evils often outweigh primary evils in their overall effect.
- The criminal law should not be based on an acceptance of a division of offences into *mala in se* (acts wrong in

themselves) and *mala prohibita* (acts wrong because the law prohibits them). An act cannot be wrong in itself; and the quality of its 'wrongness' emerges only from its consequences. Where there is a high probability of an act producing harm, it ought to be prohibited by legislation; where it is unlikely to produce harm, there can be no justification in its prohibition. Society enacts laws prohibiting, say, assault, and theft, and punishes those found guilty of this type of offence, not because assault and theft are wrong in themselves, but because evil consequences have been created.

6.8 The fundamentals of punishment under the criminal law

A censorial jurisprudence demands, in its consideration of the punishment of criminals, an investigation of the reasons behind such punishment. Bentham bases his investigation on the principle of utility.

6.8.1 Essence of punishment

To punish is to inflict suffering on an offender; this increases the sum of 'evil'. But the overall object of the criminal law ought to be an increase in the community's total happiness. Therefore, if, in the name of the community, punishment is to be administered, it must be demonstrated that the resulting pain will help to prevent greater general pain. Hence, punishment is 'valuable' or 'useful' only if its eventual outcome results in greater happiness for the community as a whole. Retribution is, in itself, without value: it merely adds to the 'units of pain' within the community.

6.8.2 Problems of punishment

There is no gain in the infliction of punishment where an offender can be ordered to give compensation.

Some punishments are too expensive and ought not to be inflicted. The quantum of punishment ought never to exceed what is required to make it effective. Extravagant punishment, which is merely wasteful, should be rejected.

It is necessary to keep in mind the relationship between the offence and the punishment to be imposed. Punishment in a given case ought to be severe enough to outweigh any profit likely to be gained by the offender. In general, the greater the offence, the greater the punishment it ought to attract.

Punishment ought to act as a general deterrent, ought to be reformatory (where that is possible) and ought to have popular support.

Practical schemes for the 'rational punishment' of offenders ought to be implemented. (Bentham drew up a variety of such schemes, some dependent on the deterrent effects of continuous surveillance.)

6.9 Opposition to Bentham's views on punishment

Jurists and others continue to condemn Bentham's analysis of the problem of punishment. In addition to objections to the reasoning which supported his view of the general happiness of society as the *summum bonum*, it is considered that he paid little attention to the root causes of crime within society and that these are certainly more complex than the utilitarian thesis suggests. Further, little is said by Bentham concerning the principles of justice which ought to determine whether or not a punishment is 'correct' in the circumstances. Hall, in *General Principles of Criminal Law* (1947), argues:

> 'If punishment is unjust, it matters not how "useful" it may be ... In the common law of crime, the primary question is not the utility of the punishment, but, instead, the justice of it.'

The effects of punishment on the minds of offenders, as perceived by Bentham, stem, it is claimed, from a naive view of human behaviour; his views on the reformation of criminals appear flawed as a result.

6.10 The discrediting of Bentham's utilitarianism

Philosophers, jurists, psychologists and political scientists have combined in condemnation of Bentham's philosophy and the jurisprudence which he fashioned from it. Among the common criticisms of utilitarianism will be found the following points.

Pleasure and pain are highly-subjective phenomena and are not capable of consideration, in any meaningful sense, as objectively assessable criteria from which 'right' and 'wrong' may be deduced. Further, the consequences of an action may not result immediately in either pleasure or pain (unless one refers in tautological fashion to 'pleasure' as 'not-pain').

6.10.1 Impracticability of measuring pleasure and pain

The entire concept of a quantitative 'felicific calculus', involving the measuring of pleasure and pain is impracticable, if not absurd, since it lacks any standard by which measurement might be made.

Men are not necessarily motivated solely by considerations of pleasure or pain, and a doctrine which denies this ends by disregarding the complexities of human motivation. Contemporary theories of motivation (a phenomenon described as 'the influence of needs and desires on the intensity and direction of behaviour') find no room for the simplistic assertions of utilitarianism.

There are, surely, *qualitative differences* between one pleasure and another, so that the precept equating 'pleasure' with 'right action' is questionable.

6.10.2 Vagueness of 'happiness'

Happiness as an objective (which features prominently in Bentham's analysis) is a vague and indeterminate phenomenon.

Nor is there a necessary coincidence of pleasure with happiness and contentment.

The relationship between individual and communal happiness is not as direct as Bentham suggests. Nor is general happiness always the *summum bonum*.

The philosopher William James (1842-1910) argues against utilitarianism by noting that it would be immoral to buy happiness for the majority of a society at the expense of the suffering of even one person.

Bertrand Russell (1872-1970) poses the paradox: 'If every man pursues his own pleasure, how are we to secure that the legislator shall pursue the pleasure of mankind in general?'

Ayer notes that 'it is not self-contradictory to say that some pleasant things are not good or that some bad things are desired'.

6.10.3 A mere restatement of natural law?

An interesting objection to utilitarianism is voiced by those who interpret it as little more than a restatement of natural law doctrine, with the defects of that doctrine, but without its moral qualities. Schumpeter, in his essay, *Scholastic Doctors and Natural Law Philosophers* (1954), refers to utilitarianism as 'the shallowest of all conceivable philosophies of life'. 'No philosophy at all in the technical sense ... it fitted to perfection the streak of materialist (anti-metaphysical) rationalism that may be associated with liberalism and the business mind.' He makes the following points:

- Utilitarianism is a philosophy of life establishing a scheme of 'ultimate values' - pleasure, happiness, the greatest happiness of the greatest number (which is perceived as an 'eternal verity'). The principle of utility has about it an aura of the 'universal and immutable values' associated with classical natural law.
- Utilitarianism is a 'normative system with a strong legal slant', as was natural law doctrine which rested upon a scheme of moral imperatives and legislative principles.
- Utilitarianism is a comprehensive system 'embodying a uniform method of analysis', as is natural law. It is possible, however, says Schumpeter, to separate from utilitarian philosophy its analytical method and use it advantageously in the social sciences. Utilitarianism may be rejected totally as a philosophy and as a worthwhile contribution to jurisprudence, but it might be possible to use aspects of its methodology as an analytical tool in the investigation of some legal problems.

Summary of Chapter 6

Utilitarianism (1): Bentham

Essence of Bentham's utilitarianism

Bentham (1748-1832) argues that the true goal of society ought to be the achievement of 'the greatest happiness of the greatest number' – a concept derived from his interpretation of the 'principle of utility'.

'Utility' is seen by Bentham as the property or tendency of an object to produce benefit, good or happiness, or to prevent mischief, pain or evil. From this concept is derived the principle that we may approve or disapprove of an action according to its tendency to increase or diminish an individual's happiness.

Pleasure is to be equated with good, pain with evil.

A 'felicific calculus' makes possible a *quantitative* comparison of the pleasure or pain which will follow on a particular course of action. A 'social total' would make it possible for an evaluation of the full effect upon a community of a particular activity. Legislators ought to bear this in mind.

Bentham's view of law

'Law' was defined by Bentham as:

> 'an assemblage of signs declarative of a volition conceived or adopted by the Sovereign in a State, concerning the conduct to be observed in a certain case by a certain person or class of persons, who in the case in question are or are supposed to be subject to his power.'

Essentially, law is viewed as the command of a Sovereign.

The task of the legislator is to study the law so as to recognise and realise 'the good'.

Legislation should have the following goals:

- To provide subsistence, or abundance.
- To provide security.
- To diminish inequalities.

Bentham and the criminal law

No action is wrong in itself, according to Bentham. Its evil arises from its consequences.

There can be no justification in prohibiting an act which is unlikely to produce harm.

The punishment of an offender should be in accordance with utilitarian principles, ie, aimed at an increase in the sum of the community's happiness. It must be demonstrated that punishment of the individual will help to prevent a greater general pain among the community. Extravagant punishment is wasteful and should be rejected. Punishment should act as a deterrent.

Objections to Bentham's utilitarianism

The main objections to Bentham's utilitarianism include the following points:

- It is impossible to make a 'quantitative evaluation' of pain or happiness. What shall be the standards of reference ?
- Men are not always motivated solely by pleasure or pain. Motivation is a much more complex phenomenon than Bentham seems to suggest.
- The relationship between individual and communal happiness is not as direct as Bentham imagined it to be.
- Ayer makes the point that 'it is not self-contradictory to say that some pleasant things are not good or that some bad things are desired'.

Utilitarianism as a species of natural law

Bentham objected to natural law doctrine as 'nonsense on stilts'. But suggestions have been made that utilitarianism may have much in common with the outlook of natural law.

Schumpeter points out some resemblances of Bentham's doctrine and the essence of natural law:

- Utilitarianism is concerned with 'ultimate values', as is natural law. The principle of utility seems to some jurists to have about it an aura of 'universal and immutable values'.
- Utilitarianism and natural law are based on 'normative systems with a strong legal slant'.
- Utilitarianism is a comprehensive philosophy which embodies a uniform method of analysis, as is the case in natural law.

Chapter 7

Utilitarianism (2): John Stuart Mill

7.1 Mill's place in jurisprudence

John Stuart Mill (1806-73), logician, economist and philosopher, has an assured place in British jurisprudence largely as the result of his important modifications of Bentham's 'fundamentalism', and his classic enunciation of the liberal approach to the rights of the individual. It is necessary to qualify his title of 'utilitarian'. In Schumpeter's words: 'In some respects he outgrew the creed; in others he refined it. But he never renounced it explicitly'. The growing interest in utilitarianism expressed by jurists during Mill's day was due in large measure to his skill in refining, in sophisticated fashion, the approach associated with Bentham. As Mill came to understand that a severe, utilitarian rationality tended to prove deficient as an analytical tool when used outside a very limited range of problems, so he proceeded to elaborate a number of qualifications to the strict Benthamite position. In this area of activity, Mill seemed to exemplify the truth of the observation that no school of thought makes any significant advance until it feels sufficiently assured to question the tenets of its founders.

7.2 Utilitarianism restated

Mill's *Utilitarianism* (1863) draws attention to the 'backward state' in which speculation on the criteria of right and wrong remains. The utilitarian creed accepts as the foundation of morals the 'greatest happiness' principle, ie, 'that actions are right in proportion as they tend to promote happiness, wrong as they tend to produce the reverse of happiness.' But to present a clear view of the *moral* standards set up by utilitarianism 'much more requires to be said; in particular, what things it includes in the ideas of pain and pleasure; and to what extent this is left an open question'.

7.2.1 Bentham's quantitative hedonism

Bentham's 'Quantitative Hedonism' viewed pleasures as of one type only - physical or sensual. The only difference among pleasures was one of *quantity* which was measurable by the felicific calculus. 'Pushpin is as good as poetry,' Bentham said, emphasising that the only real test for 'goodness' is the amount of pleasure an act produces. A 'moral thermometer' could measure degrees of happiness or unhappiness.

7.2.2 Mill's qualitative approach

Mill sought to substitute a *qualitative approach* to the problem. Pleasures differ one from the other in kind and quality, not merely in quantity. Qualitative descriptions among pleasures might render small amounts of high-quality pleasures much more 'valuable' than large amounts of qualitatively inferior pleasures. Bentham's unqualified theory would appear to suggest that it might be better to be a happy pig than a miserable human being. Mill argues:

> 'It is better to be a human being dissatisfied than a pig satisfied; better to be a Socrates dissatisfied than a fool satisfied. And if the fool or the pig are of a different opinion, it is because they only know their own side of the question. The other party to the comparison knows both sides.'

When a *choice* has to be made between competing pleasures, the quantity of pleasure produced is of secondary importance. A person who prefers one pleasure to another is ascribing to it a superiority in quality 'so far outweighing quantity as to render it, in comparison, of small account'. It is absurd, said Mill 'that the estimation of pleasures should be supposed to depend on quantity alone'.

The *qualitative difference* between pleasures was grounded, according to Mill, in the very structure of human nature; hence the full use of one's faculties (rather than mere pleasure) was the test of true happiness and goodness. 'Few human creatures would consent to be changed into any of the lower animals for a promise of the fullest allowance of a beast's pleasures.' The qualitative value of intelligence will offset the quantitative value of base pleasures. Let pleasures be graded, not for their quantity but their quality. If this be accepted, mere pleasure ceases to be the standard of morality. It is the full employment of our *higher faculties* that will lead to our true happiness.

7.3 Altruism and Utilitarianism

Bentham believed that people should help others to achieve happiness because in so doing they would secure their own happiness, thus adding to the total happiness. Mill agreed generally to this proposition but placed emphasis upon the significance of altruism (regard for others as a principle of action). 'The happiness which forms the utilitarian standard of what is right in conduct is not the agent's own happiness, but that of all concerned.'

7.3.1 The golden rule

'As between his own happiness and others, utilitarianism requires [each one of us] to be as strictly impartial as a disinterested and benevolent spectator.' Mill is interpreting utilitarianism as demanding not one's personal optimum happiness, but that of all individuals involved with that one person.

> 'In the golden rule of Jesus, we read the complete spirit of the ethics of utility. To do as one would be done by, and to love one's neighbour as oneself, constitute the ideal of utilitarian perfection.'

7.3.2 Social and legal practices

Mill, wishing to translate general principles into social and legal practices, suggests that:

> 'laws and social arrangements should place the interest of every individual as nearly as possible in harmony with the interest of the whole; and secondly that education and opinion ... shall so use that power ... that a direct impulse to promote the general good may be in every individual one of the habitual motives of action.'

7.4 Justice and utility

Bentham was, characteristically, dismissive of the concept of 'justice': it was a 'phantom ... feigned for the convenience of discourse, whose dictates are the dictates of utility applied to particular cases'. Mill perceived justice in a different light, referring to it as implying something 'which is not only right to do, and wrong not to do, but which some individual can claim from us as his moral right'.

7.4.1 Justice as a rule of conduct

The idea of justice suggests for Mill a rule of conduct and a sentiment which sanctions the rule. The rule is common to all mankind and is intended for their good. The sentiment is a desire that those who infringe the rule ought to be punished.

Additionally, when we consider justice, we may have in mind some definite person suffering as the result of the violation of his rights.

7.4.2 The widening of justice

The sentiment of justice is based on 'the animal desire to repel or retaliate a hurt or damage to oneself, or to those with whom one sympathises'. But this should be widened so as to include all persons:

> 'by the human capacity of enlarged sympathy and the human conception of self-interest. From the latter elements, the feeling derives its morality; from the former, its peculiar impressiveness and energy of self-assertion.'

7.5 Equality and utility

Bentham had written of the need to ensure that 'everybody should count for one, nobody for more than one'. The right to *equality of treatment* was vital for society. Mill comments on the growth of ideas of equality as follows:

- All social inequalities which have ceased to be considered expedient 'assume the character not of simple inexpediency, but of injustice'. People wonder how these inequalities could ever have been tolerated.
- The entire history of social improvements is a series of transitions by which customs and institutions pass from the status of supposed primary necessities of social existence 'into the rank of a universally stigmatised injustice and tyranny'.

- This is how it has been with the distinctions of slaves and freemen, nobles and serfs. 'And so it will be ... with the aristocracies of colour, race and sex.'

7.6 Mill's concept of liberty

In his celebrated essay, *On Liberty* (1859), Mill makes a strong plea for a balance of interests between government and individual citizens. A precondition for the development of the entire range of human nature is liberty. 'What more or better can be said of any condition of human affairs than that it brings human beings themselves nearer to the best thing they can be?' Is it, then, a task of government to make every citizen the best he can be? Mill's answer embodies the essence of libertarian thought. There are limits to the right of a State to interfere in the life and conduct of a citizen. His own good, either physical or moral, is not a sufficient warrant. Liberty emerges from no 'natural law'; rather ought it to be perceived as a relationship between justice and the principle of utility.

7.7 Liberty and compulsion

There is but one purpose, according to Mill, which justifies a State in seeking rightfully to exercise power over a citizen against his will: this is the prevention of harm to others. Let the citizen do as he wishes even though his physical or moral good be adversely affected. A government has no right to compel a citizen 'to do or forebear' merely because it is 'better for him' to do so or because his happiness will be increased thereby.

7.7.1 Limit to compulsion

One may remonstrate or reason with the citizen. But he must not be forced to act in a particular way. He is not accountable to society for his actions 'in so far as these concern the interests of no person but himself'. Advice and instruction may be offered in such a case so as to express society's dislike of his conduct. But no more than that.

7.7.2 Accountability of the citizen

The citizen is, however, accountable for any actions that are prejudicial to the interests of others, and he may be subjected to social or legal punishment if society feels this to be necessary for its protection. To justify interference by the State, 'the conduct from which it is desired to deter him must be calculated to produce evil to someone else'. The only part of the conduct of a person for which he is answerable to society is that which concerns others. In the part which merely concerns himself, his independence is 'of right' absolute. *'Over himself, over his own body and mind, the individual is sovereign.'*

> 'It is proper to state that I forgo any advantage which could be derived to my argument from the idea of abstract right, as a thing independent of utility. I regard utility as the ultimate appeal on all ethical questions; but it must be utility in the largest sense, grounded on the permanent

> interests of man as a progressive being. Those interests, I contend, authorise the subjection of individual spontaneity to external control, only in respect to those actions of each,which concern the interest of other people ...'

It is essential to remember the permanent interests of man 'as a progressive being'. It is these interests which authorise the subjection of man's individual spontaneity to external control only in respect of the actions of the individual which concern the interests of others.

7.8 The appropriate region of human liberty

'Liberty' implies for Mill liberty of conscience in the most comprehensive sense, liberty of thought and feeling, absolute freedom of opinion 'on all subjects, practical or speculative, scientific, moral or theological', liberty of expression and publication, liberty of tastes and pursuits, liberty to unite for any purpose not involving harm to others. A society in which these liberties are not generally respected is not free; no society is completely free unless these liberties exist 'absolute and unqualified'. Two vital precepts in this context are formulated by Mill.

7.8.1 Pursuit of one's own good

The only freedom deserving of the name is that of pursuing one's own good in one's own way, provided that others are not deprived thereby of their freedoms.

7.8.2 Self-guardianship

Each person is the proper guardian of his own health, whether bodily or mental or spiritual. No one has the right to say to another human creature of ripe years 'that he shall not do with his life what he chooses'.

7.9 Freedom of expression

Arguing in terms which have been used as points of reference by many jurists and legislators in recent years, Mill asks for complete freedom to express one's opinions except 'when the circumstances in which they are expressed are such as to constitute their expression a positive instigation to some mischievous deed'. (It is of interest to interpret the Public Order Act 1986, s 18, in the light of Mill's comments.)

7.9.1 Essence of free expression

Mill is emphatic: if all mankind minus one are of one opinion, there is no more justification in silencing that one person than he would be justified in silencing the rest of mankind. Who can measure, asks Mill, what the world loses if it is deprived of 'the clearer perception and livelier impression of truth produced by its collision with error'

7.9.2 Case for freedom of opinion

The case for freedom of opinion and the expression of that opinion rests, according to Mill's analysis on four grounds:

- An opinion which is silenced may, for all we know, be true. If we deny this we assume that we are infallible.
- A silenced opinion may contain a portion of truth. Since the generally accepted opinion on any subject is never (or very rarely) the entire truth, it is only 'by the collision of adverse opinions' that the remainder of the truth might be discovered.
- Unless a received truth is contested vigorously by its opponents it will be held as mere prejudice with little understanding of its rational grounds.
- In the absence of argument, a doctrine is in danger of becoming enfeebled and degenerating into dogma, preventing the growth of conviction from reason or personal experience.

Where the expression of opinion takes the form of acting upon that opinion, men must be left free to do so without any physical or moral hindrance, provided that it is at their own risk and that others do not suffer in any way as a result. There ought to be a variety of experiments in living, allowing the advantages of differing modes of existence to be properly investigated.

7.10 The rightful limits to society's authority

Mill poses a fundamental question: 'How much of human life ought to be assigned to individuality, and how much to society?' His answer is as follows:

- To the individual should belong that part of his life in which he is interested; to society, the part which chiefly interests it.
- Society is founded upon no 'contract' and there is no advantage to be derived from inventing one in order to provide a myth from which man's social obligations might be deduced. Those who enjoy the protection of society owe a return for benefits received. That return includes the obligation 'to observe a certain line of conduct toward the rest'. Not to ignore the interests of another, and to bear one's share of the labours and sacrifices found necessary to defend society and its members from injury and molestation, are duties which society is justified in enforcing at all costs.
- If a citizen offends by acts which hurt others but which do not violate constituted rights, society may punish by opinion, though not by law.
- Where a citizen's conduct affects prejudicially the interests of others, society has jurisdiction over it.

- This is not to say that citizens ought not to be concerned with one another's activities. There is, indeed, need of 'a great increase of disinterested exertion to promote the good of others'. 'But disinterested benevolence can find other instruments to persuade people to do good than whips and scourges, either of the literal or metaphorical sort ...'

7.11 Governmental policy

Mill suggests that, given the legitimate role which government might play in the lives of citizens, three principles ought to be considered carefully by legislators.

7.11.1 Encouraging self-development

Legislators ought to examine whether the proposed course of action might be undertaken better by individuals than by the government and its servants. Those who are personally interested in the performance of a task should have the opportunity of assisting in the determination of how and by whom an undertaking ought to be conducted.

Legislators ought to consider whether the social development and responsibilities of citizens could be intensified by their being involved in government projects.

7.11.2 Danger of bureaucracy

Legislators ought to consider whether or not their interference will result in the growth of a bureaucracy. For Mill – and this point constitutes the final paragraph of *On Liberty* – the worth of a State is, in the long run, the worth of the citizens composing it, and a State which dwarfs its citizens in order that they may be more docile tools, even for beneficial purposes, will find that '*with small men no great thing can really be accomplished*'.

7.12 Stephen's criticism of Mill

Liberty, Equality and Fraternity (1873), by James Fitzjames Stephen, Queen's Bench judge and jurist, constitutes a fundamental attack on Mill's arguments in favour of liberty of the individual. At the basis of Stephen's jurisprudential philosophy are the beliefs that the interests of human beings are necessarily in conflict, so that they will have different perceptions of what is meant by 'the good', that the social order requires the restraining effects of religion, morality and law, that liberty is of value only insofar as it contributes to the totality of society's well-being. 'Ordered liberty under the law' is Stephen's goal for society.

Mill, according to Stephen, failed to understand that 'the human condition' is much too complex for the acceptance of Mill's concept of liberty. That concept would involve, in practice, an absence of restraint which would result in the weakening of social cohesion, since liberty which is not backed by the sanctions of communal opinion would develop into little more than licence. Above all, perhaps, the application in practice of Mill's ideas on liberty would result in the subversion of morality because (in the words of Stuart Warner),'morality is instantiated through the coercive opinions of others'.

Stephen seeks to reduce Mill's theory of liberty to its simplest elements. He produces the following summary: 'On the one hand, we have the external world, which in its relation to men may be regarded as a mass of the materials of happiness. On the other, an enormous number of human creatures substantially equal, substantially alike, substantially animated by the same ideas and impulses. Divide the materials of happiness equally between them, and let them do as they like. They will live in peace and collectively increase each other's happiness to an indefinite or indefinitely increasing extent ...'. Such a view of the world seems to Stephen to be totally untenable. Supporters of Mill would condemn the summary as a gross caricature of Mill's principles which he did not present in over-simplified terms, and which are almost invariably based upon a careful analysis of and concern for the human condition. (Note the Hart-Devlin debate at Chapter 22, which has overtones of the Mill-Stephen controversy.)

Summary of Chapter 7

Utilitarianism (2): John Stuart Mill

Bentham's utilitarianism revised

Mill urged greater enquiry concerning ideas of pain and pleasure as used in Bentham's statement of utilitarian philosophy.

Mill denied the possibility of a 'moral thermometer' by which degrees of happiness or pain might be measured and compared. Pleasures and pains differ from one another in kind and quality.

Where choices are made among competing pleasures, those choices may depend on something other than mere estimates of the quantities of likely pleasures.

It is the full employment of our higher faculties that will bring true happiness. Mere pleasure can never act as a standard of morality.

Altruism may be a significant principle of action in some individuals.

Justice and utility

Justice, for Mill, was not to be dismissed, in Bentham's phrase, as a 'mere phantom'. It gives rise to moral rights and rules of conduct common to all mankind and designed for the good of individuals.

Justice moves beyond mere considerations of utility; it is concerned with matters such as sympathy and self-interest.

Liberty and compulsion

In his essay, *On Liberty* (1859), Mill argues for liberty as an expression of a balance of individual and government interests. There are limits to the right of a government to interfere with an individual's conduct.

The argument that the government has a right to interfere with the individual in his own interests is not acceptable.

One may argue or remonstrate with a citizen – but no more than that. This is a general suggestion, to which there are exceptions.

Where a citizen's course of action is likely to produce evil for others, the government has the right – even the duty – to intervene.

Freedom of expression

There is no justification in depriving an individual of his right to self-expression. An opinion which is silenced may, in fact, be true, or may contain a proportion of truth. Silencing an opinion will result in doctrine degenerating into mere dogma.

But where the expression of opinion instigates mischief, society may be right to prevent such expression.

Society's authority over the individual

Society is not founded upon any 'contract', but those who derive benefit from membership of society have social obligations which include the bearing of one's share of necessary labours and sacrifices. Society has the authority to ensure that these obligations are carried out.

To act to the prejudice of others cannot be tolerated by society in general.

Persuasion is to be preferred to 'whips and scourges, either of the literal or metaphorical sort'. But, in the final analysis, society, acting through government and its legal organs, must intervene where injury to others is likely to attend an individual's failure to observe a duty.

Criticism of Mill

Stephen, judge and jurist, criticised Mill for building his arguments concerning liberty upon a failure to take into account the inevitable conflicts among individuals and the necessity for restraint and order within communities.

Chapter 8

Legal Positivism

8.1 The choice

Fuller's *The Law in Quest of Itself* (1940) contains an exposition of the claims of legal positivism and natural law and suggests that for all persons associated with the law there is a choice to be made between these opposing and competing doctrines of legal thought. Natural law is described as 'denying the possibility of a rigid separation of "is" and "ought", and tolerating a confusion of them in legal discussion'. Legal positivism is described as 'that direction of legal thought which insists on drawing a sharp distinction between "the law that is" and "the law that ought to be"'. Jurisprudential thought remains largely polarised in this area; bridges have been fabricated, but, in general, adherents of the two schools remain far apart. Fuller, a vigorous opponent of legal positivism, believes that it is vital that a choice be made, particularly in view of his contention that the positivists have lost sight of the very purposes of positivism (thereby falling into the error described by Nietzsche as 'the commonest stupidity' of forgetting what one set out to do).

8.2 Use of the term 'legal positivism'

In *The Concept of Law* (1961), Hart (see Chapter 11) enumerates five common usages of the word 'positivism' in Anglo-American jurisprudence:

- To describe the concept of law favoured by Austin and Bentham (see Chapters 6, 10) in which laws are perceived as the commands of superiors.
- To explain the view, as propounded by Kelsen (see Chapter 12) and others that there is no necessary link between morals and the law.
- To name the idea of analysis or study of meanings of legal concepts.
- To denote the view of a legal system as a 'closed logical system' in which decisions from pre-determined legal rules are made by logical means.
- To suggest the theory that moral judgments cannot be established, as can statements of fact, by any type of rational argument, or evidence or other proof.

For purposes of this chapter, legal positivism is considered as a view of law which takes into account *the positive law only*, ie, the judicial norms established by the authority of the State, to the total exclusion of any concept of law as transcending the empirical reality of the existing legal system.

8.3 Antecedents of legal positivism

The word 'positive', as used in jurisprudence, is derived from *positum*, the past participle of *ponere = to put*. It refers to that which is formally laid down, or affirmed by man. Thus, Abelard (1079-1142) wrote of 'positive law' as that instituted by men 'for their honour or use'.

8.3.1 Philosophical positivism: the early empiricists

Sextus Empiricus (c 200 AD) taught that the laws of society were neither transcendent nor metaphysical: they were based on the facts of experience. The observation of phenomena could provide the basis for scientific investigation. Empiricism grew as a doctrine, holding that all knowledge of fact must be validated in sense experience or be inferred from propositions derived unambiguously from sense data. This doctrine stands in total opposition to metaphysics (described by Jaspers as 'contemplation of the whole (the totality) and the absolute (the ultimate reality)').

8.3.2 Locke and Berkeley

Locke (see Chapter 3) and Berkeley (1685-1753) taught the significance of interpreting reality through the senses. For Locke, the ultimate source of all ideas was sensation. Berkeley stressed that nature could only be perceived and analysed by man through his senses.

8.4 Hume and Comte

Hume (1711-1776) and Comte (1798-1857) rejected metaphysics completely. Their teachings paved the way for a systematic version of a positivist approach to problems of comprehension and analysis, which would be mirrored in the concepts of legal positivism.

8.4.1 Hume: the significance of sense impressions

Knowledge originated, according to Hume, solely in our sense impressions; what uniformity might be discovered in our perceptual experience is derived from the mind's 'associating qualities'. Our belief in cause and effect stems solely from our mental habits which are the product of repeated connections in the mind. The notion of cause and effect is the fundamental element in knowledge. Metaphysical explanations of reality which lack reasoning concerning quantity or number, or experimental reasoning concerning matters of fact and existence, are 'nothing but sophistry and illusion'.

> 'All the objects of human reason or enquiry may naturally be divided into two kinds, to whit, relations of ideas and matters of fact. Of the first kind are the sciences of geometry, algebra, and arithmetic, and, in short, every affirmation which is either intuitively or demonstratively certain ... Propositions of this kind are discoverable by the

mere operation of thought, without dependence on what is anywhere existent in the universe ... Matters of fact are not ascertained in the same manner, nor is our evidence of their truth, however great, of a like nature. The contrary of every matter is still possible, because it can never imply a contradiction ... All reasonings concerning matters of fact seem to be founded on the relation of cause and effect.'

8.4.2 Comte: the law of the three stages

The evolution of human thinking comprised, according to Comte, a movement in three stages. The *first*, 'theological', stage was characterised by explanations of phenomena couched in supernatural terms. The *second*, 'metaphysical', stage concentrated upon 'ultimate ideas and principles' as the explanation of reality. The *third*, and final, stage will involve a 'positivist approach' to reality and the discovery of systematic laws. *A priori* speculation (ie, that which is logically independent of experience) will be abandoned; knowledge will be acquired solely through scientific method based on observation.

'In the positive stage, the human mind, recognising the possibility of arriving at absolute notions, renounces the quest for the origin and destiny of the universe, and the attempt to know the underlying causes of phenomena, and devotes itself to discovering, by means of a judicious combination of reason and observation, their actual laws, that is, their invariable relations of succession and similitude. The explanation of facts, thus reduced to their real terms, is henceforth nothing but the relation established between the various particular phenomena and a few general truths whose number the advances of science tend increasingly to diminish' (*Cours de philosophie positive* (1839-45)).

8.5 Logical positivism

Based upon the work of philosophers, such as Carnap and Ayer, this doctrine supplied an important component of legal positivism, as evident in the writings of Hart. Propositions and the use of words must be examined if reality is to be understood. A sentence has literal significance if, and only if, it expresses something which is either tautologous or empirically verifiable. 'A contract is characterised by *consensus ad idem* and the desire to create legal relations' is, in this sense, tautologous. 'Parliament can only commence its deliberations at the time appointed by the Queen' is an *empirically verifiable statement*. 'The phenomenon of contract represents an advance in Western civilisation', is a 'metaphysical assertion' which does not satisfy the criteria of meaning set out by the logical positivists.

8.6 The essence of legal positivism

This doctrine carries within its principles and methodology many of the views favoured by the philosophical and logical positivists. It is, essentially, an aspect of analytical jurisprudence: it examines particular legal orders and generally utilises in its investigations the inductive method (ie, proceeding from observation of particular facts to generalisations concerning all such facts). It eschews, during its investigations, matters of ethics, social policies and morality. In Stone's words, it is concerned primarily with 'an analysis of legal terms, and an enquiry into the logical interrelations of legal propositions'. The search for 'ultimate values' is rejected. Law is seen as source-based, ie, the validity of legal norms is held to be derived from sources determined by the community's rules and conventions.

8.6.1 The rejection of metaphysics

Logical positivism involves a deliberate attempt to demonstrate the worthlessness of metaphysics, ie, those attempts to interpret the nature of reality in terms beyond the physical or experiential. Metaphysical statements, by their nature and mode of expression, are cognitively meaningless, and metaphysical speculation is mere 'pseudo-speculation'. 'Metaphysicians ... believe that their sentences assert something, represent some state of affairs. Nevertheless, analysis shows that these sentences do not say anything, being instead only expressions of some emotional attitude': Carnap. The object of all philosophy, according to the logical positivists, is the logical classification of thoughts. In principle, all knowledge can be expressed in statements of science.

8.6.2 The principle of verifiablity

It is of the essence of logical positivism that to understand a proposition is to know *what would be the case in circumstances in which the proposition were true*. One knows what one 'means' by assertion *A* as long as one knows how to discover whether *A* is true. Hence if there exists no procedure for verifying *A*, it is a 'meaningless' statement. (Students might wish to apply the 'principle of verifiability' to the following statements: (a) 'There are 30 women only among a total of 510 circuit judges'; (b) 'Discrimination on grounds of gender appears to characterise appointments to the bench'; (c) 'Prejudiced attitudes may often constitute unconscious motives in those recommending appointments to the judiciary'.)

8.7 Methodology

The positivist approach necessitates an objective investigation of the structure of the legal order so as to reveal its foundation. Functions are studied, analysed and classified and legal concepts are constructed. Hence, the legal positivist seeks to answer questions, such as: What is the law? What are its sources? What are its functions in a given society? What is the function of terms such as 'ownership', 'possession', in legal discourse? This approach determines the mode of investigation - clear delineation of the boundaries of enquiry and a concentration upon objective reality.

8.8 The exclusion of value considerations

In Kelsen's words: 'The concept of law has no moral connotations whatsoever'. The positivist must set aside values and similar considerations during his investigation of law. A social statistician, for example, investigating the incidence of homelessness within a community must confine himself strictly to his terms of reference, leaving others to consider whatever moral issues may be involved. The jurist should act in a similar fashion.

8.8.1 Holmes' view

Holmes (1841-1935) (see Chapter 18) illustrates in graphic style, in *The Path of the Law* (1897), the essence of the positivist approach: 'You see how the vague circumference of the notion of "duty" shrinks and at the same time grows more precise when we wash it with cynical acid and expel everything except the object of our study, the operations of the law'. To understand, say, the legal concept of 'duty', demands concentration upon its essence and the removal of all 'contaminating irrelevancies'. The moral significance of 'duty' is, for Holmes, irrelevant to a consideration of its 'true meaning'.

This is not to suggest in any way that the legal positivist is uninterested in moral problems: this is demonstrably not so. Legal positivism calls for a study of *essential features* only and a relegation of other matters to specialists, such as political scientists.

8.9 Positive law and 'the law'

It is of the essence of legal positivism that positive law alone is considered to be 'the law'. The judicial norms laid down by the State, case law, statute, regulations and other orders, constitute the basic material which is the foundation of juristic enquiry. The legal positivist will be aware of, but will ignore in principled fashion, questions of what the law *ought* to be.

8.10 'Is' and 'ought'

Legal positivism follows Hume and his successors in declaring: 'One cannot deduce validly "ought" from "is".' Normative statements cannot be inferred validly from merely factual statements. The very term 'ought' is not free from difficulties of interpretation arising from ambiguity. Consider its 'meaning' in statements such as: 'You *ought* not to steal'; 'If you kick this ball it *ought* to move'; 'Those who drive dangerously *ought* to be punished according to law.' (Carnap, a founder of the logical positivist movement, stated in an argument which was to achieve notoriety: 'From the statement "killing is evil' we cannot deduce any proposition about future experiences. Thus the statement is not verifiable and has no theoretical sense, and the same is true of all other value-statements'.)

8.11 Legal positivism exemplified

The influence of legal positivist doctrine may be noted in the arguments of the following jurists.

8.11.1 Austin

Austin (see Chapter 10) in his *The Province of Jurisprudence Determined* (1832):

> 'The existence of law is one thing: its merit or demerit is another. Whether it be or be not is one enquiry; whether it be or be not conformable to an assumed standard, is a different enquiry. This truth when formally announced as an abstract proposition is so simple and glaring that it seems idle to insist upon it.'

8.11.2 Kelsen

Kelsen (see Chapter 12) in his *The General Theory of Law and State* (1945):

> 'Pure theory of law' is so-called 'because it only describes the law and attempts to eliminate from the object of the description everything that is not strictly law: its aim is to free the science of law from alien elements.'

8.11.3 Hart

Hart (see Chapter 11) in his *The Concept of Law* (1961):

> 'The lawyer will regard this book as an essay in analytical jurisprudence, for it is concerned with the clarification of the general framework of legal thought, rather than with the criticism of law or legal policy.'

8.12 Some general criticisms of legal positivism

The doctrine of legal positivism has been attacked from all sides. For some jurists it is a mere embodiment of gross error. Indeed, Adler (see Chapter 4) sees as an essential task for jurisprudence the demolition of positivism as a legal philosophy so as 'to win the moral sceptic to the path of reason'. Fuller suggests that the doctrine is responsible for erecting barriers which have retarded man's reason. The Humean foundations of positivism have been denounced as false, so that legal positivism is considered by many to be flawed basically.

8.12.1 A mere search for facts

The positivist approach is condemned as a mere search for facts without any unifying frame of reference. The positivist reply stresses that the search for facts is guided by the motive of classification and interpretation in order that general, even universal, concepts might emerge. Without a basis of facts there can be no valid analysis of the legal concepts which should form the basis of disputation.

8.12.2 The exclusion of the wider context of law is fatal

Law, argue the critics, can exist only within a wider social setting. It is a product of history, inextricably intertwined with man's social needs, and reflecting social and religious *mores*. 'Law is a product of human effort, and we risk absurdity if we try to describe it in disregard of what those who brought it into being were trying to do': Fuller, in *Anatomy of the Law* (1967). What is the value of a positivist analysis of, say, the Children Act 1989 or the Sunday Trading Act 1994, without a consideration of the community's aims which produced this legislation? Fuller:

> 'We must be sufficiently capable of putting ourselves in the position of those who drafted a rule to know what they thought "ought to be". It is in the light of this "ought" that we must decide what the rule is.'

The positivist reply is that man's history and society's aspirations are of great importance, but their consideration belongs to the realm of investigation by the historian and the social scientist. Only when law is freed, for purposes of enquiry, from its context does fundamental examination become possible.

8.12.3 'Ought' in the law should not be ignored

The dictates of an absolute morality often bind and guide communities. It is because communities may share a deep concern for values that societies are coherent units, and legislation reflects that cohesion. Positivists reply by accepting the significance of 'ought', but stress that there are no *absolute standards* of morality. Standards change: consider, for example, variations in social (and legal) attitudes to incest, suicide, homosexuality. Investigation of the so-called 'absolute of the ought' is not always possible.

8.12.4 Justice downgraded

It is the 'justice downgraded' reproach which is levelled continuously against the legal positivists. The arbitrary division of law and morality, of law and concepts of 'right' and 'justice', can lead, it is argued, to acceptance of evil. If justice be relative, how important should it be in the affairs of mankind? Is it coincidence that the downgrading of justice as a concept ('bourgeois nonsense', 'liberal decadence') has accompanied the rise of totalitarian regimes? The positivist reply is firm.

8.13 The positivist reply

Positivists do not advocate the acceptance of evil or injustice any more than, say, econometricians, in their study of the labour market, accept the evil of unemployment.

Separation of the concept of justice from other phenomena in an investigation of law does not lead in any way to a rejection of its significance. In the event, many positivist jurists have played an important role in the history of social and political progress. Bentham's work in the field of social progress is of historical significance. John Stuart Mill's powerful advocacy of liberty, women's rights, and constitutional reform, is well-known. (Nor is it correct to suggest by implication that the opponents of positivism are, invariably, supporters of liberty and justice. Del Vecchio's apologia for Italian fascism is an example of natural-law doctrine, reduced to narrow certainties, placed at the service of despotism.)

8.14 A comment on the contribution of legal positivism to jurisprudence

The following points have been made.

Positivism has stressed the *autonomy of the law*, with the result that jurisprudence may be studied to advantage as a subject in its own right and not necessarily as an aspect of a 'wider sociology'.

Positivism has emphasised rati*onal investigation*. It calls for a utilisation of the methodology of the social sciences and argues for the application of logical thought and empirical investigation in the pursuit of answers to general problems of law within society.

Summary of Chapter 8

Legal Positivism

Usages of the term 'positivism'

The word is derived from *ponere, positum* = to put. 'Positive law' is that which is man-made, ie, formally laid down.

Hart, in *The Concept of Law* (1961), enumerates the following common usages of the term as applied to law:

- To describe the idea of law as a command of a superior (as favoured in the explanations of law by, eg, Austin and Bentham).
- To describe the view that there is no necessary link between law and morals.
- To name the idea of analysis of legal concepts.
- To denote the concept of a legal system as a closed logical system.
- To denote the theory that moral judgments cannot be derived from rational argument as such.

The term is used in this book to indicate a view of law as comprising the positive law *only* to the total exclusion of those concepts of law based upon transcending the empirical reality of the legal system.

Background

The early philosophical positivists, such as Hume and Comte, rejected metaphysics, believing that explanations lacking reasoning related to number or experimental conclusions were mere illusion. The discovery of systematic laws was the aim of enquiry.

The logical positivists, such as Carnap and Ayer, examined the problems of language. Sentences had literal significance if and only if they expressed that which was tautologous or empirically verifiable. Metaphysical assertions were meaningless.

Methodology of legal positivism

Legal positivism involves an analytical and objective approach to the legal order, its structure and functions.

Value considerations, 'contaminating irrelevancies', are removed from the process of investigation of the legal order.

'Ought' cannot be deduced from 'is', so that normative statements may not be inferred validly from merely factual statements.

Thus:

- Austin writes: 'The existence of law is one thing: its merit or demerit is another.'
- Kelsen sees as his aim in investigation, 'the freeing of the science of law from alien elements'.
- Hart stresses the essence of analytical jurisprudence as concerned with 'the clarification of the general framework of legal thought, rather than with the criticism of law or legal policy'.

Some criticisms of legal positivism

Legal positivism, it has been argued, is concerned merely with a search for facts and lacks any unifying frame of reference.

To exclude the wider context of law in any investigation of the nature of law is to disregard the very aims of those who brought the law into existence.

To ignore 'ought' in the context of the law is to ignore the motivation of much legislation. The result is an inadequate picture of the essence of the law.

Legal positivism results in the downgrading of the 'ideal' and the concept of justice.

The contribution of legal positivism to jurisprudence

Positivism has emphasised the autonomy of the law and stressed the importance of a study of law as a subject in its own right.

Positivism has pointed to the need for rational investigation of legal phenomena.

Chapter 9

The Hart-Fuller Debate

9.1 Occasion of the debate

A discussion, which began in the late 1950s between Hart and Fuller, highlights some of the fundamental differences between the legal positivists and advocates of natural law. Essays by Hart and Fuller, which appeared in the Harvard Law Review 1958, set out their reactions to certain events in Germany following the end of the Second World War, which appeared to revive the question of the links between law and morality. Fuller took the general view that *law and morality must not be separated* and that a law which is totally divorced from morality ceases to be 'law'. Hart insisted that *the law is the law* even though it may not satisfy the demands of morality.

9.2 Background to the debate (1): German law during the era of dictatorship

Law under the National-Socialist régime in Germany (1933-45) was put totally to the service of the dictatorship. The German Criminal Code was amended in 1935 so as to introduce the concept of 'healthy popular feeling' as a factor in the determination of 'criminality'. Punishment could be inflicted:

> 'on any person who commits an act declared by the law to be punishable, or which, in the light of the basic purpose of the criminal law and according to healthy popular feeling, deserves to be punished. If there is no specific criminal law applying directly to such an act, it is to be punished according to whatever law in its basic purpose best applies to it.'

In similar vein, a regulation of 1936 effectively placed the German secret police above the law: no court was permitted to interfere with that organisation's operations. The result was that law became the willing servant of a tyranny.

9.3 Background to the debate (2): German law during the post-war period

The defeat of Germany in 1945 led to a vigorous effort on the part of German jurists and others to rid the legal system of its associations with the dictatorship. Its structure was dismantled and a deliberate attempt was made to encourage modes of legal thought based on the concept of 'overriding justice'. The 'conversion' of the German jurist, Radbruch (see Chapter 5), which appeared to involve a shift in his thought from relativism to natural law, had a considerable effect upon German jurisprudence. He wrote:

> 'Preference should be given to the rule of positive law, supported as it is by due enactment and State power, even when the rule is unjust and contrary to the general welfare, unless the violation of justice reaches so

> intolerable a degree that the rule becomes "lawless law" and must therefore yield to justice.'

9.4 The case of the wife-informer

Hart drew attention to the prosecution in 1949 of a German woman by a West German court on a charge (under the German Criminal Code of 1871) of 'depriving a person illegally of his freedom'. It was alleged that during the war she had denounced her husband, in pursuance of a personal grudge, under a statute of 1934, for having criticised Hitler's conduct of the war. The husband was tried under laws of 1934 and 1938 and sentenced to death, that sentence being commuted to service on the Russian front. The wife's defence was the 'legality' of her action; her husband's behaviour had contravened a law which was valid at the time of the denunciation. She was found guilty, the court stating that the statute under which her husband had been sentenced was 'contrary to the sound conscience and sense of justice of all decent human beings'. (It should be noted that there is a dispute as to the precise facts of the case: see *Validity of Judicial Decisions* by Pappe (23 MLR 260). But the dispute does not alter the essence of the debate.)

For a consideration by the House of Lords of Nazi race laws, see *Oppenheimer v Cattermole* (1976), in which Lord Cross noted that 'legislation which takes away without compensation from a section of the citizen body singled out on racial grounds all their property ... and deprives them of their citizenship ... constitutes so grave an infringement of human rights that the courts of this country ought to refuse to recognise it as a law at all.'

9.5 Hart opens the debate

The German court's decision was interpreted by Hart (writing in 1958) as favouring natural law doctrine and as opposing positivism. He took issue with Radbruch's new stance and its effect upon German legal thought.

Hart sympathised with Radbruch's support for a revision of German attitudes concerning the relationship between State power and law.

9.5.1 The law is the law

Hart insisted, however, that *the law is the law*, and that it remains law even though it might not meet the demands of external moral criteria. If a law be considered so evil that it ought not to be obeyed, this is a separate, though worthy and relevant, issue. In *Positivism and The Separation of Law and Morals* (1958), he wrote:

> 'This is a moral condemnation which everyone can understand and it makes an immediate and obvious claim to moral attention. If, on the other hand, we formulate our

objection as an assertion that these evil things are not law, here is an assertion which many people do not believe, and if they are disposed to consider it at all, it would seem to raise a whole host of philosophical attitudes before it can be accepted.'

He criticises Radbruch in uncompromising terms:

'It is not, I think, uncharitable to say that we can see in [Radbruch's] argument that he has only half digested the spiritual message of liberalism which he is seeking to convey to the legal profession. For everything that he says is really dependent upon an enormous overvaluation of the importance of the bare fact that a rule may be said to be a valid rule of law, as if this, once declared, was conclusive of the final moral question: "Ought this rule of law to be obeyed?" ... Law is not morality; do not let it supplant morality.'

When we have the ample resources of plain speech, said Hart, we must not present the moral criticisms of institutions as propositions of a 'disputable philosophy'.

9.5.2 A confusion of the real issue

It must be stressed that Hart is not showing any sympathy whatsoever with Nazi law of the 1930s. (He refers in the 1958 article to Nazi Germany as 'a Hell created on earth by men for other men.') He is pointing out that the advocates of natural law appear to be confusing the real issue. The 1934 statute was a valid law, and it is not possible to deny this. Its inherent evil, and how one ought to react to this, are separate – but very important – issues. It is confusing to say of a law that, because it rests on a stratum of evil and results in atrocities, it is not, therefore, a law.

9.6 Fuller's response

Fuller insists that the attitude of the German post-war court was absolutely correct, and that Hart is in error. His argument, set out in *Positivism and Fidelity to Law – A Reply to Professor Hart* (1958), is couched in emphatic terms.

9.6.1 The necessity of inner morality of law

Law must possess certain characteristics if it is to be classified correctly as 'law'; the most important characteristic is 'inner morality' which must command respect. Where there is no such morality in an enactment there is no law. The 'tinsel of the legal form' with which the Nazis sought to disguise evil required to be analysed for what it really was.

Hart failed to realise, according to Fuller, that under the Nazi regime, *nothing* existed to which the title of 'law' might be applied correctly.

9.6.2 Lawlessness exemplified

Fuller saw the essence of the lawlessness of the dictatorship exemplified in the retroactive decree by which Hitler validated the execution without trial, in 1934, of a group of dissident party members. The total indifference to human rights and civilised conduct, which was characteristic of this incident, destroyed any claim that there was a legal regime, as such, in Germany at the time. Hart appears to ignore the inherent inability of the Nazi regime to provide the bare essentials of what might be recognised as a legal system.

9.6.3 Positivism basically flawed

Fuller widens the attack and argues against the basic theory of positivism:

> 'I do not think it is unfair to the positivistic philosophy to say that it never gives any coherent meaning to the moral obligation of fidelity to law ... The fundamental postulate of positivism - that law must be strictly severed from morality – seems to deny the possibility of any bridge between the obligation to obey law and other moral obligations.'
>
> 'As we seek order, we can meaningfully remind ourselves that order itself will do us no good unless it is good for something. As we seek to make our order good, we can remind ourselves that justice itself is impossible without order, and that we must not lose order itself in the attempt to make it good.'

9.7 Hart's reply

Hart's *The Concept of Law* (1961) contained a reaffirmation of his stance. It may be that a legal system ought to show some conformity with justice or morality; but it does not follow that a criterion of legal validity must include, expressly or by implication, any reference to justice or morality.

9.7.1 Law and morality not interchangeable terms

Law and morality are *not* interchangeable terms. A rule of law may be morally iniquitous, but it is still law; one may not impugn its validity solely on the ground of its lack of morality.

The German court was confronted with the question: 'Ought we to punish those who did evil things when they were permitted by evil rules then in force?' Within this question may be discerned different problems (of morality and justice) and they do require consideration independently of each other. Hart insists that the problems cannot be solved by a once-for-all refusal to recognise an evil law as 'valid' for any purpose. 'This is too crude a way with delicate and complex moral issues.'

9.7.2 Choice between evils

In a general response to Fuller's comments on positivism Hart states:

> 'At least it can be claimed for the simple positivist doctrine that morally iniquitous rules may still be law, that this offers no disguise for the choice between evils which, in extreme circumstances, may have to be made.'

9.8 The minimum content of natural law

In the chapter on 'Law and Morals' (in *The Concept of Law*) Hart concedes that there are 'certain rules of conduct which any social organisation must contain if it is to be viable'; further, such rules may be considered as constituting a common universal element in law within societies. The 'human condition' suggests certain basic characteristics which necessitate the creation of rules so as to protect persons and property and to insist upon the keeping of promises.

- Human vulnerability

  We are occasionally prone to, and normally vulnerable to, bodily attack. The use of violence must, therefore, be restricted.

- Approximate equality

  This makes obvious 'the necessity for a system of mutual forbearance and compromises which is at the base of both legal and moral obligation'.

- Limited altruism

  'Human altruism is limited in range and intermittent, and the tendencies to aggression are frequent enough to be fatal to social life if not controlled.'

- Limited resources

  We need food, clothes and shelter, but they are scarce. A minimal form of the institution of property 'and the distinctive kind of rule which requires respect for it' are needed.

- Limited understanding and strength of will

  Sanctions are required as a guarantee that persons who would usually obey rules must not be sacrificed to those who will not. 'What reason demands is voluntary co-operation in a coercive system.'

9.8.1 Core of good sense in natural law

These are 'simple truisms' which disclose 'the core of good sense in the doctrine of natural law'. It is upon their recognition and understanding that human beings and the world they inhabit will retain their 'salient characteristics'.

9.9 Fuller's response

In *The Morality of Law* (1963), Fuller intensified and expanded his attack on Hart's position. In the book he gives a detailed exposition of the 'morality' which must characterise an acceptable legal system. It is important to note that in spite of Fuller's concern for morality, he does not personally accept all the doctrines associated with classical natural law. He rejects the Christian approach to natural law, does not accept concepts of 'absolute values' and 'natural rights', and places no value on the religious interpretation of 'nature as the grand legislator'. Fuller's espousal of natural law reflects his basic belief that law is a collaborative effort to aid in the satisfying of mankind's common needs. Each rule of law has a purpose related to the realisation of a value of the legal order. 'Purpose' and 'values' are closely connected and a purpose may be considered as 'at once a fact and a standard for judging facts'. There is no dualism of 'is' and 'ought'.

9.9.1 The governance of rules

A legal system must be instrumental in 'the enterprise of subjecting human conduct to the governance of rules'. Such a system's 'external morality' is a morality of 'aspirations and ideals'; an aspiration to legality is one of its aspects. It is the 'internal morality' - 'a procedural version of natural law' - which is, for Fuller, of great significance as a test of 'the lawfulness of law'.

9.10 The 'internal morality' of law

Eight qualities which, according to Fuller, must be present in a legal system if it is to deserve to command allegiance from citizens, are enumerated as follows:

- Laws must be in existence: they must not 'exist' merely as *ad hoc* settlements of disputes.
- Laws must be promulgated publicly: they must be made known to persons who will be bound by them.
- Laws must not be retroactive: they must not affect adversely persons who relied upon the law as it was.
- Laws must be intelligible and clear.
- Laws must be internally consistent through time, ie, they must not change so that citizens are unable to orient their actions by them.
- Laws must be free from contradictions.
- Laws must not require the impossible.
- Laws must be administered so that there is no failure of congruence between the rules as promulgated and their administration in practice.

9.10.1 Criticism of Fuller's desiderata

Some critics, such as Friedmann, have noted that, in fact, Fuller's desiderata could have been used to 'approve' of the Nazi legal regime, which complied with each of the above requirements, save, perhaps, that calling for public promulgation.

9.11 Fuller and the 'lawless regime'

Given the principles which constitute the external and internal morality of a regime, Fuller goes on to declare that any departure from them is an affront to the dignity of the citizen as a responsible agent. How ought citizens (including judges and lawyers) to react to a regime which ignores these principles as and when it wishes? How ought individuals to behave when the legal regime under which they live assists in the systematic denial of rights to groups of citizens?

9.11.1 Lack of internal morality negates the essence of true law

Fuller's answer is simple, although highly-controversial. The regime which is based upon, or which actively assists in the spread of, injustice has forfeited any right to expect allegiance from its citizens. Even though the law be formulated and promulgated in traditional, formal fashion, its lack of internal morality deprives it of the nature of 'true law':

> 'When a system calling itself law is predicated upon a general disregard by judges of the terms of the law they purport to enforce, when this system habitually cures its legal irregularities, even the grossest, by retroactive statutes ... it is not hard for me, at least, to deny to it the name of law.'

9.11.2 Questions of law and morality inseparable

Questions of law and morality must not – indeed, cannot – be separated, particularly on the basis of the arguments enunciated by Hart.

D'Amato (*Jurisprudence* (1984)) suggests that an answer to the Hart-Fuller controversy must be found in moral, not legal, philosophy: 'Unless they are infused with basic, normative concepts, present legal theories cannot resolve such issues'. (Note Dworkin's argument that 'jurisprudential issues are at their core issues of moral principle, not legal fact or strategy'.)

9.12 The main issues in the debate: a brief recapitulation

Both Hart and Fuller are united in their abhorrence of the Nazi regime and in their approval of efforts to cleanse the succeeding regime from its past taint. They are separated, however, by basic disagreement on the relationship of law and morality. For Hart, the immorality of a law cannot constitute the basis of a denial that it is, and will continue to be, law until properly repealed. For Fuller, the immorality of a law, vitiates, or destroys, its right to be called 'law'. Specifically, a law founded upon a denial of the principles of the 'inner morality of the law' is not entitled to any respect: it is mere evil disguised by the language, ceremonies and formalities associated with rational law. Hart answers that morality is not law, and must not seek, therefore, to supplant it. Fuller retorts that law and morality cannot be separated, and a law that flies in the face of morality is no law.

9.13 An inconclusive debate

Critics have suggested that, by its very nature, the Hart-Fuller debate was doomed to inconclusiveness. Terms such as 'justice', 'morality', 'law', which were fundamental to the discussion were not defined. There appeared to be little 'give and take' in the discussions. The questions which prompted the debate remain. Societies continue to exist and prosper (in a sense) although some are totally immoral in Fuller's sense. Respect for human dignity is markedly absent from some regimes in which complex legal institutions exist. In some societies, law and elementary freedoms do not co-exist.

What, then, is the real nature of the relationship of law and morality? Is the positivist refusal to mingle law and reality tenable? Should our definitions of law mirror some moral ideal? Perhaps most important, in the words of Gross, in his *Philosophy of Law* (1980):

> 'Is there an indispensable minimum moral foundation for any legal system determined by certain universal features of the human condition and by principles of procedure that cannot be systematically ignored?'

Summary of Chapter 9

The Hart-Fuller Debate

Background to the debate

A discussion in the 1950s between Hart (b 1907) and Fuller (b 1902) concerning legal events in Germany, following the Second World War, led to a debate in which some fundamental differences between the advocates of legal positivism and the natural law were restated.

Hart was to argue that law is law even though it fails to satisfy the demands of morality.

Fuller maintained that a law divorced from morality ceases to be 'law'.

The post-war legal system in Germany was designed deliberately so as to rid itself of all vestiges of thought and procedures associated with the former regime. This was helped by the influence of the German jurist, Radbruch, who had abandoned 'legal relativism' in favour of a move towards the doctrines of natural law.

In 1949 the German courts sentenced a woman who had denounced her husband during the war because of his criticism of Hitler. The woman pleaded that her action was 'lawful' under the terms of a law then in force. The court ruled in 1949 that her action was contrary to the sound conscience and sense of justice of decent human beings.

Hart opens the debate

Although Hart was sympathetic to the attempts of the German legal system to cast aside all remnants of the dictatorship period, nevertheless, he argued, law remains law even though it does not meet the requirements of morality .

Whether a bad law (such as that allowing the denunciation of the husband) ought to be obeyed is a significant, but entirely separate, question.

Fuller's response

Hart, Fuller claimed, was in error. A law must possess certain characteristics if it is to be classified correctly as 'law'. There was nothing in the legal system of the dictatorship which remotely resembled true law.

Hart's error arose from the general positivist position which demanded a separation of law from questions of morality.

Hart and the 'minimum content of natural law'

Hart responded by stressing his belief that 'law' and 'morality' were not interchangeable terms, so that one should not impugn a law solely on the grounds of its lack of morality.

Hart suggested that the 'human condition' necessitated the creation of minimum rules designed to protect persons, property and rights created by promises. The 'human condition' revealed vulnerability, approximate equality, limited altruism, scarce resources and a general, limited understanding and strength of will. It was the recognition of these matters which formed the core of good sense in the doctrine of natural law.

Fuller's response

Fuller argued further that a legal system must aim at the subjection of human conduct to the governance of rules.

Law must have its own 'internal morality'. It must be more than the mere *ad hoc* settling of disputes; it must not be retroactive; it must be intelligible, free from contradictions, must not require the impossible and must produce congruence of its declared aims and the actions of administrators.

The dictatorship in Germany had produced an essentially 'lawless' regime which had forfeited any right to expect allegiance from its citizens.

Hart's arguments illustrate the results of attempting to separate law from morality.

An inconclusive debate

In spite of Hart's nod in the direction of 'the core of good sense' in the natural law, the parties to the debate remain widely separated. For Hart it is the confusion of 'law' with 'morality' which blurs the fundamental issue: law remains law until repealed or otherwise replaced. Fuller sees this as an inevitable, and regrettable, result of positivist doctrine; for him man-made law which lacks an inner morality has no claim to be recognised as 'true law'.

It has been suggested that the inconclusive nature of the debate followed inevitably from a failure to define terms such as 'law', 'morality', 'lawlessness'.

Chapter 10

Positivism: Austin

10.1 Background

John Austin (1790-1859), the first professor of jurisprudence at London University, and a friend of Bentham and JS Mill, was a positivist scholar who, in *The Province of Jurisprudence Determined* (1832), attempted to ascertain the general limits of jurisprudence. All that now remains of his legacy of legal thought is a much-criticised concept of law as 'a species of command', and an analysis of sovereignty. His theories were widely condemned because his critics felt that he had not understood the significance of the social functions of law and had failed to separate the concepts of legal authority and political power in his work. Hart demolished the essence of this theory in *The Concept of Law* (1961). Austin remains, nevertheless, a figure of significance in any account of the *historical development* of positivist jurisprudence.

10.2 The essence of Austin's thought

Austin was, fundamentally, a utilitarian (see Chapter 7). For him, 'the proper purpose or end of a sovereign-political government is the greatest possible advancement of human happiness'.

10.2.1 Jurisprudence is concerned with positive laws

Jurisprudence was concerned, he believed, solely with 'positive laws or with laws strictly so-called, as considered without regard to their goodness or badness'.

Positive law is *law set by political superiors to political inferiors.* The 'glaring truth' is, said Austin, that the existence of law is one thing; its demerit is another. 'Whether it be or be not is one enquiry; whether it be or be not conformable to an assumed standard is a different enquiry. A law which actually exists is a law, though we happen to dislike it, or though it vary from the text by which we regulate our approbation or disapprobation.'

10.2.2 Law is the command of a Sovereign

Law is the command of a Sovereign - hence the term applied to Austin's doctrine, 'the imperative theory of law'.

Analytical jurisprudence necessitates a strict, formal analysis of existing legal institutions. The consideration of ethical matters had no place in this method of investigation.

10.3 Austin's concept of 'law'

For Austin:

> 'A law, in the most general and comprehensive acceptation in which the term, in its literal meaning, is employed, may be said to be a rule laid down for the

guidance of an intelligent being by an intelligent being having power over him.'

Law may be classified as *'laws improperly so-called' and 'laws properly so-called'*.

10.3.1 Laws improperly so-called

Laws improperly so-called comprise the following:

- Laws by analogy

  These are 'rules set out and enforced by mere opinion by an indeterminate body of men in regard to human conduct, such as the law of honour'. Austin included under this heading 'much of what is usually termed "international law"'.

- Laws by metaphor

  These are laws such as are 'observed by the lower animals, or laws determining the movements of inanimate bodies'.

  'For where intelligence is not, or where it is too bounded to take the name of reason, and, therefore, is too bounded to conceive the purpose of a law, there is not the will which law can work on, or which duty can incite or restrain.'

10.3.2 Laws properly so-called

Laws properly so-called are 'general commands' and may be divided as follows:

- Laws of God, set to his human creatures.

- Laws set by men to men. These 'human laws' are made up of 'laws strictly so-called' and 'laws not strictly so-called'.

  Laws not strictly so-called consist of laws set by men not as political superiors, nor in pursuance of a legal right. They do not involve the commands of a Sovereign, nor do they involve legal sanctions. An example is the set of rules made by a father for his children. (Constitutional law is placed by Austin under this heading, since he did not believe it to be capable of enforcing the sanctions emanating from a Sovereign.)

  Laws strictly so-called comprise laws set by men to other men in the relationship of a political superior to political inferiors and laws set by men as private individuals in the pursuance of legal rights. The aggregate of the first group is the appropriate matter of jurisprudence.

10.4 Austin's concept of sovereignty

Sovereignty involves the positive exercise of ultimate authority over persons and groups within a State's territory. Bodin (1530-1597) had referred to it as 'the highest power over citizens and subjects unrestrained by laws'.

10.4.1 Sovereignty and superiority

The essence of the exercise of sovereignty is the demand for obedience. Austin distinguishes sovereignty from other kinds of 'superiority':

> 'The bulk of the given society is in the *habit* of obedience or submission to a determinate and common superior; let that common superior be a certain individual person, or a certain body or aggregate of individual persons.'
>
> 'That certain individual or that certain body of individuals is not in the habit of obedience to a determinate human superior.'
>
> 'If a determinate human superior, not in the habit of obedience to a like superior, receives habitual obedience from the bulk of a given society, that determinate superior is sovereign in that society, and the society (including the superior) is a society political and independent.'

10.4.2 Sovereignty and obedience

The 'base of sovereignty' is, according to Austin, the fact of obedience, which involves a relationship of sovereignty and subjection. 'The power of the Sovereign ... is incapable of legal limitation', nor is it divisible.

Where there is no law there is no Sovereign; where there is no Sovereign there is no law.

10.4.3 The essence of law

Law is, therefore, *a command issued by a political superior to whom the majority of members of society are in the habit of obedience, and which is enforced by a threatened sanction.*

10.4.4 Austin's theory anticipated

Austin's theory had been anticipated in part in the writings of other jurists.

- Bodin wrote, in his *Six Books of the Republic* (1576), of the Sovereign as 'he who makes law for the subject, abrogates the law which is already made, and amends obsolete law'.
- Hobbes wrote, in *Leviathan* (1651), of the Sovereign as 'the sole legislator ... having power to make and repeal laws ... when he pleaseth'.
- Bentham referred to law as 'conceived or adapted by the Sovereign in a State'.

10.5 Sanctions in Austin's doctrine of law

Sanctions are based, according to Austin, on motivation by the fear of 'evil':

> 'If you express or intimate a wish that I shall do or forebear from some act, and if you will visit me with an evil in case I comply not with your wish, the expression or intimation of your wish is a *command*. A command is distinguished from other significations of desire not by the style in which the desire is signified, but by the power and

> the purpose of the party commanding to inflict an evil or pain in case the desire be disregarded.'
>
> 'Being liable to evil from you if I comply not with a wish which you signify, I am bound or obliged by your command or I live under a duty to obey it ... Command and duty are, therefore, correlative terms: the meaning denoted by each being implied or supposed by the other.'
>
> 'The evil which will probably be incurred in case a command be disobeyed or ... in case a duty is broken, is frequently called a sanction, or an enforcement of obedience.'

10.6 Criticisms of Austin's doctrine

Criticism of Austin mounted steadily during his lifetime. He was accused of a 'sterile verbalism' which had produced a mere travesty of reality. His alleged narrowness of perspective was said to have stemmed from a 'naive empiricism', allowing him to ignore the real complexities of law within societies. He was said to have confused 'law' with the product of legislation and to have failed to understand that 'law' was much more than Parliamentary enactments. Specifically, the following criticisms were levelled at his work.

10.6.1 Linguistic looseness

Linguistic looseness was said to have produced ambiguities in the formulation and expression of his doctrine. Thus, the term 'command' has precise connotations, suggesting an individual who issues orders in peremptory fashion. It was difficult to employ with precision a term of this nature in referring to the content of some legislation.

10.6.2 The absolute Sovereign is rare

The untrammelled, absolute authority of the Sovereign, which Austin postulates, is rarely found in practice. There are almost always limitations on the exercise of power by most persons and bodies. Thus, Dicey, writing in *An Introduction to the Study of the Law of the Constitution* (1885), noted two limiting factors on the actual exercise of authority by a Sovereign. *First*, the possibility or certainty that a Sovereign's subjects, or a large number of them, will disobey or resist his laws; and, *second*, the nature of the Sovereign's power itself, which would be moulded by the moral feelings of the time, thus setting bounds to what the Sovereign could do in practice.

10.6.3 Law is not always a command

Is law valid merely because it is the command of a Sovereign? Law may owe its validity to the fact that it expresses the community's feelings for natural justice, or that it is perceived as embodying a people's wishes. Is the term 'command ' appropriate as a description of all laws? Is the law of contract, for example, based on 'command'? Is the source of law to be interpreted *solely* in terms of a Sovereign?

10.6.4 Confusion of sovereignty *de facto* and *de jure*

Is there a confusion of sovereignty *de facto* and *de jure*? The Crown is the *de facto* Sovereign to whom subjects owe allegiance; but Parliament is the *de jure* Sovereign, invested with a monopoly of legislative powers.

Is habitual obedience a requirement of law? Some laws dealing with relatively trivial matters may be ignored in practice by large numbers of a Sovereign's subjects, but they remain a part of 'the law'.

10.6.5 Narrowness of the theory

Austin was criticised particularly for his excluding from his enquiry all law save that of England and Rome. It has been suggested that, as a result, his theories have few roots in general historical facts. Maine, the legal historian (see Chapter 13), notes that the maxim, 'No law, no Sovereign', is not correct in relation to some early Asiatic States, and that 'No Sovereign, no law' has no application to some early regimes in, eg, Tibet. Much of early law, argues Maine, results from religion and custom, not from a political Sovereign.

10.7 Vinogradoff's criticisms

In *Commonsense in Law* (1913), Vinogradoff (1854-1925) noted certain 'weak points' of Austin's doctrine.

10.7.1 Theory uses a formal approach only

The doctrine approaches law from its formal side only; it does not admit of any examination of the contents of legal propositions, so that a harsh, unjust enactment is considered to be as 'valid' a rule as 'the most righteous law'.

The legal process does not wait until a community has definitely established a sovereign authority before it recognises the existence of laws.

10.7.2 Agreement, not command, is at the basis of much law

The basis of law is often provided, not by one-sided command, but by agreement.

It may well be asked whether law is binding only on persons who receive the command or on those who give it as well. Even if the King 'can do no wrong', yet he is bound to respect the laws.

10.7.3 Coercion alone does not explain law

There is a balance between justice and force in most systems of law; it is impossible, therefore, to give an adequate definition of law based solely on coercion by the sovereign power.

10.7.4 The theory ignores the essence of common law

English common law, which is fundamental to the legal system, 'stands or falls with the admission of legal principles obtained not by command, but by retrospective estimates of right and justice.' Judge-made law, which figures considerably in the development of the common law, does not emanate from the command of a Sovereign. Maine (see Chapter 13) rejected Austin's argument that judge-made law reflected, in practice, the tacit command of the sovereign power, as 'a mere artifice of speech' and 'a straining of language'. Austin was insistent, however, that the work of the judges in this area was highly advantageous to society as a whole. 'Unless the work of legislation had been performed mainly by subordinate judges ... then with regard to a multitude of most important subjects, society would have lived without law, and, with regard to a multitude of others, the law would have remained in pristine barbarity.'

To look upon international law merely as a form of 'positive morality' (by consigning it to the category of 'laws by analogy') is going too far: international legal rules carry a great weight of practical authority. In their real content they seem similar to ordinary laws and often have little to do with ethics.

10.8 Hart's criticisms

In *The Concept of Law* (1961), Hart writes of the importance of furthering the understanding of 'law, coercion, and morality as different but related social phenomena'. His criticisms of the theory of 'law as command' are directed against the following aspects of Austin's doctrine.

10.8.1 Law as orders backed by the threat of application of sanctions

The modern criminal law is said to provide many examples of the Austinian doctrine in practice. Thus, the Computer Misuse Act 1990 creates the offence of obtaining unauthorised access to computer material; the offender is liable to fine or imprisonment, or both. This is a specific 'order' backed by the threat of an application of 'sanctions'. Hart notes, however, that there are many laws in which there is neither 'order' nor 'threat'. Failure to comply with the Wills Act 1837 as it relates to the necessary number of witnesses to a will is no 'offence'. To deliberately ignore the provisions of the Law of Property (Miscellaneous Provisions) Act 1989 as they relate to the necessity for writing in a contract for the sale of land, is not to invoke the imposition of 'sanctions' in Austin's sense. The concept of law as 'order plus threat' is an inadequate explanation of the basis of much of the law as we know it today.

10.8.2 The law-maker is above the law

Hart notes that Austin had in mind a sovereign law-maker who himself is not bound by the rules he promulgates and is, therefore, 'above the law'. But this does not reflect the reality of the legal system as we know it. Thus, the House of Lords is *bound* by the provisions of the Parliament Acts 1911 and 1949, relating to legislation concerning money matters. The Queen is *bound* to summon Parliament to meet every year. The House of Commons is *bound* by its own strict rules of procedure. Austin's view of the legislature as being subject to no rules is not correct when applied to a consideration of 'the Queen in Parliament'.

10.8.3 The origins of the law in 'order plus threat'

Hart points out that it is not possible to understand correctly the origins of our law merely in terms of orders and sanctions. The existence of custom as a source of law is not given sufficient prominence in the Austinian explanation. Thus, some important specific rules which are now embodied in mercantile law originated in custom long before they were 'recognised' by the legislature. The customs of merchants in relation to early types of the bill of exchange possessed the force of law well before the legislature enacted the Bills of Exchange Act 1882. The existence, and observation by the mercantile community, of codes of practice which, to a very large extent, had the force, if not the regular format, of an enactment, cannot be explained satisfactorily in terms of a command theory of law.

10.8.4 The habit of obedience among subjects

The Sovereign is obeyed, according to Austin, as the result of general, habitual patterns of obedience among the community. The citizens of a parliamentary democracy are conditioned by habit and long experience to obey the 'demands' of the Queen in Parliament, as made known in statutes, regulations and orders. Hart asks us to suppose that the ruler of a State, (R1), is followed by another, (R2), say, because of the death of R1. In general there will be a continuity of obedience: citizens who are habituated to obeying R1 will 'transfer' their obedience to the person R2. On the death of George VI, 'obedience' of the citizens of the UK was given immediately to his lawful successor, Elizabeth II. But when can it be said that the citizens 'became habituated' to the position and power of the new Sovereign?

Hart's answer necessitates an examination of the rules which ensure that there will be an uninterrupted transfer of power from R1 to R2 in circumstances which are understood and accepted by their subjects.

There are fundamental *rules* concerning the right to legislate. Parliament's legislation is accepted by citizens, not because of habits or procedures of conditioning, but because of acceptance of the rules. Austin's 'habituation theory' is, in the circumstances, too simplistic.

10.8.5 The omnipotent Sovereign

Austin's concept of a Sovereign with unlimited powers has no application to our style of democracy, for example. Parliament's 'sovereign powers' are limited, for example, in reference to the extension of its life beyond a period of five years. Further, actions purporting to have been carried out under power of prerogative may be challenged in the courts if, for example, the rights of an individual are directly and adversely affected. *Per* Diplock LJ in *BBC v Johns* (1965):

> 'The limits within which the executive government may impose obligations or restraints on citizens of the United Kingdom without any statutory authority are now well settled and incapable of extension.'

Parliament's apparent surrender of a portion of its sovereignty, because of the entry of the United Kingdom into the EEC, is well-known (see, eg, *Factortame Ltd v Secretary of State for Transport (No 2)* (1991)). Attempts to resolve the dilemma of a less-than-omnipotent Sovereign within the Austinian framework have not been successful. Even if it be accepted that the electorate is 'the true sovereign power', it must be noted that the powers of the electorate, too, are limited as the result of the delegation of the exercise of its sovereignty to its representatives in the House of Commons.

10.9 The influence of Austin

Allen suggests, in *Law in the Making* (1958), that the vitality of Austin's doctrine, which has lain in its simplicity and consistency, is 'still far from exhausted'. 'For a systematic exposition of the methods of English jurisprudence we still have to turn to Austin.' Many other jurists, however, see the 'command theory' as devoid of any relevance for our day. In Hart's words:

> 'The simple idea of orders, habits and obedience cannot be adequate for an analysis of the law. What is required is the notion of a rule conferring powers, which may be limited or unlimited, on persons qualified in certain ways to legislate by complying with a certain procedure.'

Further criticism of Austin is voiced by Professor Raz in his article, *HLA Hart* (1907-92), in which reference is made to Austin as having opened a gap between jurisprudence and general philosophy. Austin paid little attention to Aristotle, Aquinas, Hobbes, Hume, Kant or Hegel with the result that, following his work, English jurisprudence moved further away from the broad issues of philosophical enquiry. A body of jurisprudence which is generally separated from a study of general philosophy loses vitality and lacks the power to link legal theory to systematic speculation.

Summary of Chapter 10

Positivism: Austin

Essence of Austin's jurisprudential thought

Austin (1790-1859) argued that the aim of government is 'the greatest possible advancement of human happiness'.

Jurisprudence was concerned solely with positive laws and not with their goodness or badness.

Positive law is law set by political superiors to political inferiors. Law is, in reality, the command of a Sovereign.

Laws may be classified as follows:

- Laws improperly so-called, comprising laws by analogy, eg, law of honour (and even, according to Austin, international law), and laws by metaphor (eg, laws determining the movements of inanimate bodies).
- Laws properly so-called which are 'general commands', comprising the laws of God, and laws set by men to men. The human laws comprise laws not strictly so-called (eg, a father's rules for his children) and laws strictly so-called, ie, laws set by political superiors to political inferiors and laws set by private persons in the pursuance of legal rights.

The basis of 'sovereignty' is the fact of obedience. The power of the Sovereign is incapable of legal limitation.

Law is, essentially, a command issued by a political superior to whom the majority of members of society are in the habit of obedience, and which is enforced by a threatened sanction.

Sanctions are based on motivation by the fear of 'evil' which will probably be incurred in case a command is disobeyed.

General criticisms of Austin's doctrine

Linguistic looseness, as in the use of the term 'command' and confusion of sovereignty *de facto* with sovereignty *de jure* were noted by critics.

Vinogradoff observed that Austin approached law from its formal side only and seemed unaware of the fact that the basis of law may be found in agreement, rather than command. Further, Austin has paid insufficient attention to the significance of 'justice' in the growth of the law and has given inadequate weight to judge-made law.

Hart's criticisms

It has been suggested that the concept of law as 'orders backed by the threat of application of sanctions' is inadequate. There are, in fact, many laws in which there is neither order nor threat.

Austin's view of the law-maker as 'above the law' is unrealistic. In the English legal system, Parliament is bound by its own strict procedural rules, for example.

Law did not originate in 'order plus threat'. The importance of custom as a source of our law is not reflected in Austin's doctrine.

Austin's suggestion that the Sovereign is obeyed because of 'habits of obedience' is too simplistic. Thus, citizens' obedience to the orders emanating from the Queen in Parliament represents, basically, an acceptance of the appropriate rules affecting legislation.

Austin's 'omnipotent Sovereign' is a fiction. Thus, Parliamentary sovereignty is limited in a variety of ways. If it be argued that the electorate in a democracy is 'truly sovereign', an examination of its powers will reveal important limitations, eg, as the result of delegation of some of those powers to its representatives in Parliament.

Chapter 11

Positivism: Hart

11.1 Essential features of Hart's view

HLA Hart (1907-1992), who was Professor of Jurisprudence at Oxford during 1952-1968, was a leading figure in the post-war movement for the revival of interest in the philosophy of law in relation to the much wider field of general philosophical enquiry. He was interested particularly in the development of the doctrines of *legal positivism* (see 8.6) and set out his view of the fundamentals of a legal system in *The Concept of Law* (1961). The essence of Hart's positivist approach emerges from the following propositions which may be derived from the text.

- 'The most prominent general feature of law at all times and places is that its existence means that certain kinds of human conduct are no longer optional, but in some sense obligatory.'
- Legal institutions and other phenomena related to the law must be studied precisely as they are.
- Law is best defined by investigating its formal features rather than the precise and detailed nature of its content.
- The concept of 'legal validity' is to be determined by reference to the source of a law within the legal system, not necessarily by its content.
- The essence of legal obligation is to be found in the phenomenon of a case covered by a law which is widely recognised as being valid.

Law ought to be studied, in general, as 'value-neutral', so that, for purposes of jurisprudential investigation, it should be kept apart from questions of morality.

Hart's goal of his jurisprudential investigation was the advancement of legal theory 'by providing an improved analysis of the distinctive structure of a municipal, legal system and a better understanding of the resemblances and differences between law, coercion, and morality, as types of social phenomena.'

11.1.1 Law as a social phenomenon

Law is a social phenomenon and its study involves recognition of 'the characteristics of the human condition' (human vulnerability, limited altruism, etc, which were noted in Chapter 9). (It is of interest to note that not all jurists accept Hart's catalogue of human characteristics. Thus, Kelly, in *A Short History of Western Legal Thought* (1992), suggests that

Hart's 'speculative anthropology' does not focus sufficiently on 'the *human* person'.)

11.1.2 The need for systematic rules

There is a need within society for a *system of rules* designed to protect 'persons, property and promises'.

It is from the analysis of the features and interrelationships of these rules that the essence of a legal system emerges for examination.

Both primary *and* secondary rules are necessary for a working legal system.

11.2 Prerequisites for the existence of a legal system

Two circumstances must be present within a community before it can be said that there is in existence a legal system.

There must be a system of 'valid obligation rules' in accordance with the legal system's ultimate criteria of validity, which are generally obeyed by the majority of members of the community.

Those who administer the affairs of the community must accept, in addition to the 'valid obligation rules', the rules of 'change', 'adjudication', and 'recognition'.

11.3 Social habits and social rules

'Rules' should *not* be viewed in the Austinian sense as 'commands'. Hart uses the term in a very specific sense.

11.3.1 Essence of social habits

Social habits may be exemplified by the phenomenon of members of a group of friends who visit the theatre every Friday evening. This is an aspect of the group's 'habitual conduct', and failure by a member to participate in one of the visits will not be considered as a 'fault' which ought to attract criticism.

11.3.2 Essence of social rules

Social rules are of much greater significance in an analysis of what is meant by 'law'. When a social rule is broken, criticism will almost invariably result, because a fault has been committed. Existence of social rules testifies to their acceptance by a social group as a whole.

Awareness of a social rule (eg, as in matters of morality, etiquette, or of obligation) and support for its significance and acceptance within the group, constitute what Hart terms 'the internal aspects' of the rule.

11.3.3 External and internal aspects of rules

The 'external aspects' of a rule refer to the possibility that an observer standing outside the particular social group could be aware of the existence of the rule.

Social habits possess only an external aspect. *Social rules* possess both external *and* internal aspects.

The 'internal aspects' of rules are of much importance: they involve 'a critical, reflective attitude to certain patterns of behaviour and a common standard'. This attitude should be reflected in criticism and self-criticism, demands for conformity with standards, and general acknowledgement that such criticism and demands are justified.

11.4 The classification of social rules

Social rules may be considered within the following categories.

Mere *social conventions*, as exemplified by the rules accepted as describing appropriate behaviour in, say, a place of public worship.

Rules constituting *obligations* are considered essential if the character and quality of a community's life are to be maintained. An example is the set of general rules forbidding theft. The rules relating to obligations are what we understand by 'law'.

11.5 Legal rules

Hart differentiates two types of legal rule: *primary rules of obligation*, which generally concern requirements to perform, or abstain from, specified types of activity; and secondary rules, which affect the operations of the primary rules. *It is the union of primary and secondary rules which constitutes 'the law'.*

11.6 The primary rules

Primary rules of obligation which, in a sense, indicate what must or must not be done in pursuance of an obligation, may be discerned in the operation of the criminal law, in particular. Thus, the Road Traffic Acts of 1988 and 1991 impose a variety of *obligations* upon those who drive motor vehicles. The Sexual Offences (Amendment) Act 1992 imposes *obligations* with respect to anonymity in connection with allegations of, and criminal proceedings relating to, certain sexual offences.

11.7 Primary rules alone will not suffice

Hart argues that if a society is to operate solely on the basis of primary rules, certain conditions arising from human nature and the very world in which we live would have to be satisfied.

11.7.1 Need for restrictions

The rules would have to contain restrictions:

> 'on the free use of violence, theft and deception to which human beings are tempted but which they must, in general, repress, if they are to coexist in close proximity to each other.'

In such a society, those who reject the rules 'except where fear of social pressure induces them to conform' must be no more than a small minority.

11.7.2 Defects of a system based on primary rules only

Only a small community 'closely knit by ties of kinship, common sentiment and belief', with a stable environment could live successfully under a regime of primary rules. There would indeed be defects inherent in a social structure based on primary rules only:

- The defect of uncertainty

  The rules could not constitute an ordered system; they would be no more than a set of separate standards. There would be no procedures for settling doubts as to the meaning, or exact scope, of a rule, and no possibility of reference to authoritative texts or to officials whose declarations might be authoritative.

- The defect of static rules

  The static nature of the primary rules would create further problems. Change in the rules would be the result of a relatively slow process. It would be very difficult to adapt the rules so as to fit changing circumstances: processes of adaptation, of eliminating old rules and introducing new ones would require a special type of rule fundamentally different from ordinary rules of obligation.

- The defect of inefficiency of the diffuse social pressure by which the primary rules are maintained

  The lack of an agency specifically empowered to ascertain authoritatively and finally whether or not a rule has been violated is an extremely serious defect of a system comprising only of primary rules. Additionally, punishments for the violation of primary rules, and other forms of social pressure necessitating the use of force, would be a matter for the individuals adversely affected, or for the entire community; but there would be no special agency capable of carrying out these tasks. Time would be wasted in unorganised attempts to apprehend offenders, and there would be the possibility of disturbance resulting from 'self-help' in the absence of an organised system of sanctions.

11.8 The secondary rules

The defects of the primary rules-only system may be remedied, according to Hart, by the introduction of a system of secondary rules which will act as a supplement to the primary rules. These secondary rules are 'parasitic' on the primary rules and will allow members of the community, by performing actions or saying things, to introduce new types of primary rules, modify old rules and control the operations and effects of the primary rules. Hart suggests that introducing remedies for each of the defects of the primary rules-only system would constitute 'a step from the pre-legal order into the legal world'.

Together, the remedies would suffice to transform a system utilising only primary rules into a full legal system. Although the remedies differ from one another, and from the primary rules, they each concern those rules and specify ways in which the primary rules might be ascertained correctly, varied, and the fact of their breach determined authoritatively.

11.9 The rule of recognition

This secondary rule is designed to remedy the defect of uncertainty. It specifies particular features, the presence of which will affirm conclusively that the rule in question 'is a rule of the group to be supported by the social pressure it exerts'.

The rule may take a variety of forms - a document, for example.

11.9.1 Essence of the rule

The important feature of the rule is that an acknowledgement of reference to the document, for example, is 'authoritative' and constitutes the proper way of removing doubts as to the existence of the rule.

11.9.2 The rule as a test

The rule of recognition involves the very idea of a legal *system* because the rules are part of a unified set and are perceived and accepted as such.

The rule of recognition may be 'the ultimate rule' of a legal system in that it is in itself the test of the system's legal validity. Thus, the rule that what is enacted formally and properly by Parliament is 'the law' provides criteria for assessing the validity of other rules within the legal system of a parliamentary democracy.

11.10 The rules of change

These secondary rules will remedy the defect of static rules. Rules of this nature may be exemplified by enactments empowering particular individuals to make changes in their legal positions by abolishing old rules and introducing new primary rules.

The rules of change may be simple or complex and the powers they confer may be unrestricted or limited. Additionally, they may specify procedures and individuals who are empowered to legislate.

11.10.1 Examples

Examples of the secondary rules of change are to be found in the law of succession, the making of contracts and the transfer of property:

- The Wills Act 1837 empowers an individual to make changes in his legal position so that his property rights will not be affected by the general rules relating to the disposition of the property of an intestate.

- Aspects of the law of contract, such as the rules concerning consideration, offer and acceptance, allow an individual to create a new relationship between himself and the other party to the agreement, and thereby to alter his position in relation to that other party.
- The Law of Property Act 1925, s 2, allows the conveyancing of certain equitable interests and powers, thereby modifying the relationships between the vendor and the purchaser of a legal estate and the owner of equitable interests or powers affecting that estate.

11.11 The rules of adjudication

These particular secondary rules remedy the defect arising from the diffuse social pressures by which the primary rules are maintained; they empower selected individuals to pass authoritative judgment where rules are broken. Rules stating who is to decide a dispute (see, for example, the Courts and Legal Services Act 1990) and the procedures to be followed (see, for example, the County Courts Act 1984) may be considered as secondary rules of adjudication.

Rules of adjudication may prohibit individuals from adopting practices of self-help in the punishment of others.

Imprisonment, the collection of fines and damages, and other sanctions of a legal system will be centralised.

11.12 The 'existence' of a legal system

Primary rules and the secondary rules of change, recognition and adjudication coalesce into 'the law' which is the very essence of a legal system. But what is meant, in precise terms, by the statement that, within a given community, 'a legal system does exist'? Are there any conditions, criteria, which allow us to say that within a community there are systems, procedures, regulations and rules from which may be deduced with accuracy the presence of a 'legal system'?

11.12.1 Fundamental conditions

Hart enunciates two fundamental conditions for the existence of a legal system: *first*, rules – in particular, the rule of recognition – must be obeyed; *second*, the secondary rules, in particular, must be accepted by the community's officials as 'common public standards' in relation to official behaviour.

11.13 Obedience to the rules

It is essential, if a legal system is to function adequately, that the mass of citizens within a community shall give general obedience to its rules and shall accept their validity in the light of the rule of recognition.

11.13.1 Pervasive obedience

The obedience required must involve more than the giving of 'lip-service': it must extend in practice to all important aspects of the daily life of the community.

The obligations and duties imposing respect for the property of others, for example, must be observed strictly if the system is to be considered as having been 'accepted' by the community.

11.13.2 Widespread obedience

Obedience must be given by a large majority of citizens (but not by all, for that would be an impossibility).

Obedience to the system's rule of recognition is of great significance in 'testing the validity' of a legal system. The rule must be understood and obeyed, so that, in a system of parliamentary democracy, for example, there shall be general agreement on the necessity to observe the binding nature of the rules and regulations emanating from legislation by Parliament.

11.14 Relationship of officials to the secondary rules

In their capacity as citizens, the community's officials must show obedience to the rules. But, says Hart, it is their attitude to the secondary rules in particular which is significant. Officials must not only obey the rules, but must 'collectively accept them'. In particular, they must understand and accept the importance of the rule of recognition as providing common standards for the making and enunciation of judicial decisions, for example. Hence, when a judge asserts that no court may enquire into the mode in which Parliament makes a law, he is indicating acceptance of the rule of recognition in relation to the power and authority of Parliament. (Note *Edinburgh & Dalkeith Railway v Wauchope* (1842), *per* Lord Campbell:

> 'All that a court of justice can do is to look at the Parliament roll ... no court can enquire into the mode by which [a Bill] was introduced into Parliament ... or what passed in Parliament during its progress.'

(See also *Lee v Bude and Torrington Railway Co* (1871).)

11.15 A Janus-faced statement

To assert that a legal system exists is, according to Hart, a statement which looks both towards obedience by the majority of citizens and to the acceptance by the community's officials of the secondary rules as providing 'critical common standards of official behaviour'. This duality is not surprising: it is a reflection of the composite nature of a legal system as compared with the relatively simple pre-legal form of social structure in a community in which only primary rules exist.

11.16 Hart's postscript

The second edition of *The Concept of Law* appeared in 1994, two years after Hart's death. In a postscript which was edited by Penelope Bulloch and Joseph Raz, fragments of Hart's notes, which had not been given their final form, were put together; what appears in the second edition is a partial reply by Hart to some specific criticisms raised by Dworkin. Hart's reply includes the following matter.

- *The Concept of Law* (first edition) attempted to provide a theory of what law was. The theory was general and descriptive; general in the sense that it was not restricted in its application to any particular legal system, and descriptive in that it sought to be morally neutral. This differs radically from Dworkin's approach to legal theory which he views as being evaluative, justificatory and tied essentially to Anglo-American culture. Hart finds Dworkin's exact reasons for rejecting descriptive legal theory difficult to follow.

- Dworkin has argued that the truth of propositions of law depends on facts which he calls 'grounds of law'. He is against the opinion that these are uncontroversial and fixed by linguistic rules; he stresses his opinion that facts of this nature have an essentially controversial basis. In effect, he has confused the meaning of 'law' and the meaning of 'propositions of law'.

- Dworkin's view of Hart as a supporter of the opinion that the purpose of the law is to justify the employment of coercive measures where they are necessary is incorrect. Nothing in Hart's exposition of the system of primary and secondary rules suggests that such a justification is the purpose of the law as a whole.

- Dworkin apparently accepts the 'objective standing' of the general status of moral judgments (upon which a judge may rely). Hart believes that the question of the objective study of such judgments ought to be left open by legal theory.

- Hart accepts the criticism of Dworkin and others that he may have ignored the importance of legal principles in legal reasoning and adjudication.

- Dworkin has argued that statements of legal rights and duties make sense in the real world only where there exist moral grounds for asserting their very existence. Hart replies that legal rights and duties constitute 'points' at which the law protects freedom or restricts it, and these 'focal points' are of great importance to individuals 'independently of moral merits of the law'.

Summary of Chapter 11

Positivism: Hart

Essence of Hart's approach

In *The Concept of Law* (1961) Hart sets out his positivist approach to investigating the phenomenon of law.

Legal institutions and their functions must be studied exactly as they are.

Matters of morality should not enter an investigation of this nature.

A society requires a system of *rules* in order to protect persons, property and promises.

The existence of a legal system presupposes a set of *primary* and *secondary rules*. Valid obligation rules must be accepted by the majority of the community including administrators.

Rules

Rules must not be viewed as 'commands'. They should be differentiated from 'social habits', a breach of which will rarely attract criticism.

Social rules are of much importance. Breach of these rules will attract criticism. They may be classified as 'social conventions', 'rules constituting obligations', eg, a set of rules forbidding and penalising theft. It is these latter rules which constitute 'the law'.

Legal rules may be classified as primary rules of obligation, and secondary rules. *A union of both types of rule is essential for the existence of 'law'.*

The primary rules

Primary rules are based on obligations to perform, or to abstain from some act. They may be discerned in the workings of the criminal law.

But primary rules alone will not suffice. Rules must contain restrictions on, eg, the use of violence, must be able to deal with those who reject them.

Specifically, a 'primary rules-only' system will suffer from the defect of uncertainty (in relation to standards), the defect of static rules (which would create problems of adaptation to new circumstances), and the defect of inefficiency of the diffuse social pressures by which the primary rules are maintained.

The secondary rules

A system of secondary rules designed to implement the primary rules is necessary if the deficiencies of the primary rules are to be remedied.

The 'rule of recognition' would specify modes of removing doubts as to the existence of a rule, thereby remedying the deficiency of uncertainty of primary rules.

The 'rules of change' would remedy the deficiency associated with static rules. Individuals would be empowered to legislate for change, thereby allowing individuals to modify their legal position in relation to others.

The 'rules of adjudication' would empower designated individuals to make authoritative judgments in cases relating to the breaking of rules. Such rules of adjudication would remedy the primary rules deficiency associated with the maintenance of those rules.

Obedience

The existence of a legal system necessitates obedience to the rules.

Such obedience involves the acceptance of appropriate obligations and duties by a large majority of citizens.

In particular, officials within the community must demonstrate acceptance of, and obedience to, the rules. The rule of recognition (in relation, say, to the power and authority of Parliament) will be of high importance.

Chapter 12

Positivism: Kelsen

12.1 Object of the pure theory, and Kelsen's methodology

Kelsen (1881-1973) was an Austrian-American jurist, committed to the doctrines of positivism, who wrote the Austrian Constitution (adopted in 1920), became a judge of the Austrian Supreme Constitutional Court and, after emigrating to the US, participated in the drafting of the Charter of the United Nations.

The object of Kelsen's theory is to assist in an understanding of positive law *in general*, not of any particular legal order. The theory attempts to explain what the law is, and not what it ought to be. It is to be accepted as a contribution to the science of law and not to legal politics. 'As a theory, its sole purpose is to know its subject.' Kelsen seeks to make a rigorous enquiry based upon a strict methodology.

A logical, structural analysis of the positive law must be made if a pure science of law is to emerge. Systems of law need to be considered in terms of their basic constituent elements.

12.1.1 Value-free judgments essential

The analysis is to be free from all ethical or political judgments concerning values as such: hence its title – 'pure theory'. Everything that is not strictly law is discarded and the science of law is considered in terms free from alien, adulterating elements; the science will be independent of the moral law and concepts of 'purpose'.

12.1.2 The study of law to be free from adulteration

The adulteration of the science of law is explained by noting how psychology, ethics, political theory, deal with some matters closely involved with law; hence law has become an uncritical mixture of methodologically different disciplines ('methodological syncretism') which obscures the essence of the science of law and obliterates the limits imposed upon it by the nature of its subject matter.

The analysis is *'positive'* because it necessitates a study of the law as it is; it is *'realistic'* because it removes from that study those illusions concerning its nature which have produced inadequate theories.

12.1.3 Metaphysics and natural law rejected

There is no place in the analysis for the metaphysical speculation which dominates the doctrines of natural law. This concept does little more than clothe with an apparently objective character claims which are insupportable. The suggestion that there are 'sacred rights' implanted in man by a divine nature 'and that positive law can neither establish nor abolish these rights but only protect them', is unacceptable.

12.2 The essence of the pure theory

Kelsen first published the outlines of his theory in 1911 in his *Chief Problems of the Doctrine of International Law*; they were further developed in his *General Theory of Law and State* (1945). Law is 'a system of coercion imposing norms which are laid down by human acts in accordance with a constitution the validity of which is pre-supposed if it is on the whole efficacious'. The theory is presented as 'pure' in that it is logically self-supporting and not dependent in any manner upon extra-legal values. It has been described as 'perhaps the most consistent expression of positivism in legal theory'. Friedmann, in *Legal Theory* (1967), states that it represents 'a quest for pure knowledge in its most uncompromising form'.

12.3 The place of 'justice' in the pure theory

Kelsen views justice as a concept which, on analysis, emerges as no more than the expression of an 'irrational ideal'. It represents the value-preferences of individuals and is not subject to cognition. It is not possible, therefore, to answer scientifically the question: What is justice? One can say that it is 'just' that a general rule be applied and obeyed where, because of its nature and content, circumstances necessitate its application. 'Justice', in this sense, is seen in the maintenance of a positive order by the conscientious application of appropriate general rules. It can be identified, therefore, with 'legality'. To pursue the question of its nature is an irrelevance for those seeking to construct a pure theory of law. 'The pure theory of law simply declares itself incompetent to answer either the question whether a given law is just or not, or the more fundamental question of what constitutes justice. The pure theory of law – a science – cannot answer these questions because they cannot be answered scientifically at all.'

But this attitude should not be taken to imply a lack of interest by Kelsen in the problem of justice. He is merely emphasising that, in relation to the *analysis* of the structure of law, the concept of justice has no place. 'The pure science of law seeks the real and possible law, not the just, and in this sense it is radically realistic and empirical. It declines to justify or condemn.'

12.4 The norms

According to Kelsen, every activity of a legal system can be traced back to an authoritative standard - a norm - which alone gives validity to the precise behaviour involved in such an activity. A norm is, therefore, the 'meaning' of an act by which a certain behaviour is commanded, permitted or authorised.

'Norms either arise through custom, as do the norms of the common law, or are enacted by conscious acts of certain organisations aiming to create law, as a legislature acting in its law-making capacity.'

12.4.1 Law as a coercive order of human nature

The legal norms do not merely prescribe certain types of behaviour; they attach to any manifestation of the contrary type of behaviour specified coercive acts, ie, *sanctions*. Thus, according to the pure theory, the law does not merely declare that the possession of specified drugs without a licence is to be avoided; it makes such behaviour an *offence* under the Misuse of Drugs Act 1971. Effective sanctions must be supported by an element of coercion, and this is, according to Kelsen, a very significant constituent of the law. Law is, in essence, *a coercive order of human behaviour*, relying not merely upon the psychological element of sanctions; when employed by the law, sanctions are 'outward' since they demand, 'in visible form' the deprivation of an offender's freedom (or his property). 'The law is a decree of a measure of coercion, a sanction, for that conduct called "illegal", a *delict*; and this conduct has the character of *delict* because and only because it is a condition of the sanction.'

12.4.2 Law as norms addressed to officials

Law may be thought of in terms of 'norms addressed to officials' (such as judges). Such norms may be interpreted as rules prescriptive of conduct to be pursued in certain specified circumstances, ie, if condition *X* exists, then legal consequence *Y* should ensue. If defendant is shown to have dishonestly obtained property by deception contrary to the Theft Act 1968, s 15(1), then the judge is obliged to consider the appropriate sanctions under the Act. The appropriate norm validates the judge's decision.

12.5 The validity of norms

A norm's validity is derived, according to Kelsen, solely from its having been authorised by another legal norm of a higher rank. Assume that an administrative order is issued under SI 1992/725, relating to hazardous substances. The order owes its validity to the powers conferred by the Secretary of State under the Planning (Hazardous Substances) Act 1990, s 41(3). This authorising statute is valid because it has been enacted in strict accordance with the rules of Parliamentary practice, which owe their validity to the provisions, practices, customs and procedures of the British Constitution, which owes its validity to ... etc.

12.6 The hierarchy of norms

There is, according to Kelsen, a *hierarchy of norms* (a 'step-structure' of the law) apparent in all bodies of law. Every norm is dependent for its authority upon a superior norm.

The legal order should not be interpreted as a system of co-ordinated norms of equal level; rather is it a hierarchy made up of *different levels of legal norms*.

12.6.1 Concretisation of norms

The norms become 'more concrete' and less abstract as one descends the levels within the hierarchy, the final (downward) level being reached, eg when the prison doors close behind an offender. The court, passing sentence on X, who has been found guilty of an offence, is 'concretising' the more general, abstract norms by which the case against X has been controlled (as embodied in, say, the Theft Act 1968). The decision of the court constitutes 'an individual norm' relating *specifically* to X.

12.7 The *Grundnorm*

'The law, or the legal order, is a system of legal norms. The first question we have to answer, therefore, is this: What constitutes the unity in the diversity of legal norms? Further: Why does a particular legal norm belong to a particular legal order?' A multiplicity of norms constitutes a unity, a system, an order, when validity can be traced back to its final source in a single norm.

12.7.1 Essential features

The basic norm (the '*Grundnorm*') is that norm, the validity of which cannot be derived from a higher one; it is the commencement of a specific chain of legal norms. Thus, in tracing the validity of, say, a procedural norm resulting in the imprisonment of an offender, we arrive at the validity of a statute which owes its validity to the essential features of the British Constitution. But this is not 'the highest norm': there is a 'final postulate' which gives validity to other norms. This 'basic norm' is presupposed by legal thinking; for legal purposes, therefore, the analysis of a legal norm cannot move beyond the *Grundnorm*, which may take the form of a proposition, such as, 'Every citizen ought to obey the Constitution'. (Note that a norm can be a part of an *unwritten* constitution which has been created by custom.)

12.7.2 Fundamentals

The basic norm is the presupposed starting point of the procedure of positive law creation. It is itself not a norm created by custom or by the act of a legal institution.

A basic norm may be discovered in any type of legal order.

A system of law cannot be established upon a foundation of conflicting basic norms.

The basic norm is not eternal: thus, a basic norm establishing autocratic rule within a society may give way to a new basic norm bestowing power upon a generally-elected assembly.

Formulation of the concept of the *Grundnorm* does not result, according to Kelsen, from any new method of jurisprudential analysis. It merely makes explicit what all jurists tend to assume, often unconsciously, when they consider the positive law as a 'system of valid norms', and not merely as a group of facts whose validity is derived from some 'natural law'.

12.8 The effectiveness of norms

It is not enough for the continued existence of a legal system that its laws be 'valid', ie, legitimate. The principle of legitimacy is restricted by the *principle of effectiveness*.

12.8.1 Acceptance

The norms of the legal order must be accepted by and large within the community. In the case of the *Grundnorm*, there must be appropriate general support for it.

12.8.2 Obedience

Universal and total obedience in relation to specific norms is not essential (even if it were possible). What is required within the community is a *sufficiency of adherence* to the essence of the basic norm allowing it to be effective in practice. Legal norms must be obeyed; a norm which is not obeyed by any citizens cannot be regarded as a 'valid norm'. Validity requires, therefore, not only authorisation by a higher norm; it requires also 'a minimum of effectiveness'. 'The efficacy of the total legal order is a necessary condition for the validity of every single norm of the order.'

12.9 The all-embracing nature of law

'Any material content whatever can be law; there is no such thing as a human activity which, because of its content, is disqualified from being embodied within a "legal rule".' From this assumption can be inferred, therefore, a variety of identities among aspects of law which are generally considered as dissimilar.

12.9.1 Identities of some aspects of law

- Subjective and objective rights

  'Subjective' and 'objective' rights are, according to Kelsen, merely personalised representations of the group of norms forbidding interference with an individual or his property in certain ways.

- Natural and juristic persons

  'Natural' and 'juristic' persons suggest a dualism which reflects the influence of ideas founded solely upon anthropomorphic views; the reality is that they personify no more than particular types of norms affecting individuals.

- Judicial decisions and administrative orders and regulations

  'Judicial decisions' and 'administrative orders and regulations' which, according to the doctrine of separation of powers, must be kept apart, are revealed by Kelsen as representing, fundamentally, aspects of the same process which is concerned with the concretisation of given norms.

- The State and law

  'The State' and 'law' are, fundamentally, identical. The State is a political organisation which expresses a particular legal order. It is 'governed by' the law. Indeed, says Kelsen, a State not governed by law is 'unthinkable'. 'The State is not its individuals; it is the specific union of individuals, and this union is the function of the order which regulates their mutual behaviour. Only in this order does the social community exist at all.'

  What is the State other than the norms which declare its structure, processes, systems and procedures? These norms are by their nature the same kind of norms represented in the legal system.

  The State may be considered, therefore, as a totality of the norms within a hierarchy; indeed, it is no more than 'the sum total of norms ordering compulsion'.

  State and law are to be thought of as co-extensive. Under the terms of the pure theory, the State is the law, and the traditional dualism of 'Law versus State' has disappeared.

12.10 Criticisms of Kelsen

Kelsen's search for an unadulterated concept of law has produced, it is argued, a theory which is arid, unreal and far-removed from the complexities of the law in action. Laski, in his *Grammar of Politics* (1925), refers to the pure theory as 'an exercise in logic and not in life'. Given its postulates, Laski argues, the theory is unanswerable. But those postulates reflect the uncompromising demands of a rigid logic, and their utilisation involves ignoring the fundamentals of the social life which creates and, therefore, colours the law.

12.10.1 Law is not an isolate

Encapsulated in Laski's statement is a major criticism of the pure theory, namely that it disregards the totality of any society within which a legal system is established. To abstract from an investigation of the law its environment of social and political factors is virtually impossible, even if it were desirable. Law does not, because it cannot, exist as an isolate; hence it cannot be considered as such. It is a part of the community and is affected by the dynamics of society. The 'meaning and significance' of, say, the Children Act 1989, reflect deeply-held communal and ethical attitudes within society to a range of social matters. To remove the inner significance of legislation from an analysis of its structure is to be left with mere 'form' which has been given primacy over 'meaning'.

12.10.2 Justice should not be excluded from a consideration of law

The exclusion of 'justice' from the pure theory has evoked considerable criticism. The concept of justice as a measure of the validity of law is rejected by Kelsen: justice is to be interpreted as no more than 'the conscientious application of appropriate general rules'. A concept which for many societies and jurists is perceived as the very end of the law should not be dismissed, it is argued, merely because it appears to be beyond the pale of cognition. The life of the law as we know it is, in many societies, built from a conscious desire that the tenets of justice shall be observed and that unjust behaviour (no matter how ill defined) shall not be tolerated.

12.10.3 Coercion is exaggerated in significance

The place of 'coercion' in the pure theory suggests to some critics an inference that the effectiveness of law is derived solely from sanctions and force, ie, an apparatus of compulsion, and that the essence of law is in duty, rather than right. It has been argued that this is a confusion of 'coercion' and 'obligation'. We are able to attach a measure of coercion to a rule only because the community considers the rule as obligatory in its nature; the rule is not obligatory simply because it is related to sanction and coercion. Thus, the rules embodied in, say, the Infant Life (Preservation) Act 1929, as subsequently amended, are considered to be of an obligatory nature; their force is not derived entirely from the threat of sanctions contained within the statute. Indeed, some critics view the pure theory as based upon the concept of formal, authoritarian commands enforced by those who have a monopoly of force at their disposal within the community - a caricature of a community in which laws are obeyed for reasons other than fear of sanctions and in which a legal system may impose duties without any threat of sanctions.

12.10.4 *Grundnorm* is unreal

The concept of the *Grundnorm* has been attacked by some critics as unreal (and, in any event, as representing the personal value-judgments of the investigator). The 'basic norm' is condemned as 'Austin's "Sovereign" in another guise', or as a mythical 'first cause' beyond which an investigator may not venture. The reasons for obedience to the law are not to be found, it is argued, in any one norm; there is a variety of complex reasons, psychological, social, political, behind the conscious response of citizens to legal duties. (Similar problems have been raised concerning international law which is based on a system of relationships apparently lacking a single basic norm and a developed apparatus of compulsion.)

It would be very difficult to test the 'minimum support' for a basic norm without an enquiry into political and social facts, thereby contradicting the methodology associated with the pure law.

12.10.5 A recognition of natural law principles?

Some jurists, eg, Lauterpacht, suggest that in spite of Kelsen's total rejection of the principles of natural law (see 12.1.3 above) there are recognisable overtones of some of those principles in his concept of a hierarchy of legal norms (see 12.6 above). Natural law theories tend to an affirmation of the principle of the existence of some 'higher norm' which is inherently superior to the positive law. 'The very conception of a definite rank between different manifestations of legal will, such as statutes and judicial decisions, implies itself a certain "social valuation" of State activity': Friedmann, *Legal Theory* (1967).

12.10.6 Failure to identify the source of the law

Fuller has criticised the pure theory for its failure to identify the source of the law: see *Law in Quest of Itself* (1940). The theory appears to assert that men assume the existence of some single source when they think and talk about the law. But it does not define that source in objectively descriptive terms.

12.11 The continuing attraction of pure law theory

In spite of the criticisms of Kelsen's theory, ranging from Allen's view of the author as having raised perception of the pure law 'to such an inaccessible altitude that it has difficulty in drawing the breath of life', to the view of the many jurists who interpret the theory as embodying almost all the inaccuracies of positivism, the theory continues to attract much interest. In particular, its emphasis on a methodology free from ideology ('politics masquerading as jurisprudence') seems to appeal to some who wish to study the legal order as an organised structure and who feel it would be useful to conduct that study free from what is perceived as the contamination of value-judgments derived, in particular, from natural law doctrine.

Summary of Chapter 12

Positivism: Kelsen

Kelsen's methodology

Kelsen (1881-1973) was concerned to explain what the law is, not what it ought to be. This involved a positivist analysis free from any ethical or political judgments. Hence the title - 'the pure theory of law'.

The appropriate mode of analysis will be from 'adulterating elements' of other disciplines. Metaphysical speculation will be rejected.

Essence of the 'pure theory'

Every activity of a legal nature may be traced back to an authoritative standard - a 'norm'.

Legal norms prescribe certain types of behaviour and, additionally, attach sanctions to any manifestation of the contrary type of behaviour.

Law is considered, in terms of the 'pure theory' as a coercive order of human behaviour.

The validity of a norm is derived from its having been authorised by another legal norm of a higher rank.

The legal order may be interpreted as a hierarchy made up of different levels of legal norms.

The basic norm is the *Grundnorm* - the presupposed starting point of the procedure of positive law creation. Such a basic norm exists in any kind of legal order. No system of law can be established on the basis of conflicting basic norms.

The effectiveness of norms

The 'principle of legitimacy' of norms within a community is restricted by the principle of effectiveness. Norms must be accepted generally within the community. Additionally, there must be appropriate general support for the *Grundnorm*.

Universal and total obedience to norms is not essential (even if it were possible). What is essential is a sufficiency of adherence to the essence of the basic norm. 'The efficacy of the total legal order is a necessary condition for the validity of every single norm of the order.'

The 'all-embracing nature' of law

There is no such thing as a human activity which, because of its content, is disqualified from being embodied within a 'legal rule'.

'Subjective' and 'objective' rights are merely personalised expressions of one group of norms.

'Natural' and 'juristic' persons are no more than representations of a type of norm relating to individuals.

'State' and 'law' are fundamentally identical. The State is the totality of norms within a hierarchy. State and law are to be thought of as co-extensive and the traditional dualism of 'Law versus State' has disappeared.

Criticism of Kelsen

Laski suggests that the 'pure theory' is 'an exercise in logic and not in life'. The theory is condemned as arid, unreal and far-removed from the complex reality of the law in action.

Because Kelsen has rejected any consideration of the context of a legal system, he has given form precedence over meaning and has failed to recognise the formative nature of the community's morality in relation to law.

The exclusion of any consideration of 'justice' from the 'pure theory' ignores the fact that for many jurists and legislators 'justice' is the very essence of the law.

The place of coercion in the 'pure theory' ignores the fact that within a community laws may be obeyed for reasons other than fear of sanctions.

The concept of the *Grundnorm* has been held to be unreal and to represent little more than personal value-judgments.

Chapter 13

The Historical Approach: Savigny and Maine

13.1 History as an aid to understanding

The 'historical movement' in jurisprudence reflects the belief that a deep knowledge of the past is essential for a comprehension of the present. A study of existing legal institutions and contemporary legal thought demands an understanding of historical roots and patterns of development. Two jurists are selected for comment, Friedrich Carl von Savigny (1799-1861) and Sir Henry Maine (1822-88). *Savigny*, a Prussian statesman and historian, viewed law as reflecting a people's historical experience, culture and 'spirit'. For him, ancient custom guides the law; the growth of legal principles is evidence of 'silently-operating forces' and not the result of deliberate decisions. *Maine*, the first professor of comparative jurisprudence at Oxford, suggested that legal ideas and institutions have their own course of development, and that evolutionary patterns of growth may be deduced from historical evidence.

13.2 Savigny: the 'spirit of the people'

Savigny lived during an era dominated by the effects of the French Revolution and the Napoleonic conquests. The destruction of the French feudal order, the spread of revolutionary ideology and the belief that, henceforth, 'the general and legislative will' of peoples was to be guided by reason, produced in Savigny and many other European jurists a deep and abiding hostility to the philosophy of the revolution. Concepts of liberty and equality were rejected in Germany, where a reaction set in; authority, tradition, 'the creative spirit' of the people's folklore, were stressed. Cosmopolitanism was rejected; the creative role of 'national character' was emphasised. The origin and essence of the law would be discovered by an understanding of the people's spirit - the *Volksgeist*.

13.2.1 Kindred consciousness

Savigny's tract, *Of the Vocation of Our Age for Legislation and Jurisprudence* (1814), written as an answer to those who urged the preparation of a civil code for a united Germany, set out the essential features of his outlook:

> 'We first enquire of history how law has actually developed among nations of the nobler races ... That which binds a people into one whole is the common conviction of the people, the kindred consciousness of an inward necessity, excluding all notion of an accidental and arbitrary origin.'

13.2.2 Custom and the people

Savigny states: 'All law is originally formed in the manner in which, in ordinary but not quite correct language, customary law is said to have been formed: ie, that it is first developed by custom and popular faith, next by jurisprudence – therefore, by internal silently operating powers, not by the arbitrary will of a lawgiver.' The customs of a people embody ('externalise') its *common consciousness* and from them law grows in an *organic, unconscious fashion.*

- A people's laws embody 'the popular genius'.
- Law seems to resemble language in some aspects.
- Law and language evolve gradually, reflecting a people's evolving characteristics.
- Law and language are essentially non-static: both flourish when the people flourish; both die when the people loses its individuality. 'For law as for language there is no moment of absolute rest.'

No laws have universal validity; they have application to specific peoples only.

13.3 The place of legislation and lawyers

Savigny suggests that historical research reveals that legislation is of subsidiary importance in the development of law. The 'living law' does not emerge from the commands of a Sovereign or the arbitrary will of a legislator; rather does it develop organically from the complex amalgam of reason, intuition, custom, instinct, etc. *'Law comes from the people, not from the State.'*

13.3.1 Legislation reflects harmony with the people

Legislation will be effective only when it is in harmony with the people's voice and deep aspirations and when it reflects the needs of the people.

This is not to decry legislation. (Indeed, Savigny was himself head of the Prussian Department for the Revision of Statutes.) He emphasises the point that a law which is in conformity with the needs of the people, which expresses their requirements at a particular stage in their historical and spiritual development, will be valuable. A law which ignores the significance of the people's developmental stage will be futile.

13.3.2 Lawyers are trustees for the people

As law becomes more technical, with the advance of civilisation, a division of labour emerges: in the sphere of matters concerning the law, the people will be represented to a growing extent by specialists - lawyers - whose task is to enunciate and elaborate legal principles in a formal style. Those principles remain rooted, however, in the consciousness of the people. Lawyers are *trustees* for the people.

13.4 Learning from the past: the significance of Roman law

Savigny was a celebrated scholar of classical Roman law. He turned to that system for material which might throw light on the true legal needs of the German people.

13.4.1 Its eternal significance

For Savigny, Roman law of the classical period seems to have 'eternal significance'. Its doctrines can constitute a fortress within which German legal tradition as nurtured by the *Volksgeist* might be sheltered from the assaults of French revolutionary doctrine. The 'profound certainties' of the Corpus Juris would provide lessons which the German people could use to their advantage.

13.4.2 Its universality

Savigny's vast *History of Roman Law in the Middle Ages* (1831) seems to suggest that there are concepts within Roman law which might reflect 'the nature of things'. Principles of a *universal nature* could be deduced from those concepts. Hence some legal rules which existed in Savigny's day were to be denounced as 'logically impossible' because they appeared to be inconsistent with Roman principles. That which is logically impossible cannot be justified legally.

13.5 Savigny criticised

Criticism of Savigny's doctrine ranges from condemnation of the concept of the *Volksgeist* as a reactionary, unscientific fiction, to a rejection of his version of the relationship of custom and legislation.

13.5.1 Highly selective investigation

Savigny's view of history appears to have been highly selective; he seems to have written history solely in terms of his own time. In particular, his hostility to the French Revolution coloured his view of historical development as a whole, leading to an undue reverence for the past with little comprehension of the forces which led to revolution in his own day.

13.5.2 *Volksgeist* a mere fiction

The *Volksgeist* is rejected by many critics as a mere fiction, cloaking a narrow and nationalistic attitude. The concept of *Volk* ('people'), which Savigny does not define, other than to state that it resembles a 'spiritual communion of people living together, using a common language and creating a communal conscience', involves a loose statement incapable of proof and of little value in jurisprudential analysis.

13.5.3 What is a 'communal conscience'?

What is 'the communal conscience'? How does the concept apply to a nation which is deeply divided on legal matters? What of important advances in the law which have arisen from political and legal conflict within a nation?

There are many examples of laws transplanted successfully (eg, as the result of conquest) from one culture to another. Law is not, in these circumstances, the result of a people's 'feeling for right and wrong'.

13.5.4 Law often based on pragmatism

Law has often been created in times past and present as the result of pragmatic reaction to immediate problems. Thus, the very important statute *Quia Emptores* 1290 was a reaction to specific problems of estates in land; it was in no sense an emanation from 'the dark well springs of the people's unconscious feelings'.

13.5.5 Custom exaggerated

Custom – elevated by Savigny into a vital source of law - can be given an exaggerated significance in the history of legal institutions. It is often of a local nature only and may affect relatively small sections of a community. It may be unresponsive to changed conditions and, when this occurs, has to be ignored or supplemented with formal legislation.

13.5.6 Gray's criticisms

The American jurist, Gray (see 18.10), criticised Savigny in colourful style. How, he asked, can law be 'the product of the common consciousness'? 'Take a simple instance … By the law of Massachusetts, a contract by letter is not complete until the answer of acceptance is received. By the law of New York, it is complete when the answer is mailed. Is the "common consciousness" of the people of Massachusetts different on this point from that of the people of New York?'

Savigny's view that lawyers are the 'trustees of the people' leads Gray to comment: 'The jurists set forth the opinions of the people no more and no less than any other specially educated or trained class in a community sets forth the opinions of that community, each in its own sphere. They in no way set forth the *Volksgeist* in the domain of law than educated physicians set forth the *Volksgeist* in the matter of medicine.'

13.6 The paradox of 'Roman law for the German people'

Although Savigny presented law as reflecting nationhood, he advocated a refined system of Roman law for the German people. There is little reason to suppose that any reception of Roman law by German legislators would have reflected in any way the 'deep desires of the *Volk*'. The suggestion that legislation based upon the spirit of the principles of Roman law would have coincided with the demands of the German 'folk spirit' is not easy to sustain.

13.7 Social pressures and legislation

The exaggerations and mystical trappings of the *Volksgeist* doctrine should not blind one to the force of social pressures in relation to legislation. Within a democracy, for example, the pressure of public anxieties, such as those which led to the Protection of Children Act 1978 (enacted by a reluctant government) may exemplify 'community consciousness'. This may be an example of what Savigny had in mind when he lauded 'a people's spirit and feelings of justice and right'. It would be mere hyperbole, however, to speak of these feelings as 'the special product of a people's genius reflecting its folk-spirit'.

13.8 Maine: the relationship of ancient law to modern legal thought

Maine's very wide knowledge of early society leads him to reject theories of law based upon 'man's rational nature'. He stresses the importance in historical development of man's deep instincts, emotions and habits, and interprets human history as providing proof of the existence of stages in the evolution of law. Law can be understood, Maine argues, as a late stage in a slowly-evolving pattern of growth. In *Ancient Law: Its Connection with the Early History of Society and its Relation to Modern Ideas* (1861), Maine adopted a systematic method of investigating early law and embryonic legal systems.

13.9 Stages in the development of law

Three distinct, yet connected, stages are discerned by Maine in his survey of the development of law within early societies: law as the personal commands and judgments of patriarchal rulers; law as custom upheld by judgments; law as code. Maine had in mind a *universal pattern* of development.

13.9.1 First stage: commands

The *first stage* involves law emerging from the personal judgments and authoritarian commands of patriarchal rulers, eg, kings. They often claimed divine inspiration and their judgments were issued separately without any reference to patterns of principle. Judgments preceded rules: essentially the judge came before the law-maker.

13.9.2 Second stage: customary law

The *second stage* begins when the power of the patriarchs declines following a weakening of belief in their charisma and sacredness. Oligarchies of a political and military nature appear, claiming a monopoly of control over the interpretation and institutions of the law. The judgments of the oligarchs evolve into the basis of customs, and, what Maine names 'the epoch of customary law', begins and develops. 'Customs or observances now exist as a substantive aggregate, and are assumed to be precisely known to the aristocratic order or caste.' At this stage, the law is largely unwritten, so that its interpreters enjoy a monopoly of explanation. But the epoch does not endure, and the spread of writing assists in the creation of a transitional period leading to the third epoch.

13.9.3 Third stage: codes

In the *third stage*, which generally includes a period during which the monopoly of exposition of the law enjoyed by the oligarchs is broken, codes are predominant. The Roman Twelve Tables and Solon's Attic Code are examples. Maine argues that codes arose at virtually similar points in the relative growth of Greece, Rome, and some parts of Western Asia. The codes state the law as it is. Henceforth law would be characterised by declared purpose, and changes would follow a conscious wish for improvement in legal procedures and aims.

13.10 Further progress and the nature of societies

There was historical proof, according to Maine, of further progress in the development of the law related to the very nature of a given society. Two types of society were considered in this context: the stationary and the progressive.

13.10.1 The stationary societies

The stationary societies (and they were the rule) did not move beyond the concept of code-based law. Reference to the code decided all legal problems. This reflected, according to Maine, a general lack of desire on the part of members of a society to effect any change in the law. An inflexible law which fettered legal and social development was the invariable result of reliance upon the certainties of the code.

13.10.2 The progressive societies

The progressive societies (they were the exception) included most societies within Western Europe. They possessed a dynamism which expressed itself in modification of the law. The gap between formal, rigid, legal doctrine and the 'untidy', urgent needs of a society in flux was narrowed significantly. The result was an expansion of legal institutions and a refinement of legal doctrine.

13.11 The dynamic stage of legal development

Maine discerned within the history of the progressive societies a characteristic use of three agencies – legal fictions, equity, and legislation (in that historical order) – each assisting in the development of the law from rigidity to flexibility.

13.11.1 Legal fictions

Legal fictions are mere suppositions or assumptions intended to overcome the rigidities of the formal law and designed to advance the interests of justice. They are used so as to conceal the fact that although the letter of the law remains unchanged, its operation and effect have been modified. Maine gives as an example the Roman fiction of adoption. Its object was to ensure the perpetuation of the family cult or name: a child was handed over by one paterfamilias, X, to another, Y, so that he would take rank as Y's descendant within Y's family.

13.11.2 Equity

The growth of a secondary system of law, such as equity, which claims a superior sanctity inherent in its principles, allows the existence side by side with the established system of law, of rules and procedures enabling the rigidities of the formal law to be smoothed out, or even displaced. The ability of the second system to 'interfere' in the established system indicates an advance on the legal fiction. Maine suggests that its existence testifies to an advance in the complexity of legal thought.

13.11.3 Legislation

In this final stage of development, the enactments of a legislature indicate a peak of legal achievement. Jurisprudential thought and political will interact so as to erect an edifice comprising various forms of law which can be systematised and unified, perhaps in the form of a legislative code.

13.12 From status to contract

'*The movement of progressive societies has hitherto been a movement from status to contract.*' Maine interprets historical development as showing a basic pattern in which man's individual legal position is gradually modified. In early times an individual's position in his social group remained fixed; it was imposed without any reference to him and could not be changed by his own efforts. A Roman slave might be 'manumitted'(ie, liberated from slavery) by the efforts of a free person; but eventually the fixed status of the slave disappeared and he was able to deal with others freely and reciprocally.

> 'Starting, as from one terminus of history, from a condition of society in which all relations of Persons are summed up in the relation of Family, we seem to have steadily moved towards a phase of social order in which all these relations arise from the free agreement of individuals.'

Maine interprets historical development as illustrating a move from slavery and serfdom, from status determined at birth. An example is the change from the master-servant link to the employer-employee contract.

13.13 Maine criticised

It should be remembered in connection with the following criticisms that Maine was writing at a time when anthropology was in its formative stage. Relatively little was understood of the techniques of field study, and there were large gaps in the known history of early ages; thus, the Palaeolithic Age was unknown. It is said, however, that Maine persistently extrapolated well beyond the data available to him.

13.13.1 Lack of evidence

Diamond, in *Primitive Law* (1935), pointed out that the very title of Maine's study, *Ancient Law*, indicated a failure to understand that the study of the origins of law demands evidence as to the beginnings of law 'both as we know of them in the past *and as we see them in the present*'.

13.13.2 Oversimplication

Maine is criticised for having presented an over-simplification of the nature and structure of early society:

- Early society does not show an invariable pattern of movement from 'charismatic judgment' through 'aristocratic interpretation' to code.
- The 'rigidity of primitive law', as portrayed by Maine, is challenged repeatedly by contemporary anthropologists

who emphasise the remarkable adaptation of primitive peoples and the flexibility of legal arrangements.

- Maine's classification of societies appears to have been superseded by the work of anthropologists such as Childe and Hobhouse, who have produced evidence supporting a classification based upon the functions of food producers and gatherers, with law emerging at the point at which ploughing and irrigation became common.
- Custom is not distinct from law in all early societies, as Maine implied. Further, the patriarchal system was not universal in those communities: matriarchal systems (which were the result of specific cultural patterns) were often widespread.

13.13.3 Status does not yield invariably to contract

There is no steady growth of the phenomenon of status yielding to contract. Critics point out that, for example, feudalism can be interpreted as embodying a move from contract to status. Additionally, contemporary Western society shows much evidence of the continuing significance of status and gives indications of the prevalence of moves from contract to status. Industry-wide collective bargaining, protective social legislation, aspects of the landlord-tenant contract and mortgage agreements, may be interpreted as the creation of novel types of personal legal relationships which carry some important features of 'status'.

13.14 Jurisprudence as the study of historically-evolving systems

Savigny and Maine are now viewed widely as having based parts of their theories upon intuition or inadequate and misinterpreted evidence. They remain, nevertheless, figures of some significance in the development of jurisprudence considered as *a study of change*. Both viewed history as a tapestry of cultures, beliefs, traditions and events; both stressed the importance of studying the law, not only as it is, but as it has evolved over time. It is, perhaps, because of the work of those who pioneered the historical movement that few jurists would now reject the warning of Michelet: 'He who would confine his thought to present time will not understand present reality.'

Summary of Chapter 13

The Historical Approach: Savigny and Maine

History and jurisprudence

The historical approach to jurisprudence is based upon the assumption that the key to an understanding of jurisprudential problems may be discovered in an analysis of the past. 'He who would confine his thought to present time will not understand present reality': Michelet.

It is the light thrown by historical study upon the interpretation of *patterns* of jurisprudential development which continues to attract contemporary jurists.

Savigny and the *Volksgeist*

Savigny (1799-1861), a Prussian statesman and jurist lived during an era dominated by the challenge of the French Revolution. He supported the reaction against this philosophy by urging a return to the doctrines of the past and by aggrandising the spirit of nationalism which he claimed to discern in historical development.

Law was interpreted as arising out of custom and popular feeling. 'Silently-operating forces' nurtured the processes which led to the growth of law.

The 'spirit of the people' - the *Volksgeist* - created the 'living law'. 'Law comes from the people, not from the State.'

Legislation will be effective only when it is in harmony with the people's needs and deep aspirations.

Lawyers are trustees for the people. Their task is to interpret needs and assist in the enunciation of those principles which embody the communal conscience.

Maine: understanding ancient law

In his *Ancient Law* (1861), Maine (1822-1888) interpreted history as providing proof of the existence of stages in the evolution of law.

Three distinct, yet connected, stages in legal development may be discerned in the records of the past.

- *First stage.* Law emerges from the personal judgments of patriarchs and rulers.
- *Second stage.* Oligarchs appear, claiming a monopoly of interpretation of the law.
- *Third stage.* The spread of writing produces 'codes of law' (eg, the Roman Twelve Tables) which state the law as it is.

Further progress in legal development depends upon the nature of society. The *stationary societies* did not move beyond code-based law. The result was inflexible legal systems. The *progressive societies* had a dynamism which expressed itself in modification of the law to meet new situations. The result was a progressive law.

Maine's 'dynamic stage of legal development'

'Progressive societies' utilised three agencies so as to move the law from rigidity to flexibility.

- *Legal fictions* were employed so as to advance the interests of justice.
- *Equity* grew in response to the need for a softening of the occasional harshness of formal law.
- *Legislation,* the 'peak of legal achievement', according to Maine, indicated a systematic approach to the needs of society in relation to law.

From status to contract

'The movement of progressive societies has hitherto been a movement from status to contract': Maine.

Maine argued that history indicated within progressive societies a pattern of development within which man's legal position was modified. Slavery and serfdom (which were generally fixed at birth) disappeared gradually and gave way in time to contractually determined social positions.

Critics of Maine suggest that 20th century developments may be interpreted as indicating a move from contract to status in some areas of society, eg, as in the case of industry-wide collective bargaining and protective social legislation.

Chapter 14

The Marxist Approach

14.1 'Up till now philosophers have merely interpreted the world ...'

Karl Marx (1818-1883), the son of a lawyer, and himself a student of jurisprudence, fashioned a theory of law in strict accord with his carefully-developed world outlook. Study was, for Marx, a means to an end: the end was the revolutionary transformation of society. An understanding of the nature of social phenomena such as economics, politics and law, would ensure that the path to revolution was charted properly. Comprehension of the origins and nature of law and of its objective role within society had to go hand in hand with a determination to change that society. 'Up till now', said Marx, 'philosophers have merely interpreted the world; *the point, however, is to change it.*' An understanding of jurisprudence demands more than a static analysis, according to Marx; it must encompass a study of the nature of law within a society in flux. Marx's world outlook, founded upon his studies in philosophy at the University of Bonn, and, later, Berlin, where he was profoundly affected by the philosophy of Hegel (1770-1831), comprises three doctrines: dialectical materialism, laws of economic production, and historical materialism. Marxist jurisprudence reflects these doctrines.

14.2 Dialectical materialism

Marx's approach to the phenomena of nature is *dialectical*; his interpretation of those phenomena is *materialistic.*

14.2.1 Dialectics

Dialectics (*dialego* = to debate, discourse) is, as a general mode of analysis, totally opposed to metaphysical speculation (so that, for example, natural law is to be rejected). Its essential features are as follows:

- Nature is a connected and integral whole: nothing exists as an isolate. Hence law cannot be understood 'on its own': it is connected with, and, therefore, dependent on, many other phenomena.
- Nature is in a state of continuous movement and change. A study of jurisprudence cannot ignore the changing character of the law.
- Development in *all* phenomena is characterised by imperceptible, quantitative changes, which become fundamental, qualitative changes, as evidenced by the decay and eventual disappearance of some jurisprudential doctrines and the appearance of new forms of theory.

- Internal contradictions are inherent in all phenomena, and 'struggles' between opposites, the old and the new, are inevitable. Thus, Marxist jurists would view some fundamental disputes within jurisprudence as reflecting a struggle between opposing modes of interpretation.

14.2.2 Materialism

Materialism stands in direct opposition to philosophical idealism and rejects metaphysics, 'the primacy of spirit', and the concept of 'rational purpose in nature'. Matter is the basis of all that exists.

- The world is material: its phenomena constitute different forms of matter in motion ('motion is the mode of existence of matter'). Hence Marxist jurisprudence requires for its methodology no 'universal spirit' and no 'categories of the unknowable': it must be able to explain in their totality the phenomena which comprise the law.
- Matter is primary, mind is secondary, derivative, because it is a reflection of matter. To divide thought from matter, in jurisprudence or in any other sphere of study, is to fall into error. (Lenin, in his *Materialism and Empirio-Criticism* (1913) stated: 'The material world perceived by the senses to which we ourselves belong is the sole reality ... our consciousness and thought, however supra-sensible they may seem, are merely the products of a material and corporeal organ, the brain. Matter is not a product of the mind, but the mind itself is merely the superior product of matter.')
- The world and its phenomena are entirely knowable: experiment and other forms of practical activity can produce authentic knowledge which has the validity of objective truth. The processes of discovering objectivity are difficult and never complete. There are no 'eternal principles' and humanity's concepts change from age to age.

14.3 Laws of economic production

Production under capitalism is regulated, according to Marx, by inexorable economic laws. Those who own the instruments of production (the capitalist class) derive surplus value from the labour of those who have nothing but their labour power to sell (the proletariat). The appropriation of surplus value is the key to an understanding of capitalism (*and the legal rules which are created so as to support that system*). In the drive for profit, the capitalist class must intensify the exploitation of the proletariat. Crises of overproduction develop and existing markets are exploited more intensively. Society is polarised; economic crisis deepens, immiseration of the workers intensifies. The workers learn from their struggles and are able to attain a level of organisation which enables them to confront the capitalist class and to 'expropriate the expropriators'. The capitalist system, says Marx, produces its own grave-diggers. Following the disappearance of bourgeois society, 'we shall have an association in which the free development of each is the condition for the free development of all'.

14.4 Historical materialism

Marx provides a brief summary of his views on historical materialism in the preface to *A Contribution to the Critique of Political Economy* (1859).

14.4.1 Mode of production of fundamental significance

The mode of production of material life conditions the general process of social, political and intellectual life. 'It is not the consciousness of men that determines their existence, but their social existence that determines their consciousness.'

14.4.2 Inevitability of conflict

At a certain stage of development, society's productive forces come into 'conflict' with the existing relations of production. 'These relations turn into their fetters. Then begins an era of social revolution.'

> 'No social order is ever destroyed before all the productive forces for which it is sufficient have been developed, and new, superior relations of production never replace older ones before the material conditions for their existence have matured within the womb of the old society. Therefore mankind always takes up only such problems as it can solve ... the problems arise only when the material conditions necessary for its solution already exist or are at least in the process of formation.'

14.4.3 Capitalism is the final antagonistic form of production

The capitalist mode of production is:

> 'the last antagonistic form of the social process of production ... the productive forces developing within bourgeois [ie, capitalist] society create also the material conditions for a solution of this antagonism. The prehistory of human society accordingly closes with this social formation.'

> 'Marx's whole canon is an attempt to show that this antagonistic character is inseparable from the fundamental structure of the capitalist system and is, at the same time the mechanism of the historic movement': Aron.

14.5 Base and superstructure

The real basis of any given social order is, according to Marx, its economic foundation, and, in particular, the relations created by the processes of production. How production is organised, who owns the instruments of production, who sells his labour power, under what conditions - these matters constitute 'the basis of production'.

14.5.1 Superstructure is a corollary to economic structure

Upon this foundation society erects a legal and political superstructure. 'The role of production of material life conditions the general process of social, political and intellectual life.' This superstructure includes ideas, theories, ideologies, philosophy; it is a corollary to economic structure.' 'Neither legal relations nor the form the State takes can be explained either by themselves or by the presumed general evolution of the human mind; both have their roots in the material conditions of life': Marx.

- *Superstructure* cannot be understood apart from its basis. A correct understanding of law and jurisprudence in a particular epoch requires an analysis of the relationships which men have entered into as a direct result of the processes of production within that epoch.
- *Ideologies*, theories of law, do not exist *in vacuo*; to trace the fundamentals of a theory is a necessary stage in understanding it. Hence, argues Marx, an appropriate method for any social study, such as jurisprudence, cannot neglect the economic fundamentals of society. Consider, for example, the significance of the fact that common law developed during the era of feudalism, and the resulting effects upon the law of tenures and estates.

14.5.2 Legal rules reflect the needs of the ruling class

Legal rules, institutions and jurisprudential theories arise, according to Marx, not accidentally, but in response to needs perceived by the ruling group within society. Religion, ethics, art, jurisprudence, perform functions which assist in the maintenance of social cohesion; their claim to reflect and portray 'eternal categories' is nonsense. As society changes, as the perceived needs of the ruling class change, so the theories of the social sciences will alter.

14.6 Class instrumentalism

Because of the very nature of capitalist society, exploitation and struggle are inevitable. Ideas concerning the law, its foundation and content, are mere reflections of the unrelenting class struggle which is at the basis of social activity. Objectively, jurists do not, because they cannot, stand aside from a struggle of which they are an integral part. Jurisprudence is to be interpreted as an aspect of the class interests served, consciously or unconsciously, by jurists.

14.6.1 Law is an instrument of class domination

Law is perceived by Marx as an instrument of class domination, allowing the ruling class to control the working class. Enactments, regulations, the legal apparatus, no matter how beneficial and disinterested they seem to be, are methods of ensuring the continuation of the economic and political *status quo*. 'Law is sacred to the bourgeois, for it is enacted for his benefit.'

14.6.2 Impossibility of a neutral jurisprudence

A 'neutral', 'disinterested', jurisprudence is a fiction. Marxist jurists have attempted to show that behind the tenets of jurisprudential movements in this century may be discerned a concern for the protection and preservation of the interests of the ruling class. Concern for 'natural rights', 'the rights of property', is a mask for intellectual activities aimed at the maintenance of a system based upon economic exploitation. Jurists become, in effect, 'hired pugilists', defending a ruling class, 'indulging in a rhetoric of self-praise and dogmatism', and attempting to perpetuate patterns of class domination.

Jurisprudential theories are not 'isolates'; they can be interpreted only within the context of economically-determined relationships. The process of unravelling these relationships demands an awareness of the historical development of classes.

In a celebrated passage from the *Communist Manifesto* (1848) – a review of the history of society, and a 'call to arms' - Marx addresses the doomed bourgeoisie:

> 'Your jurisprudence is but the will of your class made into a law for all, a will whose essential character and direction are determined by the economic conditions of existence of your class ... Behind your jurisprudence is your concern for the maintenance of your economic superiority. Your law is a mere expression, a rationalisation, of that concept.'

14.6.3 Jurisprudence as legitimisation

Because law and jurisprudence implement what is required by the dominant economic group within society, jurisprudential ideas tend, according to Marx, to 'legitimise' the existing social structure. Property rights are exalted, attempts by the exploited to combine and improve their bargaining position are anathematised as interference with 'natural forces', and the withdrawal of labour, in the form of strikes, is categorised as 'anarchical'. The favoured form of jurisprudence is that which views the *status quo* as the result of the workings of an 'invisible hand', guiding society towards freedom and prosperity. So runs the Marxist view of 'legitimisation'.

14.7 State and law

In spite of its outward trappings of power and the support given to it by legal theories which tend to sanctify the basis of its operations, the State is viewed in Marxist jurisprudence as no more than an aspect of superstructure, resting upon an economic basis whose contradictions it mirrors.

The State did not exist, according to Marxists, before the emergence of classes; its subsequent growth mirrors the burgeoning of a class system.

14.7.1 The State as the executive committee of the ruling class

Within capitalist society, the State is merely 'the executive committee' of the bourgeoisie, ruling on its behalf and utilising a legal apparatus which is based upon the threat of coercive action against those who seek to overturn the existing order. In the words of Marx's collaborator, Engels (1820-95), the State is 'the form in which the individuals of a ruling class assert their common interests, and in which the whole civil society of an epoch is epitomised'.

14.7.2 Jurisprudence assists the State's role

Jurisprudence assists the State by providing an ideology which, under the guise of an objective analysis of the role of the State, underpins its dominant, exploitative role and objectives.

14.8 The withering away of the State

All phenomena are affected by change and eventual decay; the State is not, therefore, eternal. Marxists have prophesied that it will wither away when a triumphant revolution replaces 'the government of persons by the administration of things'. When classes disappear, following the revolution, there will be no need for a legal apparatus which is the expression of class rule. Exploitation and poverty – the root causes of criminal conduct – will vanish in the classless society.

14.8.1 Gradual disappearance of the State

The State will disappear gradually. During the transitional period from capitalism to socialism, new forms of law and a new jurisprudence will be required. As man develops into 'a group creature', he will have no need of codes and rules, and the very need for an institutionalised law will vanish.

14.8.2 Soviet revision of the doctrine

Jurists within the USSR found it difficult to accept the implications of this doctrine. According to Vyshinsky, a leading Soviet jurist, writing in 1938, the construction of socialist society rendered it necessary to consolidate law and the State:

> 'In the society which emerges from the womb of exploitation it is essential to retain law as an administrative law, as a means of regulating social relationships and as a method of controlling and fixing the quotas of work and consumption.'

14.8.3 Pashukanis

Pashukanis (1891-1937), an early Soviet jurist and Vice-Minister for Justice, argued in his contribution to the debate in the early days of the Soviet Union on the materialist critique of legal forms, *Law and Marxism: a General Theory* (1924, corrected version 1930), that bourgeois law would continue during the period of transition to socialism even though capitalist exploitation had disappeared. So-called 'proletarian law' was a meaningless abstraction because all law would die away as the State itself withered away. Pashukanis was attacked by party legal theoreticians who reminded him that, according to official Marxist theory, the State creates its own law so as to protect the dominant class and that there could be no law independent of the State. 'Law is nothing without a mechanism capable of enforcing observance of the norms of law.' Bourgeois law would disappear when the victorious proletariat and peasantry finally broke the power of the exploiters, but until that was achieved, a new, proletarian law was needed which would strengthen the power of the new State, including its punitive organs. Pashukanis disappeared in the purges of the 1930s following his denunciation as an 'ideological wrecker'.

14.8.4 Vyshinsky's definition of law

Vyshinsky defined law in terms which are in line with Marx's thesis of class instrumentalism:

> 'Law is the totality of rules of conduct which express the will of the ruling class and are laid down in a legislative manner, along with the rules and practices of communal life which are sanctioned by the power of the State. The application of these rules is backed by the coercive power of the State in order to secure, reinforce, and develop the social relationships and conditions which are agreeable to the interests of the ruling class.'

14.9 Law as fetish

In recent years, Marxist jurists have criticised some lawyers and social reformers who are accused of having made a 'fetish' of the legal process. The term 'fetish' is borrowed from anthropology, where it is used to refer to an object of extreme and irrational reverence.

14.9.1 A diversion from revolutionary struggle

To concentrate revolutionary struggle on the objective of improved social rights is to confuse means with ends. Successful agitation for, say, an extension of union rights or equal pay, can be, in Marxist terms, no more than a diversion from the overriding historical task of transforming society. To strive for changes in the law aimed at an amelioration of the conditions of the workers is to ignore the fundamental purpose of *all* law within bourgeois society, which is to buttress the existing social structure.

Reverence for law as standing, somehow, 'above society', is condemned as a virtual superstition, a 'fetishising of law'.

14.9.2 The point is to change society

Concentration upon the maintenance or extension of 'the rule of law' is criticised as based upon a misunderstanding of the reality of law in a capitalist society. Such a stance indicates a failure to discern what is behind the so-called 'neutrality of the law' and 'apolitical jurisprudence'. The result is a neglect of the basic demands of the class struggle in favour of temporary, opportunist gains. 'The point is to change society', not to come to terms with it. 'Law as fetish' obscures this historical necessity.

14.10 Jurisprudence at the service of the State

The history of Marxist jurisprudence in the post-1917 era is the story of legal theory used to shore up regimes characterised by an absence of human rights and a denial of freedoms, in the name of 'historical necessity'. The recent collapse of the Marxist regimes has drawn attention to what is widely perceived as an essentially-flawed theory of law.

Dialectical materialism has been condemned as built upon false foundations, so that a theory of law derived from that philosophy is inherently false. Historical materialism is viewed by many jurists as a one-sided interpretation of a very complex set of events which are not explained fully in terms of the class struggle.

The excesses of legal systems which were fashioned from Marxist theory took place in political environments from which the rule of law and the rights of the accused had been banished as 'remnants of bourgeois dominance'. The result was, in practice, a failure to generate a theory of human rights, a denial of human dignity and the growth of legal theories which were often little more than *ex post facto* justification of the State's political practices. (For a documented account of the excesses associated with Chinese Marxist jurisprudence, see Professor Ladany's *Law and Legality in China* (Hurst, 1992).)

Summary of Chapter 14

The Marxist Approach

Marx and jurisprudence

Marx (1818-1883) had studied jurisprudence at German universities. He viewed legal theory in the light of his own world outlook. An understanding of jurisprudence necessitated awareness of the class struggle and the class structure within bourgeois (capitalist) society.

Jurisprudence reflected the aspirations and needs of the dominant class.

Marx's world outlook

There are three separate, but connected, strands of thought within Marx's philosophy. Each strand is reflected in Marx's attitude to jurisprudence and legal structure.

- Dialectical materialism

  This is a mode of thought based upon a materialist conception of the universe and the dialectical method, which examines the interconnections of, and contradictions within, all phenomena. All things are in flux; to understand the laws of change is essential.

- Laws of economic production

  Production under capitalism is based on exploitation of the workers, who have only their labour power to sell, by the capitalists, who own the instruments of production. Crises are endemic and result in the workers intensifying their organisation so that, eventually, their very experiences in the productive apparatus teach them how to overthrow their exploiters.

- Historical materialism

  The history of society is the history of the class struggle. The mode of production within society conditions the general process of intellectual life. Revolution will occur only when the contradictions created by the capitalist mode of production cannot be solved.

Base and superstructure

The basis of society is its economic foundation. Upon this base, society erects a political and legal superstructure. Ideas, theories, ideologies reflect economic activity. Jurisprudence is no exception to this rule.

Legal institutions, rules, procedures, theories, arise in response to the needs perceived by the ruling class. Under capitalism, jurisprudence guards and advances the interests of the bourgeoisie.

Class instrumentalism

Because law is an instrument - a 'tool' - of the dominant class, it is neither neutral nor standing above the class struggle. It is a part of it. Marx, addressing the bourgeoisie, in the *Communist Manifesto* (1848) said:

> 'Behind your jurisprudence is your concern for the maintenance of your economic superiority. Your law is a mere expression, a rationalisation, of that concept.'

Jurisprudence 'legitimises' the activities of the dominant economic class by providing intellectual support for the *status quo*.

State and law

The State came into existence, according to Marx, only when classes appeared within society. In capitalist society, the State is effectively, the executive committee of the ruling class. Jurisprudence assists the State by providing theories concerning the 'neutrality' of government and the law.

After the socialist revolution, classes will disappear and, therefore, the need for a State and its legal apparatus of repression will also disappear. The government of persons will give way to the administration of things. Bourgeois law will be rendered obsolete. The State will have withered away.

Criticisms of the Marxist approach

The philosophical basis of Marxist jurisprudence has been criticised continuously by those who argue that dialectical materialism is flawed, that there is no proof of the validity of Marx's interpretation of history, and that the 'class-struggle concept' of social development is a simplistic view of a very complex phenomenon.

Attention has been drawn, in recent years, to the quality of the legal systems erected in Marxist States on the basis of Marxist jurisprudence. Common to those States has been a rejection of the rule of law and a continuous abuse of human rights. Critics suggest that this is not accidental; Marxist jurisprudence, it is argued, contains within its tenets the seeds of an intolerance from which totalitarianism will inevitably burgeon.

Chapter 15

The Sociological Approach (1); Jhering, Ehrlich, Durkheim

15.1 Sociology and the law

Sociology is defined by Faris as:

> 'a branch of the science of human behaviour that seeks to discover the causes and effects that arise in social relations among persons and in the intercommunication and interaction among persons and groups.'

15.1.1 Law as a social institution

Human beings are more dependent, sociologists point out, on social organisation than is any other species; hence institutionalised social forms (law, State, etc) are of considerable significance in the life of a community. The study of law in its social setting, as a *social institution*, is the basis of the sociological approach to jurisprudence.

15.1.2 Comte

Comte (1798-1857) invented the word 'sociology'. He believed that society developed according to certain principles, the pattern and essence of which could be discovered:

> 'Sociology itself depends upon preliminary study, first of the outer world, in which the actions of humanity take place; and, secondly, of man, the individual agent.'

15.1.3 Methodology of sociology

The methodology of sociology, in relation to the study of law, involves a close analysis of the structure, functions, effects and values of a legal system; this necessitates an investigation of persons, institutions, rules, procedures and doctrines, so that hypotheses and principles might be formulated and tested. Field surveys (such as the collection of data relating to the functioning of aspects of the judicial system), comparative observation and statistical analysis, should feature in the work of sociological jurists.

The essence of the sociological view is that law is a social phenomenon reflecting human needs, functioning as an organised system, and embodying within its fundamental principles and substantive rules the basic values of a society. The discovery of principles governing the law *as a social phenomenon*, remains the key task of sociological jurisprudence.

Pound, in his *Mechanical Jurisprudence* (1908) wrote of the sociological movement in jurisprudence as 'a movement for pragmatism as a philosophy of law; for the adjustment of principles and doctrines to the human conditions they are to govern rather than to assumed first principles; for putting the human factor in the central place and relegating logic to its true position as an instrument.'

Three theoreticians are selected for comment: *Jhering* (1818-1892), a German jurist; *Ehrlich* (1862-1922), an Austrian jurist; and *Durkheim* (1858-1917), founder of the French school of sociology.

15.2 Jhering: law as a social mechanism for the balancing of purposes and interests

Jhering's doctrine of law was based upon 'social utilitarianism'; law's essence could be expressed by reference to its very *purpose*, which was *social*. Law existed to protect the interests of society and of the individual by coordinating those interests, thus minimising the possibility of social conflict. Jhering in *Law as Means to an End* (1873) said:

> 'Law is the sum of the conditions of social life in the widest sense of that term, as secured by the power of the State through the means of external compulsion.'

15.2.1 Rules reflect purpose

Social values, social utility, are all-important in an understanding of the concept and functions of the law.

There is, according to Jhering, no single legal rule which does not owe its origin to some purpose, ie, some practical motive. Indeed, law emerges from social struggle concerning purposes; it is a direct social response to perceived needs and methods of satisfying them. Its sole purpose is to achieve desired objectives by *guiding and protecting social interests.*

15.2.2 Interests dictate purpose

Interests dictate purpose: interests need to be studied if the purposes of the law are to be comprehended fully.

- *Individual interests* ought to be linked to the interests of others so that social purposes might be fulfilled.
- The law should ease the pursuit of the *common interest*, and the legislator should keep in mind the principle that 'every person exists for the world, and the world exists for everybody'.

15.3 The reconciliation of interests

The object of a society, the very purpose of its existence, is essentially the securing of the satisfaction of human wants. There are, according to Jhering, 'levers of social motion' which can be used to this end. The 'egoistical levers' of reward and coercion, ie, private gain, and the threat of sanctions where undesirable conduct takes place, may be utilised in combination with the 'altruistic levers', such as the sentiment of duty. A coordinated use of these levers makes the achievement of social ends possible through the *balancing of purposes and principles*, and the law assists to this end.

15.3.1 Law aims at equilibrium

The true aim of the law is *the realisation of an equilibrium of individual and social principles and purposes*. The law is, in effect, 'the realised partnership of the individual and society'. Competing interests must be resolved by the impartial mediation of the law. Let legislators and judges seek to bring interests into harmony: the legislator will keep in mind the essential purpose of society, while the judge will be aware of the true social purpose behind the law he seeks to enforce.

15.3.2 Purpose is all and purpose is relative

Society's purposes and standards will change from time to time; hence to rely upon concepts of an 'immutable natural law' as an absolute guide to social and legal activity would be difficult. 'Purpose is all and purpose is relative.'

There is not necessarily an opposition of individual and social interests: the individual is interested in the maintenance of effective social institutions; while society is interested in the protection of individual rights.

15.3.3 Law aims at creating unity from diversity

Above all, the law aims at the good of society in its entirety and, in attempting to achieve that goal, it creates a *unity from diversity*, allowing individuals to realise their purposes, and, in so doing, creating a strong social fabric. Legal institutions enable man to add to the very quality of his being; individually, man may be able to achieve only relatively limited objectives, but in collaboration with his fellows within society his capacities for self-realisation are greatly increased. The law will provide the institutional framework within which the individual's life can be enhanced. *Law is the mediator, the balancer, the harmoniser.*

15.4 Ehrlich: the centre of gravity of legal development

'At the present as well as at any other time, the centre of gravity of legal development lies not in legislation, nor in juristic science, nor in judicial decision, but in society itself': *Fundamental Principles of the Sociology of Law* (1912). Ehrlich recognises two vital and complementary sources of law: legal history and jurisprudence, and 'the living law' (derived from currently-acknowledged custom and the creation of norms by members of society).

15.5 Ehrlich's analysis of norms

Ehrlich differentiates norms for decision and norms for conduct.

15.5.1 Norms for decision

Norms for decision are equivalent to what are generally understood as 'laws' and comprise those legal norms embodied in statutes, codes or common law doctrines and intended for the adjudication of disputes. They may be considered as the rules and regulations for persons whose business is the settling of disputes. Thus, in our day, the Social Security

Administration Act 1992 sets out appropriate 'rules' allowing the courts to adjudicate on claims and payments relating to social benefits.

15.5.2 Norms of conduct

Norms of conduct are self-generating social rules, dependent upon no superior sanctioning authority, but effectively governing many groups and relationships within society. They form 'the inner order of associations' and are accepted by society. They may often stand in contrast to rules enforced by the State.

15.6 The 'living law'

This concept dominated Ehrlich's jurisprudential thought. 'Living law' grows within society and may dominate its conduct even though it does not possess the authority of legal formality. *It reflects the true values of society.*

Because the 'inner order' of society's life (its 'culture-pattern') reflects changing values, the 'living law' can never be static.

15.6.1 The gap between 'living' and 'positive' law

There is, necessarily, a gap between 'the living law' and 'the positive law'. Ehrlich cites the private financial practices within commercial communities as illustrating this gap. However, the law often bridges gaps of this nature, as in the case of the Bills of Exchange Act 1882 and, in our day, the Law of Property (Miscellaneous Provisions) Act 1989 (in relation to practices involving the sealing of deeds).

15.6.2 Importance of the gap

Legislators and judges must be aware of 'the gap' and must accept the necessity of giving expression to the community's innermost feelings.

Ehrlich defines society as 'the sum total of the human associations that have mutual relations with one another'. 'The living law' reflects that which binds individuals within associations. Where legislators fail to recognise the potency of the law in relation to social ends, enacted law will cease to mirror social aspirations.

15.7 Discovering 'the living law'

This vital task for legislators, judges and jurists involves, according to Ehrlich, continuous analysis not only of judicial decisions and formal regulations, but also of the perceptions and activities of members of society in their daily lives.

If we wish to understand 'the law' as it relates, say, to the mortgage, it is necessary to study the legislation embodied in the Law of Property Act 1925, the development of the equitable right to redeem and the equity of redemption, together with decisions concerning foreclosure, tacking, etc. See, eg, *Knightsbridge Estates v Byrne* (1940); *Multiservice Bookbinding v Marden* (1979).

15.7.1 'Living law' as an amalgam

But a much more comprehensive study is required. What is revealed by the formal language of the mortgage deed? What of social attitudes to the repossession of mortgaged property? What of the political and economic concepts of 'ownership' of mortgaged property? Ehrlich calls for a study, in this context, of the mortgage *in its entirety*. Thus and only thus would 'the living law' be revealed as an amalgam of formalities, current social values and perceptions.

15.8 The Czernowitz experiment

In a celebrated example of unusual field work in the realm of sociological jurisprudence, Ehrlich organised a 'seminar of the living law' at Czernowitz (now in the Ukraine). Groups of his students were asked to discover 'the practical realities of the law' in that area. Data were collected and analysed and contrasted with private documents, local customs and practices, particularly in relation to the rules of succession within family groups. The investigation revealed a profound gap between the customs and behaviour of a variety of ethnic groups and the formal legal code under which they lived. This intensified Ehrlich's belief in the necessity of investigating extra-legal data when one is examining any aspect of law; jurisprudence required, therefore, strong links with the social sciences in particular.

15.8.1 Boundless jurisprudence

The province of jurisprudence, declared Ehrlich, must be *boundless* because the vital facts of 'the living law' are the facts of social life in its entirety.

15.8.2 Megalomaniac jurisprudence

Allen, in *Law in the Making* (1958), refers to Ehrlich's concept of jurisprudence as a 'science of observation' and points out that a boundless jurisprudence might be 'a megalomaniac jurisprudence'. Indeed, if every legal dispute were to be subjected to the processes suggested by Ehrlich, 'scientific justice might perhaps be achieved ... but the parties would certainly be dead before the forensic process was complete'.

15.9 Durkheim and 'social solidarity'

Durkheim viewed the phenomenon of law in remarkable fashion - as an 'index to the level of development' within a community. Hence the study of law was essential for a fully-fledged science of society. Investigation of the development of early societies revealed varying degrees of social cohesion which Durkheim spoke of in terms of 'solidarity'. *Different types of solidarity produced their own forms of law*: see *The Division of Labour in Society* (1993).

15.9.1 Mechanical solidarity

Within early, undeveloped society, men recognised the need for mutual assistance and the combining of their aptitudes. Cohesion of a kind existed – *'solidarity by similitude'* or '*mechanical solidarity*'. In such a society values would be uniform and, because of an absence of division of labour and the consequent need for a collectivist attitude, individualism would exist only at a low level.

15.9.2 Organic solidarity

In more advanced societies in which the division of labour was widespread, collectivism was replaced by individualism. A strong social conscience would produce an '*organic solidarity*' which reflected the functional interdependence of producers.

15.9.3 Division of labour

> 'Division of labour appears to us in a different light than it does to economists. For them it consists essentially in producing more. For us this increased productivity is only a necessary consequence, an after-effect of the phenomenon. The reason we specialise is not to produce more, but to achieve the new living conditions that are provided for us': *The Division of Labour in Society*.

15.10 Law as an 'external index'

Because law tends to reflect in its concepts and modes of procedure types of social cohesion, Durkheim suggests that it ought to be possible to deduce from the evidence of a given form of law the type of social organisation within which it flourishes. it flourishes. Writing on Durkheim in *Main Currents in Sociological Thought* (1965), Aron states:

> 'Repressive law is, as it were, the index of the collective consciousness in societies with mechanical solidarity, since by the very fact that it multiplies punishments it reveals the force of common sentiments, their extent, and their particularisation. The more widespread, strong, and particularised the collective conscience, the more crimes there will be – crime being defined simply as the violation of an imperative or prohibition'. See 15.11 below.

15.10.1 Law indicates social norms

Within societies characterised by mechanical solidarity, the law appears strict, repressive, and its sanctions are applied with severity when social norms are disregarded. In Durkheim's phrase, there is a 'passionate reaction' by such a society to those deviations from the norm which offend the collective social conscience.

Within societies characterised by organic solidarity, restitution tends to replace mere vengeance as an aim of the legal process and social norms are embodied within legislation. The objective is not to punish but to re-establish the state of things as it should have been in accordance with justice.

15.10.2 Law symbolises morality

Because law is derived from the morality of society (according to Durkheim), it comes to symbolise it. Law and morality produce an amalgam of ties, binding individuals to society and producing unified, coherent groups. That which is a source of 'social solidarity' is, in essence, 'moral'; the morality of a society is as strong as the ties among its members. *'Everything which forces man to take account of other men is moral.'*

15.11 Law, crime and punishment

An act is considered 'criminal', says Durkheim, when it is generally perceived as offending the collective conscience (which he describes as 'a totality of beliefs and sentiments common to average citizens of the same society'). The phenomenon of crime affects 'society's upright consciences' and acts as a focus for them. Members of society are not shocked and angered by conduct merely because legislation has rendered it criminal; such conduct is criminal because society's collective conscience is shocked. Our abhorrence of one who deliberately poisons another reflects not our outrage at his offence under the Offences against the Person Act 1861, s 23, but rather our detestation of his actions in terms of our estimate of their effects upon *society's general cohesion.*

The purpose of punishment is, says Durkheim, not to deter, but rather to satisfy the common consciousness: the punishment of an offender is a 'reparation' offered to the feelings of members of the community.

15.12 Durkheim criticised

Durkheim's approach to the essence and function of law fails to satisfy many jurists; in particular, his neglect of the wide-ranging field work which would be necessary to substantiate his theories is considered as having vitiated the force of his conclusions. Some specific criticisms run as follows:

- The concept of 'social solidarity' seems not to possess, in reality, the significance attributed to it by Durkheim. Other factors in the life of the community may possess an even greater significance - the drive to survival, for example, which certainly colours attitudes to deviations from social norms. Further, there is no necessary correlation of 'solidarity' and level of civilisation: some of the repressive régimes of our century have lauded the concept of social and national solidarity while destroying basic human rights.
- There is doubt as to the universality of the 'mechanical solidarity' which Durkheim suggests to be characteristic of primitive societies. Recent field work by anthropologists has produced evidence of non-repressive regulation of social activities (together with a rudimentary division of labour) among some undeveloped peoples.
- Attitudes within a society to retribution and vengeance through the criminal law are not always as clear-cut and indicative of the development of society as Durkheim

suggests. Thus, the High Court judge, Sir James Stephen, writing in *Liberty, Equality and Fraternity* (1873) (see 7.12), at the height of the Victorian era, mentions one of the functions of the criminal law as 'gratifying a feeling of hatred - call it revenge, resentment, or what you will - which the contemplation of such [criminal conduct] excites in healthily constituted minds'. Some of today's jurists and sociologists perceive in current attitudes to capital punishment within highly-developed societies distinct vestiges of the ancient *lex talionis*. Attitudes of this type are not easy to explain satisfactorily merely by reference to Durkheim's thesis of development and solidarity.

Summary of Chapter 15

The Sociological Approach (1); Jhering, Ehrlich, Durkheim

Sociology and the law

Sociology is defined by Faris as:

> 'a branch of the science of human behaviour that seeks to discover the causes and effects that arise in social relations among persons and in the intercommunication and interaction among persons and groups.'

The sociological approach to jurisprudence suggests that law is a *social phenomenon* reflecting human needs, functioning as an organised system, and embodying within its fundamental principles and substantive rules a society's basic values.

The appropriate methodology of jurists who favour this approach is based on a systematic analysis of the structure, functions and values of legal systems.

Jhering: the balancing of interests

Jhering (1818-1892) was a 'social utilitarian' who believed that the essence of law could be expressed by reference to its very *purpose*, which was social. Law existed to protect the interests of individuals and society by balancing and coordinating interests.

'Law is the sum of the conditions of social life in the widest sense of that term, as secured by the power of the State through the means of external compulsion': Jhering (*Law as a Means to an End* (1873)).

Interests dictate purpose; they need to be studied if the purposes of the law are to be understood:

- The law should attempt to achieve an equilibrium of individual and social principles and purposes.
- The creation of unity from diversity demands an effective law which will reflect social purpose and contribute to a partnership of individuals within society.

Ehrlich: the 'living law'

'At the present as well as at any other time, the centre of gravity of legal development lies not in legislation, nor in juristic science, nor in judicial decision, but in society itself': Ehrlich (*Fundamental Principles of the Sociology of Law* (1912)).

Ehrlich (1862-1922) differentiated 'norms for decision' (formal laws and other regulations) from 'norms of conduct' (self-generating social rules). The norms of conduct are often in contrast to the rules enforced by the State and constitute the 'living law', which reflects the true values of society.

A vital task for legislators, judges and jurists is to discover the 'living law'; this involves studying much extra-legal data when investigating a legal problem.

The province of jurisprudence must be 'boundless' because the facts of the 'living law' are the facts of social life in its entirety.

Durkheim: social solidarity

Durkheim (1858-1917) saw social cohesion ('social solidarity') as fundamental to society. Mechanical solidarity' (which seemed to exist in societies in which there was an absence of the division of labour) was contrasted with 'organic solidarity' (which reflected the functional interdependence of producers).

Law could be perceived as an external index to the type of society in which it flourished. A strict, repressive law was characteristic of societies dominated by a mechanical solidarity; a more flexible legal structure characterised societies in which organic solidarity prevailed.

Law symbolises society's morality. That which assists in the creation and maintenance of social solidarity is 'moral', and the morality of society is as strong as the ties existing among its members. 'Everything which forces man to take account of other men is moral.' Law and morality cannot be divorced.

Chapter 16

The Sociological Approach (2): Weber and Pound

16.1 Systematisation and sociological jurisprudence

Weber (1864-1920) and *Pound* (1870-1964) pioneered the analytical, systematic approach to jurisprudence. Law was to be studied as a *social institution* and the legal order would be investigated in its setting in relation to other social phenomena. A sociological review of law would be undertaken. Weber, a German jurist, economist and sociologist, evolved a synoptic view of legal development which he interpreted as characterised by systematic changes in the legal order and in the growth of authority. Sociology was, for Weber, a comprehensive, wide-ranging science of social action. Pound, Dean of the Harvard Law School, enunciated the aim of law as the balancing of the security of society and the individual life. To this end he wished to construct a 'theory of social interests which courts may use, just as in the past they have used the scheme of individual interests which we call theories of natural rights'. He attempted to make an inventory and classification of interests, believing that such a systematisation was necessary if interests were to be balanced correctly.

16.2 Weber: law as legitimate authority

Law within society could be comprehended, according to Weber, only through an appreciation of the significance of 'social order'. In *Law in Economy and Society* (1891), Weber emphasised that the essence of social order is to be found in norms and the power to enforce them. The law cannot be effective in the absence of power. By 'power', Weber has in mind the ability of persons or institutions to affect the will and behaviour of others by coercion or the threat of such coercion. Underlying the exercise of power must be an acceptance by members of society of *legitimate authority*, and such an authority exists only where those persons accept their rulers as a living embodiment of the idea of 'power through authority'.

It is important to note that Weber deliberately rejected Marx's work on the nature of society and social change. Marx's historical determinism and the economic interpretation of history were unacceptable. 'In my opinion,' wrote Weber, 'the view of historical materialism frequently espoused, that the economic is in some sense the ultimate point in the chain of causes is completely finished as a scientific proposition.' Weber's interpretation of history gave no support to the Marxist view of history as the expression of class struggle.

Historical change, social progress, changes in law and jurisprudence required investigation in a rigorous fashion which would, by its nature, exclude the world-view of Marx.

16.3 The types of legitimate authority

Weber's investigation of the legal history of societies suggested to him three types of 'legitimate authority', each having its own special attitudes to the concept of law and the purposes of legal institutions and procedures, each defined in terms of relationships built on obedience, or by the kind of legitimacy claimed by a leader.

16.3.1 Traditional authority

Traditional authority existed as the result of a community's long habituation to the concept of legitimacy as deriving from the sacred quality of age-old powers. Obedience of the ruled was required, not on the basis of enactments, but rather through the belief that the rulers had an authority conferred by ancient tradition.

Rule by patriarchs and elders epitomised the exercise of authority of this nature.

New rules, having the force of law, were legitimised by the very form of their enunciation which often reaffirmed ancient, traditional rules. Law was rarely created in open fashion in these circumstances.

16.3.2 Charismatic authority

(*Charisma* = the gift of grace.) Norms of social conduct upon which systems demanding obedience will rest, are revealed or ordained by some extraordinary person - a hero, prophet or god-king - who seems endowed with superhuman powers.

Revolutionary leaders tend to wield authority of this nature in the first years following their victorious revolutions.

Weber notes that the charismatic type of authority is enforced easily in the initial period of revolutionary victory, but becomes difficult to maintain in later years when it produces conflict with rules of a routine and mundane nature.

The authority of the charismatic leader may be transmitted to a successor so that legitimate authority then rests on descent and inherited status. The original 'charisma' becomes institutionalised and results in the creation of legal forms and other power structures.

16.3.3 Rational legal authority

Rational legal authority tends to be impersonal. Belief in the legality of enacted rules is widespread, and there is an acceptance of authority as resting upon a credible legitimacy. 'Be it enacted by the Queen's Most Excellent Majesty ...' (the enactment clause which introduced a statute) epitomises a command which will be obeyed not because of the charismatic qualities of the Monarchy, but because of general belief in the *legitimate basis* of Parliamentary supremacy, which authorises the exercise of supreme power within our society.

Authority within this context is justified by the obviously-rational nature of the rules promulgated by Parliament.

Authority attaches, under a legal order of this type, to the office rather than to the person. Thus, the authority of the Court of Appeal rests upon its position in the hierarchy of the courts rather than the personal reputation enjoyed by a particular Lord Justice of Appeal.

Weber viewed this type of authority, and structure, as being particularly appropriate for the development of a capitalist society: it provided an environment of certainty and predictability within which a law of contract (essential for the development of commercial activity) might develop.

The rational legal order is the conceptual basis of Weber's description of law as rules promulgated and externally guaranteed by the probability that physical or psychological coercion to produce uniformity (or to avenge violation) will be applied by appropriate groups of persons.

16.4 A systematised view of procedures within legal systems

Weber suggested that legal systems might be considered in terms of their 'rationality' or 'irrationality'; a sub-division would take into account the 'substantive' or 'formal' nature of legal procedures within the systems. This typology produced the following classification.

- Substantively irrational systems

  Disputes tend to be decided upon their individual merits: there is no set of general legal principles. *Ad hoc* and intuitive decisions predominate.

- Formally irrational systems

  Decisions result from tests 'beyond control of the human mind'. Intuitive decisions are replaced by the results of tests, such as ordeals. Basic irrationality is masked by formality, as in the case of appeals to Divine judgment through ordeal by fire or water.

- Substantively rational systems

  Morality and law are combined totally, as in theocratic systems in which the revealed Divine word is law. Justice is administered in the name of the Divinity.

- Formally rational systems

  Weber views this system as epitomised by the codes of civil law derived from Roman classical law. The system seeks to apply principles of logical consistence and of a general nature to the construction of rational and impersonal norms. Rules may be codified and sets of principles evolved which will assist in the solution of all types of legal problem.

16.5 Weber's typology and English law

Weber showed special interest in the characteristics of English law as epitomising the rules necessary for a developed capitalist society. He concluded that England was an exception to his generalised typology: capitalism had burgeoned there *before* the establishment of a rational legal system. The important, formative common law was a mixture of substantive and formal irrationality, while vestiges of the charismatic style of law-making remained in an era which was characterised predominantly by formally rational patterns. In Boyle's words, in his introduction to *Critical Legal Studies* (1992):

> 'Instead of rationalised administration [Weber] found tradition, pomp and ceremony. Instead of universal, general rules, there was a mass of particular doctrines, each keyed to a different procedural form. Where was the necessary connection between legal form and social form?'.

16.5.1 The problem of 'the Queen in Parliament'

The concept of 'the Queen in Parliament' is an interesting example of an amalgam of different types of legitimate authority and procedures. England's supremacy as a capitalist power seemed, to Weber, to have been achieved in spite of its legal system and procedures.

16.6 Pound: the essence of his jurisprudential thought

Law was, for Pound, a *social institution*, created and designed to satisfy human (individual and social) wants:

> 'by giving effect to as much as we may with the least sacrifice, so far as such wants may be satisfied or such claims given effect by an ordering of human conduct through politically organised society.'

The essential feature of the legal order was the securing and protection of a variety of interests, and this necessitated the modification of traditional, inherited legal codes with existing social conditions in mind. It was a task of sociological jurisprudence to ensure that social facts were noted and analysed so that they might be considered in the formulation, use and interpretation of law. The end of juristic study should be a contribution to the achieving of the purposes of the law; where justice was considered as one such purpose, this would necessitate the study of 'impersonal, equal, certain administration' and of social-legal precepts of general application.

16.7 Interests

Pound defines an interest (in his *Outlines of Lectures on Jurisprudence* (1943)) as:

> 'a demand or desire or expectation which human beings either individually or in groups or associations or relations, seek to satisfy, of which, therefore, the adjustment of human relations and ordering of human behaviour through the force of a politically organised society must take account.'

The recognition and definition of interests demand: an inventory and classification of interests; decisions on the selection of interests to be legally recognised; systematic study of the means of securing recognised interests.

It is the balancing of interests - individual, public, social - which constitutes the principal problem for legislators and jurists.

16.8 Individual interests

Individual interests are 'demands or desires involved in or regarded from the standpoint of the individual life'. They comprise the following:

- Personality

  This involves those interests pertaining to an individual's physical and spiritual existence, eg, physical security, health, freedom of will, privacy and sensibilities, beliefs and opinions.

- Domestic relations

  This relates to the interests of parents and children and the protection of marriage.

- Substance

  This concerns interests of property, succession and testamentary disposition, freedom of industry, contract and association, ie, those claims or demands 'asserted by individuals in title of the individual economic existence'.

16.9 Public interests

Public interests are 'demands or desires involved in or looked at from the standpoint of life in a politically organised society, asserted in title of political life'. They comprise the following:

- Interests of the State considered as a *juristic person*, ie, its integrity, freedom of action, security.
- Interests of the State as the *guardian* of social interests.

16.10 Social interests

Social interests are 'those wider demands or desires involved in or looked at from the standpoint of social life in civilised society and asserted in title of social life'. They comprise the following:

- General security, including claims to peace and order (against those actions likely to threaten the very existence of society), safety, health, security of transactions and acquisitions.
- Security of social institutions (domestic, religious, political and economic).
- General morals, ie, security of social life against acts offensive to general moral sentiments.
- Conservation of social resources, eg, use and conservation of natural resources, protection and education of dependants and defectives, protection of the economically-dependent.
- General progress, ie, the self-assertion of the social group toward higher and more complete development of human powers, including economic progress (freedom of property, trade, industry), political progress (freedom of criticism), cultural progress (freedom of science, improvement of education and aesthetic surroundings).
- Individual life is, perhaps, the most important interest of all, involving the claim or demand of each individual to live a full life according to society's standards.

16.11 The balancing of interests

From a *functional* point of view, argues Pound, law is really an attempt to reconcile, harmonise or compromise overlapping or conflicting interests:

> 'either through securing them directly and immediately, or through securing certain individual interests ... so as to give effect to the greatest number of interests, or to the interests that weigh most in our civilisation, with the least sacrifice of other interests.'

16.11.1 A problem of 'social engineering'

The appropriate 'balancing process' is related to problems of 'eliminating friction and precluding waste in human enjoyment of the goods of existence'. It is a kind of 'social engineering', the brunt of which falls upon the legal order.

Interests must be balanced 'fairly' and this involves examining a conflict of interests on *an appropriate plane*. Thus, an individual interest ought not to be weighed against a public interest.

16.11.2 The process of balancing interests

The process of balancing may necessitate reference to the following forms of law:

- *Rules*, ie, 'precepts attaching a definite, detailed legal consequence to a definite, detailed statement of facts'.

- *Principles*, ie, 'authoritative starting points for legal reasoning employed continually and legitimately where cases are not covered or are not fully or obviously covered by rules "in the narrower sense"'.
- *Conceptions*, ie, 'authoritative categories to which ... cases or situations are referred, in consequence of which a series of rules, principles and standards become applicable'. (Pound suggests that these are chiefly the work of law teachers and writers.)
- *Standards*, ie, 'the general limits of permissible conduct to be applied according to the circumstances of each case'.

16.12 The recognition of new interests

As society advances and changes, so claims to 'new interests' will emerge. Recognition of a new interest will involve its being 'tested' by reference to 'the jural postulates' of a civilised society. These postulates encapsulate a given society's underlying *values*. Reference to the postulates will allow legislators to consider the modification of values and the enunciation of new ones so as to conform with basic general values. These are the postulates as set out by Pound.

16.12.1 Pound's 'jural postulates'

The citizens of a civilised society are entitled to assume:

- that others will commit no intentional aggression upon them;
- that they may control for beneficial purposes what they have discovered, created and acquired;
- that promises will be carried out in good faith and that unreasonable and unjust enrichment will be prevented as far as possible;
- that persons engaged in a course of conduct will act with due care so as not to create unreasonable risk of injury to others.

16.12.2 Additional postulates

In his later writings Pound added the following to his list of postulates:

- that citizens shall be entitled to assume that the burdens incident to social life shall be borne by society;
- that, as a minimum matter, 'a standard human life' shall be assured to every citizen.

Summary of Chapter 16

The Sociological Approach (2): Weber and Pound

Weber: law as legitimate authority

Weber (1864-1920) viewed the essence of 'social order' in terms of norms and the power to enforce them. The exercise of power within a society involves an acceptance by its members of 'legitimate authority'.

Weber enumerates three types of 'legitimate authority':

- *Traditional,* epitomised by the rule of patriarchs and arising from the belief that the rulers' authority was conferred by ancient tradition.
- *Charismatic,* involving obedience to some extraordinary person (hero, prophet).
- *Rational legal,* involving impersonal authority and widespread belief in the legitimacy of enacted rules.

Weber analysed procedures within legal systems and produced the following classification:

- *Substantively irrational* systems - *ad hoc* and intuitive decisions predominate.
- *Formally irrational* systems - decisions result from tests (such as ordeals) 'beyond control of the human mind'.
- *Substantively rational* systems - morality and law are combined totally, as in a theocracy.
- *Formally rational* systems - attempts are made to apply logically consistent principles to the solution of a wide type of legal problem.

Pound: the balancing of interests

Pound (1870-1964) defined an interest as:

> 'a demand or desire or expectation which human beings either individually or in groups or associations or relations, seek to satisfy, of which, therefore, the adjustment of human relations and ordering of human behaviour through the force of a politically organised society must take account'.

A principal task for legislators, judges and jurists is the balancing of individual, public and social interests.

Individual interests comprise: personality; domestic relations; substance (interests of property, etc).

Public interests comprise: interests of the State considered as a juristic person; interests of the State as the guardian of social interests.

Social interests comprise: general security; security of social institutions; general morals; conservation of social resources; general progress; individual life.

Balancing of interests involves a process of reconciliation, harmonisation and compromise, with the object of eliminating friction and precluding waste in 'human enjoyment of the goods of existence'. Rules, principles, conceptions and standards must be referred to, and a conflict of interests must be examined on an appropriate plane.

The *recognition of new interests* involves their being tested by reference to the 'jural postulates' of a civilised society. Such postulates are: that citizens will commit no intentional aggression against one another; that citizens may control for beneficial purposes what they have discovered, created and acquired; that promises will be carried out in good faith and unjust enrichment prevented; that due care must be exercised so as not to create unreasonable risks of injury; that a 'standard human life' shall be assured to every citizen.

Chapter 17

Scandinavian Realism

17.1 Background and essential features

The name 'Scandinavian Realism' is generally applied to the writings of the Swedish philosopher *Hägerström* (1868-1939), his compatriots and disciples, *Lundstedt* (1882-1955) and *Olivecrona* (1897-1980), and the Danish jurist, *Ross* (1899-1979). They were concerned, as were the American realists, to explain the law 'as it is'; but unlike the Americans, the Scandinavians did not concentrate on the workings of the courts, and their explanations of the basis of law were often couched in the vocabulary of psychology. The essential features of their approach are as follows:

- Metaphysical speculation is to be rejected. It comprises mere pseudo-concepts and is, therefore, a sham. (It is, in the words of Boltzmann, 'a migraine of the human mind'.) Reality may be discovered and analysed only through an investigation of the 'fundamental facts' of the legal system. Assertions which are incapable of proof are nonsense. Hence, if a jurisprudential proposition cannot be verified through the experience of the senses, it is unacceptable.
- Our morality is created by the law; our law does not emerge from our morality.
- Values such as 'goodness' are no more than the embodiment of reactions expressing approval of a stimulus.
- Natural law is an illusion, and the jurisprudential arguments derived from it are unacceptable.
- Law can be understood in terms of sets of the brain's responses to groups of stimuli.
- Legal ideas are merely the rationalisation of social facts.
- Commands reflect illusions ensuring obedience by their mandatory forms.

17.2 Hägerström

The founder of the Scandinavian movement, Hägerström, believed that empirical analysis, which involves the acceptance of sense-data as the sole source of valid information, would provide answers to questions concerning the origin, nature and functions of the law.

17.2.1 Rights as meaningless concepts in themselves

'Rights', 'duties', 'obligations', are, in themselves, meaningless concepts. Indeed, a 'right of ownership' lacks any empirical significance until particular states of affairs are challenged. The term 'rights' has meaning only when associated clearly with remedies and legal enforcement procedures.

17.2.2 Justice a mere evaluation

The term 'justice' represents, in reality, no more than a personal, highly-subjective evaluation of some states of affairs of which we generally approve.

'Rights' as a concept, may have originated in a belief 'in certain forces which exist quite apart from our own natural powers: forces which belong to another world than that of nature and which are brought into operation by legislation or other forms of law-giving: *Inquiries into the Nature of Law and Morals* (1933).

17.2.3 Significance of conditioning

People are persuaded as the result of conditioning, and society accepts because of long historical periods of 'training', that certain rights 'exist' as the result of a series of particular types of event, eg, X transferring property to Y, so that the mental states created in X and Y result in their belief (shared by others in the community) in 'valid rights and duties'. This is the extent of the 'reality' of concepts such as 'right', 'duty' and 'obligation'.

17.3 Hägerström and 'word-magic'

Hägerström's studies in Roman law and, in particular, the significance of the *obligation* (defined in *The Institutes* as 'the legal bond whose force compels us to perform something in accordance with the laws of our State'), convinced him that the use of a legal form was linked, in ancient days, with magical incantations. A party to the Roman ceremony of *mancipatio* (a fictitious sale used as a mode of transfer of ownership), who struck a bronze balance with a coin in the presence of witnesses, was invoking supernatural powers in reciting the formula: 'This thing I state to be mine by quiritary right ...' Similarly, in our own day, the words of the marriage ceremony might be interpreted by Hägerström as indicating a belief in the supernatural modification of reality through incantation ('With this ring I thee wed ...'). Word-magic, he argues, remains embedded in the procedures of the law. It is the *objective form* of law which creates the illusion of objectivity.

17.4 Lundstedt

Lundstedt, a jurist and member of the Swedish legislature, followed Hägerström in rejecting the pretensions of metaphysical interpretations of the law. That which can never be proved can be no foundation for the investigation of legal phenomena. Linguistic looseness and ambiguities are responsible for the appearance of many worthless arguments concerning the nature of law.

17.4.1 Rights are illusory

'Judicial concepts' of, eg, 'rights', 'justice', are illusory; there is no scientific method of evaluating their basis. 'Rights', so-called, are mere phantasma which act only as 'labels' pertaining to consequences of certain legal procedures.

17.4.2 The law directs justice

'Feelings of justice' do not direct law. On the contrary, they are directed by law. Lundstedt argues that feelings of 'justice' are often little more than subjective reflections of economic interests (see his *Legal Thinking Revised* (1956)).

Law should be interpreted as 'simply the facts of social existence: all else is illusion'. The legal order is essential to the continued existence of society.

> 'I only establish as a fact that which can be observed in general, namely, that the overwhelming majority of human beings (in Sweden as well as in other countries of comparable cultural development) wish to live and develop their lives' possibilities ... It is obvious that the interest in legislation and the abstraction of law is indissolubly united with these aspirations.'

17.5 Olivecrona

The exploration of 'rights' is the principal concern of Olivecrona's jurisprudential thought. Rights, he claims, may have originated in psychological feelings which initiate individual actions. He notes the paradox of individuals referring to 'rights' as though they have an existence 'in reality'. But rights have no existence in the empirical sense. The individual feels, on the basis of his perception of events, that he does possess 'rights' and 'duties'; he is aware, also, of the existence of institutions which will adjudicate on disputes arising from a failure to carry out duties or to observe 'rights'. But, asks, Olivecrona, where is the empirical reality of 'rights' and 'duties' ?

17.5.1 Rights in terms of feelings of strength

A right may be understood also in terms of 'feelings of strength' and 'sensations of power'.

The existence of a document creating, say, a mortgage of real property will create, according to Olivecrona, 'feelings of strength' in the minds of the mortgagor and mortgagee: the mortgagor is aware of his rights embodied in his equity of redemption, and the mortgagee is aware of the power arising from his rights in relation to the agreed payments of capital and interest.

17.6 Olivecrona's 'independent imperatives'

The rules of law, Olivecrona argues, are not 'true commands', although issued in the imperative form. *Law as Fact* (1971):

> 'Whatever words are used, the meaning of rules is always: this action *shall* be performed under such and such circumstances, this right *shall* arise from such and such facts, this official *shall* have this or that power, etc.'

17.6.1 Comparison with commands

Imperative statements found in the law must be distinguished from 'commands' in the accepted sense of that term. A 'command', properly called, implies, according to Olivecrona, some personal relationship arising where X gives an order directly to Y in the form of words, gestures, intended to affect Y's will and subsequent actions. Even in the absence of a personal relationship between X and Y, the words may have a similar intention and effect as compared with those used when a personal relationship does exist. Thus, the Charities Act 1993 is not 'issued' by any individual, nor is it addressed specifically to any one person. It is an imperative statement issued independently of the context of a mere 'personal command' of X addressed to Y. It functions as an 'independent imperative', ordering actions and attracting obedience.

17.6.2 Significance of immediacy

It is not always simple to distinguish clearly a 'command' from an 'independent imperative', such as an Act of Parliament. Olivecrona suggests that the 'command' assumes the nature of an independent imperative' as the distance between those involved increases. Thus, there is a different perception, in terms of *immediacy*, of the essence of the situation arising when a police officer asks an individual to account for his possession of recently stolen property, and the 'independent imperative' of statute and common law authorising that action. Habits (and ambiguities) of language enable individuals to reconcile 'commands' and 'independent imperatives' and to think of them in equivalent terms.

17.6.3 Rules of law

The 'rules of law' within a legal system are now, largely, 'independent imperatives' that have passed through a series of recognised, formal activities, eg, the Royal Assent, official promulgation.

Citizens assume 'independent imperatives' to be orders which demand obedience because individuals have been conditioned and trained to think and respond in this manner. The perceived power of the State 'is surrounded by august ceremonies and met with a traditional and deep-rooted reverence'. This has a profound impact upon the individual's mind so that he takes to heart the commands of the law as objectively binding. Custom, tradition, feelings of social solidarity and duty, and the residue of generations of historical development, combine to assure the 'binding, non-optional character' of 'independent imperatives'.

The effect of citizens' attitudes towards the constitution of their State is that:

> 'the constitutional law-givers gain access to a psychological mechanism through which they can influence the life of the country; secondly, that only they gain access to this mechanism ... The effect of legislation is conditioned by the psychological attitude which we ourselves and the millions of others maintain ... Because of this attitude, the law-givers can play on our minds as on a musical instrument.'

17.6.4 Morality is founded by the law

From the earliest days of our lives, says Olivecrona, we are in the grip of the law and our moral views are moulded by its influence. Imperatives result from psychological conditioning, and are inculcated directly by parents and teachers; they are underlined by our awareness of the consequences, often of a stigmatic nature, which attend the failure to act in accordance with an imperative. Hence, our morality is formed by the law - and not the other way round.

17.7 Ross

Jurisprudence is, according to Ross, an empirical social science. Law takes the form of a system of normative rules. The 'validity of law' does not rest upon any transcendental notions, but merely upon the possibility of one's being able to predict that the rules are likely to be applied appropriately in future disputes.

17.7.1 Justice as an expression of emotion

'Justice' is a mere expression of emotion, the transformation of one's demands into an absolute postulate. It may simply express the view that a judge ought to apply the rules of the law correctly and impartially: *On Law and Justice* (1958).

17.7.2 Significance of legal rules

Legal rules ('quasi-commands': see *Directives and Norms* (1968)) govern the entire set of institutions and agencies through which actions ascribed to the State in its legal capacity are undertaken:

- The *primary rules*, which are followed with regularity, and which may exist as psychological facts only, informing citizens as to how they are expected to behave, become binding.
- The *secondary rules* specify sanctions and the conditions under which they will operate. Predictability of the operation of the rules ('the experience of validity') induces confidence in them. 'To know the secondary rules is to know everything about the existence and content of law.'

17.7.3 Rights as a psychological reality

Ross followed the general pattern of interpretation of rights which was enunciated by Hägerström. The term 'rights' suggests 'a power of an incorporeal nature', resembling, to some extent, 'magic-thought'. But Ross accepts that statements concerning 'rights' which are made in the course of judicial proceedings can, and do, testify to the concept having acquired 'a realistic content'. The 'reality of rights' is, then, a *psychological reality*; the concept of 'rights' is a tool which assists in presenting, in simplified form, the facts and consequences of states of affairs based upon rules of law.

17.8 Criticisms of Scandinavian Realism

The Scandinavian movement has been criticised in general terms for its apparent failure to adopt the rigorous methodology associated with 'realist jurisprudence'. Thorough investigation has been replaced by 'armchair speculation', and, although the movement stresses the psychological explanation of some legal phenomena, the type of disciplined enquiry which characterises psychological research in other fields is conspicuously absent from Scandinavian theorising. Specific criticisms include the following comments:

- Although the movement has abandoned formal metaphysical interpretations of the law, it seems to have substituted its own neo-metaphysics. Its search for 'essential characteristic features of the law' appears to presuppose a transcendental phenomenon in the same category as 'the ultimate essence of law' associated with some natural law doctrine.
- An excessive concentration on semantics and the inherent problems of the use of words is a hallmark of much Scandinavian speculation. But words are much more than 'emotive sounds' (as suggested by Olivecrona); they have their generally accepted meanings and they are essential to the vast amount of effective communication which takes place within the procedures of the law. The use of words such as 'rights' is often a reflection of a precise awareness of legal events in which the speaker or writer participates. The suggestion that the word 'justice' is meaningless (or, in Ross' interpretation, the equivalent of 'banging on the table') ignores the widely-accepted rational significance of the term and the history of powerful movements for social and legal reform mounted in its name.
- There is little evidence of the prevalence of feelings related to 'word-magic' in contemporary legal procedure. 'This is my deed ...'; 'This is my last will and testament ...' These phrases exemplify, not belief in the magical potency of words, but rather an understanding and expectation of events likely to follow on the execution of a deed or will, or an awareness of the changes which will occur in the status, rights and duties of those to whom the

documents refer. The words used in the documents are, in effect, an acknowledgement of the creation and content of new interests.

- Olivecrona's suggestion of a 'right' as involving a 'feeling of power' is a highly-subjective interpretation of legal events which is not always supported by appropriate evidence. It would be difficult to conceive of statutory rights, such as those arising from the Land Registration Act 1925 or the Children Act 1989, as creating 'feelings of power'.
- The view that 'law creates morality' seems to be contrary to historical evidence. The widespread abhorrence of murder, and the moral imperatives which this reflects, have resulted in strict legal rules relating to the consequences of unlawful homicide - and not the other way about. The history of law contains many examples of legislatures bowing to the pressure of strong, morally-inspired feelings of citizens. This is not to deny the educative function of law; but this is far removed from the Scandinavian movement's assertion that 'morality is the creature of the law'.

Summary of Chapter 17

Scandinavian Realism

Background

The Scandinavian realists are opposed fundamentally to any metaphysical speculation in jurisprudential argument; they are in favour of the investigation only of that which can be verified by the experience of the senses.

- Law creates our morality.
- Natural law is mere illusion.
- Law can be viewed as arising from the brain's responses to stimuli.

Hägerström

Hägerström (1868-1939) viewed legal concepts as meaningless unless their interpretation is associated with remedies and other legal procedures.

'Justice' was no more than a highly-subjective evaluation of states of affairs of which we approve.

A belief in the 'magic' potency of words may be found at the basis of many legal procedures. Incantation can modify reality - this primitive belief has affected the growth of some legal concepts.

Lundstedt

Lundstedt (1882-1955) insisted on the illusory nature of judicial concepts such as 'right' and 'duty'. These are little more than labels.

Law is 'simply the facts of social existence: all else is illusion'. A legal order is essential for the maintenance of society.

Feelings of justice do not direct the law; on the contrary they are directed by the law.

Olivecrona

Rights may be understood as having originated in feelings of strength and sensations of power; they have no existence in the empirical sense.

Rules of law are not true 'commands' although issued in the imperative form. A command implies a personal relationship. An Act of Parliament is an imperative statement issued independently of the context of a personal command. It functions as an 'independent imperative' ordering actions and attracting obedience.

From our earliest days, argues Olivecrona (1897-1980), we are affected by the law and our moral views come to be moulded by it. Our morality is formed by the law, and not the other way round.

Ross

Ross (1899-1979) believes that jurisprudence is an empirical social science and law takes the form of a system of normative rules.

'Justice' is a mere expression of emotion, taking the form of a view that rules ought to be applied correctly and impartially.

Legal rules, which govern the system, comprise 'primary rules', informing citizens how they ought to behave, and 'secondary rules', specifying sanctions and the conditions of their operation. 'To know the secondary rules is to know everything about the existence and content of the law.'

Criticism of the Scandinavian movement

Critics point out that the Scandinavian realists lack a rigorous methodology. Speculation replaces thorough investigation and there is a general lack of the disciplined enquiry which characterises much psychological research (which the Scandinavians appear to favour).

'Rights', 'justice' are powerful, real concepts which do affect the law and its administration. To relegate them to the sphere of 'non-verifiable concepts' is to downgrade them.

There is little proof of law creating and conditioning morality. The widespread, almost universal, abhorrence of some acts, such as murder, suggests that there is a morality which, in turn, forms the law.

Chapter 18

American Realism (1): Holmes, Frank, Gray

18.1 Philosophical roots of American realism

Essentially, realist jurists envisage a science of law as built upon a study of law in action. 'Law is as law does.' The philosophical roots of this approach are to be found in the teachings of the American writers, *William James* (1890-1922) and *John Dewey* (1859-1952). In broad terms, the basis of 'realism' rests on the belief that when we perceive, we are aware of things existing independently of us; implicitly, therefore, this belief involves a rejection of the view that what is perceived is no more than private sense-data. The investigation of a phenomenon such as law necessitates an application of objective procedures uninfluenced by sentiment or idealism.

18.1.1 James

James expounded the theory of *'pragmatism'* (*pragma* = action), a positivist doctrine which rejected 'closed systems and pretended absolutes and origins' and favoured 'facts and action'. 'It means the open air and the possibilities of nature as against dogma, artificiality and the pretence of finality in truth.'

Anything that is meaningful or real must, in some way, influence practice; anything having a practical effect is 'real'. A theory which lacks a consequential result is nonsense. 'Meaningless' is synonymous with 'inconsequential'.

If an idea works when applied to the facts of experience, it is a 'true idea'. That which does not work cannot be 'true'; 'true' is to be equated, therefore, with 'useful'.

18.1.2 Dewey

Dewey urged jurists to remember that 'knowledge is successful practice'.

Jurists should adopt a logic 'relative to consequences rather than to antecedents'. Old principles should be revised, adapted and altered. 'The problem is one of continuous, vital re-adaptation.'

In his *Logical Method and Law* (1924), Dewey demanded 'the infiltration into law of a more experimental and flexible logic as a social as well as an intellectual need'.

18.2 The realist approach to jurisprudence

Law is, according to the realist jurists, *what officials (judges) do*; it is not to be found in, and cannot be deduced from, the mere rules by which those officials are guided. An investigation of the unique elements of cases, an awareness of irrational and non-logical factors in judicial decision-making, an assessment of rules of law by an evaluation of their practical consequences – these are some characteristics of the realist approach.

18.2.1 Llewellyn

Llewellyn (see Chapter 19) argues that realism 'is not a philosophy, but a technology ... What realism was, and is, is a method and nothing more'. In his article, *Some Realism about Realism* (1931), he enumerates the following themes as common to the general realist approach to method:

- Law is not static, and should be considered and investigated as if in flux.
- Law is to be considered as a means to a social end.
- Because society is in a continuous process of change and is often 'ahead of the law' in its attitudes, continuous re-examination and revision of the law is essential.
- 'Is' and 'ought' must be divorced - if only temporarily - for purposes of legal study. 'After the purely scientific problem has been solved ... the hour of ideals and value judgments occurs.'
- Traditional concepts and legal rules cannot provide a full description of what the courts do.
- Law has to be evaluated in terms of its impact and effects on society.

18.2.2 Objectivity in investigation

Objectivity in investigation is emphasised by the realists. Llewellyn comments that although ideals are valuable, once a problem is set, 'every effort must be bent on keeping observation uncontaminated by other value judgments than the desirability of finding out, of being objective and accurate'. In *Facts, Opinions and Value-Judgments* (1932), Oliphant suggests that the jurist needs 'some of the humility of the experimental physicist or chemist who wastes no time in worrying about the absence of ultimates and abstract rational structures'.

18.3 Holmes, founder of the American realist movement

Holmes (1841-1935), who was for 30 years a justice of the US Supreme Court, founded and inspired American realism. Fundamental to his jurisprudential thought is the dictum: 'We must think things, not words, or at least we must consistently translate our words into the facts for which they stand if we are to keep to the real and the true.' The examination of facts must be the basis of jurisprudence: jurisprudential concepts incapable of verification must be rejected.

18.3.1 The life of the law is experience

The life of the law is, essentially, experience. The pragmatic and empirical aspects of law are all-important. Indeed, although the language of judicial decision is largely the language of logic, behind the logical form may often be detected an 'inarticulate and unconscious judgment ... the very root and nerve of the whole proceeding'. Hence the apparent 'certainty of the law' is mere illusion: 'repose is not the destiny of man'.

Far more important than the trappings of formal logic in determining the legal rules by which men ought to be governed, are moral and political theories, intuitions of public policy and 'even the prejudices which judges share with their fellow-men'. These 'have had a good deal more to do than the syllogism in determing the rules by which men should be governed'.

18.3.2 Analysis must exclude moral questions

Holmes urged the deliberate exclusion from one's study of law of 'every word of moral significance'. This was not a rejection of the significance of society's moral standards in the creation of law; these standards are to be regarded as of little consequence in any analysis of operational matters. The jurist ought to attempt to use only words which will convey legal concepts uncontaminated by extra-legal ideas. Thus, to introduce into discussion of the law of contract a concept such as 'irrefragable undertakings', with its lofty overtones of moral significance, is to muddy the waters of scientific examination.

> 'The law is the witness and external deposit of our moral life. Its history is the history of the moral development of the race. The practice of it, in spite of popular jests, tends to make good citizens and good men. When I emphasise the difference between law and morals I do so with reference to a single end, *that of learning and understanding the law.*'

18.4 What is the law? The 'bad man' test

'The prophecies of what the courts will do in fact, and nothing more pretentious, are what I mean by the law': Holmes (*The Path of the Law* (1897)). Essentially, therefore, the object of jurisprudential study is no more than 'the prediction of the incidence of public force through the instrumentality of the courts'.

> 'When we study the law we are not studying a mystery but a well-known profession. We are studying what we shall want in order to appear before judges, or to advise people in such a way as to keep them out of court.'

18.4.1 Consequences require study

Law is for Holmes a *set of consequences* emerging from the practices of the courts. It is not a system of reason, it is not an amalgam of deductions from ethical principles; it is the consequences of the mode of operation of the courts.

> 'General propositions do not determine concrete cases ... I always say in conference that no case can be settled by general propositions, that I will admit any general proposition you like and decide the case either way.'

18.4.2 The 'bad man's' point of view

If we wish to know 'the real law', and nothing else, we should consider it from the point of view of 'the bad man' who cares only for the material consequences of the courts' decisions.

> 'He does not care two straws for the axioms or deductions, but he does want to know what the Massachusetts or English courts are likely to do in fact. I am much of his mind.' The concept of 'legal duty' as interpreted by 'the bad man' is 'a prophecy that if he does certain things he will be subjected to disagreeable consequences.'

The point of view of 'the good man' is not relevant in this context because he may find reasons for his conduct in 'the vaguer sanctions of conscience'.

The events which follow on a breach of the criminal law, regarding, say, making off without payment (see the Theft Act 1978, s 3(1)), exemplify 'the law'.

18.5 Restraining judicial law-making

Holmes draws attention to the significance of a judge's interpretation of the public policy underlying the law, the judge's 'inarticulate major premise'. He emphasises, as a counter-balance, the need to insist upon the process of law-making as the business, not of the court, but of the legislative bodies within the community. The tendency towards judicial law-making has to be restrained; citizens have the right to make, through their elected representatives, whatever laws *they* consider to be necessary. Judges must be reminded of their duty to 'weigh' considerations of 'social advantage' when enunciating or interpreting rules.

18.6 Holmes and legal theory

Holmes' views should not be interpreted as implying a rejection of legal theory. The pragmatism which he embraced is, in itself, a theoretical interpretation of perceived reality. He believed that 'we have too little theory in the law, rather than too much'. His insistence upon the continuous re-examination of rules and procedures and the rejection of that which is outworn is not an attack on theory as such. 'Theory,' he wrote, 'is the most important part of the dogma of the law'. One cannot predict correctly save on the basis of valid principles and theory. He who wishes to master the law 'must look straight through all the dramatic incidents ... to discern the true basis for prophecy'. Hence, when Holmes states that 'general propositions do not decide concrete cases', he is not calling for the abandonment of the theoretical investigation of those propositions. Some jurists (see, for example, Yntema's *American Legal Realism in Retrospect* (1960)) suggest that the significant achievement of American legal realism has been 'to imprint in legal thinking the concept of relativity in the adaptation of positive law to social change'. This reflects the influence of Holmes' work and his insistence upon a conceptual approach to legal data – the hallmark of applied theory.

18.7 The essence of Frank's realism

Frank (1889-1957), a jurist and judge who served on the US Court of the Second Circuit, followed the path charted by Holmes. He counted himself a 'constructive fact-sceptic', who found legal certainty as arising from the elusiveness of 'facts', in contrast to the 'rule-sceptics' who found legal uncertainty to be a product of the law's formal rules. 'Law' could not be separated from the decisions of the courts; hence it was necessary to understand the bases of judicial decisions, and this required an investigation of a variety of factors, often of an 'irrational nature', such as emotions, hunches.

18.7.1 The courts and facts

The law is, in relation to a set of facts, a decision of the court relating to *those* facts. Until the court has given its decision, no law concerning those specific facts is in existence. *Law and the Modern Mind* (1930):

> 'No one knows the law about any case or with respect to any given situation, transaction or event, until there has been a specific decision (judgment, order or decree) with regard thereto.'

Before the making of such a decision, the only 'relevant law' available is a lawyer's opinion - a mere guess as to what the court will decide.

18.7.2 Uncertainty in the law

The law is essentially uncertain. Frank was attracted to an analogy presented by Heisenberg's Principle of Uncertainty (1927) (a hypothesis of quantum mechanics) which considered 'the impossibility of complete definiteness'. Indeterminacy affects *all* phenomena. If lack of certainty was fundamental to the natural sciences, it was absurd to expect even approximate certainty or predictability in the law.

18.7.3 The search for certainty

Why do we seek an 'unrealisable certainty' in the law? How has the 'basic myth' of 'law's certainty' arisen? Frank turns to Freudian psychology for an answer. The search for certainty arises fundamentally from the search for a 'father figure' and reflects the childish need for an authoritative parent. Allen attacks this explanation, pointing out that it is unnecessary to turn to Freud if one wishes to understand why those who are uncertain as to their rights would prefer to be freed from their doubts.

Frank urged jurists to reject 'the infantile search for a father figure' and to follow 'completely adult jurists', such as Holmes.

18.8 Rules as the basis of prediction

Rules, according to Frank, are 'no more law than statutes are law'. Rules are mere words, and, in any event, the court will indicate what rules mean, whether contained within a statute or implied in the opinion of some other court. Rules are not to be found at the basis of a judge's decisions: those decisions may be arrived at before he finds a reason for them. The reasons he gives later may be no more than a rationalisation of his intuitive feelings.

18.8.1 The significance of prejudices

Since knowledge of the rules alone is of limited value in predicting the outcome of a trial, it is necessary to turn for guidance to a study of other matters. Thus, the prejudices of a jury may be of disproportionate significance in the outcome of legal proceedings.

> 'Opinions disclose but little of how judges come to their conclusions. The opinions are often *ex post facto*; they are *censored expositions*. To study those eviscerated expositions as the principal bases of forecasts of future judicial action is to delude oneself. It is far more unwise than it would be for a botanist to assume that plants are merely what appears above the ground, or for an anatomist to content himself with scrutinising the outside of the body.'

18.8.2 The 'judicial hunch'

Frank argues that 'the concealed and highly idiosyncratic basis' of a judge's personality must be taken into account by those who wish to investigate the workings of the courts. The 'judicial hunch' as to what is fair or expedient, and the personality of the judge, cannot be described in terms of legal rules and principles.

Complex, inspired guesses may explain the nature of the basis of a court's decision. The realist approach must include a study of this phenomenon.

The judge, 'naturally disinterested', and trained in the neutral, objective approach to legal facts, is, nevertheless, a sentient being, with beliefs, prejudices and a general background, all of which reflect his class, education, religion, etc. He does not, because he cannot, approach a hearing with a mind emptied of emotion and sentiment. The 'spasm of an incalculable intuitionism' which constitutes 'the judicial hunch' may explain more of the basis of a decision than the apparent interpretation of rules. (Judges who deny this are indulging in a form of self-deception.)

18.9 The unblindfolding of justice

In spite of Frank's scepticism as to the reliability of trial procedures in the process of discovering the essence of law, he was concerned with the question of attaining justice as the end of those procedures. He urged, therefore, the enlargement of the bounds of judicial discretion so that rules might be made more flexible in individual cases. Every legal hearing is, in a sense, unique, and a judge ought not to be tied to the demands of 'rigid universals and abstract generalisations'. This is essential if justice is to be 'unblindfolded'.

18.10 Gray and the significance of rules

The American jurist, Gray (1839-1915), set out in *Nature and Sources of Law* (1909), his views on the significance of rules in the legal process. He defined jurisprudence as 'the science which deals with the principles on which courts ought to decide cases ... it is the statement and systematic arrangemnent of the rules followed by the courts and of the principles involved in those rules'. The 'law of the State' or of any organised body of men 'is composed of the rules which the courts, that is, the judicial organs of that body, lay down for the determination of legal rights and duties'.

18.10.1 Judicial interpretation

According to Gray, the judges settle what facts exist 'and also lay down rules according to which they deduce legal consequences from facts. These rules are the rules of law.' Gray cites with approval the words of Bishop Hoadly, preaching in 1727 before George I: 'Whoever hath an absolute authority to interpret any written or spoken laws, it is he who is truly the law-giver to all intents and purposes, and not the person who first wrote or spoke them'.

18.10.2 State, rules, law

Gray sums up his views on rules, thus:

> 'The State exists for the protection and forwarding of human interests, mainly through the medium of rights and duties. If every member of the State knew perfectly his own rights and duties, and the rights and duties of everybody else, the State would need no judicial organs; administrative organs would suffice. But there is no such universal knowledge. To determine, in actual life, what are the State's and citizens' rights and duties, the State needs and establishes judicial organs, the judges. To determine rights and duties, the judges settle what facts exist, and also lay down rules according to which they decide legal consequences from facts. *These rules are law.*'

18.11 Holmes, Frank, Gray criticised

The uncompromising nature of American realism produced a reaction in the form of intense criticism of the philosophy upon which the movement was based and the validity of some of the proposals made in its name.

18.11.1 Oversimplification

Holmes and his followers have been reminded by jurists such as Lucey (see *Natural Law and American Legal Realism* (1942)) that to rid law of moral terms is to take from it all significance. Pragmatism and empiricism are, he argued, in the final analysis, abnegations of the search for truth. Further, to regard law as 'what the courts will do in fact', is oversimplification which disregards the phenomena of legal error and appellate review. Indeed, if the law is merely what the courts do in fact, then those same courts may freely ignore 'the law'. And is the aphorism 'law is what the courts do' any more satisfactory than the statement that 'medicine' is what the doctors give you, or 'religion' is what the churches preach?

18.11.2 The ignoring of the law's certainties

Frank's followers have been urged to consider the fact that judges may have common standards, that they may be aware of 'secret, private norms' which they consciously attempt to disregard, that there are many areas within systems of law in which discretion may not be exercised and in which statute and precedent may exclude 'creative law-making' by the judges. Those who attempt, during legal proceedings, to present pleadings in a highly-unusual fashion, to adduce evidence based entirely on hearsay, to disregard the rulings of the judge, will become aware swiftly of a body of firm and important rules. Frank's general concept of law as lacking certainty is difficult to reconcile with, for example, the existence and workings of the vast world of commerce, based, in large measure, upon awareness of regularity and certainty in the operations of the law. Without the 'relative certainties' of contract law, for example, commercial activity as we know it would be impossible throughout the world. And so it is with many other 'certainties' in other areas of the law.

18.11.3 Uncertainty

Gray was criticised by Cardozo, in *The Nature of the Judicial Process* (1921) on the grounds of the uncertainties inherent in his view that statutes are merely sources of law which judges utilise in the exercise of a law-making function. In that view, says Cardozo, even past decisions are not law. The courts may override them. 'Law never *is*, but is always *about to be* ... There are no such things as rules of principle; there are only isolated dooms.'

Summary of Chapter 18

American Realism (1): Holmes, Frank, Gray

The 'realist' approach

'Law is as law does.' A science of law should be built upon a study of the law in action.

Realism is based upon pragmatism (a positivist doctrine which rejects 'pretended absolutes and origins' and favoured 'facts and action'). True ideas are those which work in practice.

Law is, essentially, 'what officials (judges) do'. It is not to be discovered in mere rules.

Llewellyn

Llewellyn argues that realism is a technology, not a philosophy. Its principles are: law is never static; it is to be considered as a means to a social end; continuous examination of law is essential; 'is' and 'ought' must be divorced for purposes of legal study; traditional concepts are rarely an adequate explanation of law in action; law has to be evaluated in terms of its social impact.

Holmes

'We must think things, not words, or at least we must consistently translate our words into the facts for which they stand': Holmes (1841-1935). The life of the law has been, not logic, but experience.

Matters concerning 'moral significance' must be excluded from an investigation of law.

'The prophecies of what the courts will do in fact, and nothing more pretentious, are what I mean by the law.'

If we wish to know 'the real law' we should consider it from the point of view of 'the bad man' who cares only for the consequences of the courts' decisions. Law is to be viewed as sets of *consequences* emerging from the decisions of the courts.

The tendency to judicial law-making should be carefully controlled, and judges must be reminded of their duty to weigh considerations of social advantage when interpreting rules.

Frank

Frank (1889-1957) argued that 'law' cannot be separated from the decisions of the courts. It is necessary, therefore, to investigate the factors - some of them of an irrational nature - which enter into the making of a decision.

The law is uncertain, and it is fruitless to seek certainty where none can exist.

Knowledge of the rules is of limited value in predicting the outcome of legal proceedings. It is necessary to take into account 'the judicial hunch', which will involve the judge's personality, background, beliefs and prejudices.

An enlargement of the bounds of judicial discretion is necessary if rules are to be made more flexible in individual cases. Rigid universals and abstract generalisations are to be avoided if justice is to be 'unblindfolded'.

Gray

Gray (1839-1915) emphasised the significance of rules in the legal process. The rules which are used by the judges in the exercise of their law-making function do effectively constitute the law as it relates to individual rights and duties.

Holmes, Frank, Gray criticised

Holmes was reminded by critics that the pragmatism and empiricism upon which he based his jurisprudential thought were considered by many philosophers and jurists to be abnegations of the search for truth. He was reminded, further, that to regard law as 'what the courts will do in fact', is to oversimplify, and to disregard the important phenomena of legal error and appellate review.

Frank's critics suggested that he had forgotten that there are important areas of the law in which judicial discretion may not be exercised and that, in the real world, a belief in the certainty of the law does guide conduct. Commercial activity as we know it could not exist in the absence of a belief in the certainties of the law of contract.

Gray's view of statutes as no more than *sources* of law was criticised because of the uncertainty which it introduces into the concept of law: even past decisions are not considered in this argument as constituting law.

Chapter 19

American Realism (2): Llewellyn, Scientific Prediction

19.1 Essence of Llewellyn's approach

Llewellyn (1893-1962), a leading figure in the American realist movement, claimed (see *The Common Law Tradition* (1960)) to have introduced the term 'realistic jurisprudence' into modern legal literature in his 1931 essay on *A Realistic Jurisprudence - the Next Step*. His enumeration of the characteristics of the realist approach was set out in 18.2.1. He stressed that there was no 'school of realists' and that the so-called 'realist movement' was merely 'a ferment' among some of those American jurists calling for 'a dynamic jurisprudence'.

Realism is, he said, a method, 'nothing more, and the only tenet involved is that the method is a good one'. 'Method includes nothing at all about whither to go.'

19.1.1 'Is' and 'ought'

His approach to the 'is' and 'ought' argument is important:

> 'The argument is simply that no judgment of what ought to be done in the future with respect to any part of the law can be intelligently made without knowing objectively, as far as possible, what the part of the law is doing ... This means an insistence on informed evaluations instead of armchair speculations.'

Realists believe that the intrusion of 'ought-spectacles' during the actual process of investigation of the facts makes it very difficult to observe exactly what is being done.

19.1.2 Inquiry into results of investigation

In relation to dealing with a legal problem, the advice which Llewellyn gives is 'see it fresh', 'see it clean', and 'come back to make sure'. 'The fresh look is always the fresh hope; the fresh inquiry into results is always the needed check-up.'

Firm links between jurisprudence and other social sciences (anthropology, for example) are essential.

19.2 The problem of rules

Llewellyn emphasised that legal rules are not as important as some legal theorists assume them to be. It is *how a rule works* that determines its significance; a rule of law thought of solely in terms of a verbal formula is mere emptiness. *Rules are what they do.*

> 'There is less possibility of accurate prediction of what courts will do than the traditional rules would lead us to suppose (and what possibility there is must be found in good measure outside these same traditional rules).'

The jurist who confines his attention *exclusively* to a study of rules, and omits a study of ideology and ideals, often implicit, ignores the reality of the law.

19.2.1 The operational significance of rules

This is not to say, however, that rules are, in themselves, of no value in a legal system; indeed, Llewellyn himself had served as a draftsman of the USA Uniform Chattel Mortgage Act. In interpreting the essence of a legal system, rules are, according to Llewellyn, of restricted value only; it is their operational significance which has to be considered.

19.3 What is 'the law'?

The Bramble Bush (1930):

> 'This doing of something about disputes, this doing of it reasonably, is the business of law. And the people who have the doing in charge, whether they be judges or sheriffs or clerks or jailers or lawyers, are officials of the law. *What these officials do about disputes is, to my mind, the law itself.*'

19.3.1 Criticism of Llewellyn's formulation

D'Amato, in *Jurisprudence* (1984), criticises this formulation. What if officials act illegally ? Would their actions form a part of the law? If Llewellyn were to answer by adding the qualification, 'law is what officials do when they act legally', then the statement would be mere tautology. But use of the term 'officials' in the original definition appears to suggest 'lawfulness and authority'. To this extent, therefore, the definition lacks any informational content.

19.3.2 Significance of standards

In his later writings, Llewellyn apparently rejected his earlier view as no more than a partial statement of the truth. His rejection was accompanied by a declaration emphasising the significance in the American legal system of *standards* aimed at the control of official conduct so as to minimise arbitrariness.

Law, for Llewellyn, was always a means to social ends: the law was 'an engine' which had to be examined in terms of *purpose* and *effect*.

19.4 Law as institution

Law, in Llewellyn's scheme of interpretation, constituted an institution organised around the performance of necessary social tasks. An 'institution', such as law, is made up of techniques, precepts, rules and ideology: its end is a contribution to the survival of society and the search for a just order. It has defined jobs to perform and its function is effective performance of those jobs. The true measure of the success of an institution will be its 'results in life'.

19.5 'Law jobs'

Llewellyn argues that, for the effective functioning of law as an institution, certain law jobs must be carried out; they are of a universal nature and, therefore, necessary in most types of social organisation. Such organisations require a 'stabilising device' which will deal with centrifugal tendencies. The overall law job is to effect organisation and to keep it effective. The level of performance of law jobs is an index to the nature of the law itself. Five such law jobs emerge:

- The disposition (ie, the adjustment) of trouble cases, perhaps the most important of the law jobs. Llewellyn refers to this job as 'garage repair work': it is work of a basic nature which must be done properly and in a sufficiently large number of cases if society is to remain a coherent unit. Work of this type - the resolution of disputes, the settling of grievances - acts as a test to decide which legal rules prevail in the real world.
- The preventive channelling of conduct and expectations in areas of actual or potential conflict. This is intended to head off 'collisions and consequent disputes'.
- The allocation and exercise of authority or jurisdiction within society, which Llewellyn refers to as 'arranging the say, and its saying'. It results in the settling of procedures which legitimise subsequent action (eg, systems of judicial decision).
- The provision of directive and incentive through the organisation of society as a whole, which involves the total effect of the three previously-listed law jobs; in Llewellyn's phrase, 'the Whither of the net Totality'.
- The provision of an appropriate juristic method, which involves 'law as technology', and embraces the maintenance and improvement of law structures and the traditions and skills of 'the official craftsmen of the law'.

19.6 Law job clusters

Around the performance of 'clusters of law jobs' will emerge specific types of activity from which 'the stuff of law' will become apparent. Specialisation in these activities will create a demand for 'the men of law'; their crafts, including advocacy, adjudication, legislation, will be transmitted through educational example to succeeding generations, in the form of organised skills.

19.7 The predictability of law

In the later stages of his researches, Llewellyn attempted to counteract a growing lack of confidence in the American system of appeal courts, as a result of what he perceived as 'the death of *stare decisis*' and a general concern with the unpredictability of decisions. He discovered in the workings of the appeal courts 'a reckonable quality': judges were not merely capricious in their use of precedent but were guided by 'a situation sense' which was producing a kind of stability in the operations of those courts.

19.7.1 Reckonability

Reckonability is determined by three 'laws' which could be deduced from the workings of the courts:

- A law of *compatibility*, under which the application of an appropriate rule is seen as 'compatible with sense', thus narrowing the spread of possible decision and increasing the reckonability of the upshot and direction which will be taken by the court.
- A law of *incompatibility*, under which use of an apposite rule is seen as 'incompatible with sense', so that reckonability of upshot and direction of a decision will depend on factors *apart* from the rule, sense, or both. In effect, the court will reject non-workable or just-workable rules.
- A law of *regularity and reason*, which applies where there is 'a rule which wears both a right situation-reason and a clear scope-criterion on its face'. Such a rule will yield regularity, reckonability and justice.

19.7.2 Style of judicial reasoning

'Style' may be discerned in the overall performance of law jobs, and not merely in legal writing. The phrase refers to the manner of doing law jobs. 'In the beginning was not a Word, but a Doing.'

- The *grand style* seeks to minimise uncertainty, to produce rules which appear to make sense, and to pay attention to principle in considering the weight to be given to relevant decisions of the past. Judges who adopt this style show good 'situation sense'.
- The *formal style* shows a keen reliance on rules of law rather than on the demands of social policy. It goes hand-in-hand with an orthodox ideology and tends to reflect 'a perverse drive for strong opinions'. The style tends to be characterised by deductive reasoning and what Llewellyn describes as 'single-line inevitability'.

Towards the end of his career, Llewellyn seems to have detected in the American appellate courts a shift in the direction of 'the grand style'. This phenomenon, plus the spread of 'reckonability' augured well for the future of law in the USA. It was the task of American jurists and lawyers to analyse movements of this nature and, given the fact that total certainty in the law cannot be attained, to assist in the discovery and application of *objective norms* by the courts.

19.8 Scientific prediction of the law

The era following the Second World War, in which technological advance in the area of electronic computation had been remarkable, saw the growth of novel techniques of prediction based upon the capacity of computers to handle large quantities of numerical data at great speed and with complete accuracy. *Schubert*, professor of political science at Michigan University, proposed the application of scientific techniques of prediction, using computerised techniques, to the task of predicting the outcome of judicial decisions.

19.8.1 Schubert

Schubert was influenced by the work of the jurist, Haines, who, in the 1920s, enumerated the personal factors likely to influence judicial decisions as: *remote and indirect* (eg, the judge's education, social position, personal and family associations); *direct* (eg, the judge's legal and political experience, opinions, traits).

Scientific prediction, according to Schubert, involved a quantification of a judge's attributes, orientation and value-attitudes towards specific issues. This information would assist in determining the probability of judges deciding issues in particular ways.

19.8.2 Scientific forecasting

In Schubert's *Judicial Analysis and Voting Behaviour* (1963), he draws attention to the success of Rodell's scientific forecast of the outcome of *Baker v Carr* (1962), a case heard by the US Supreme Court. Rodell analysed, in quantitative terms, the Supreme Court judges 'individually as whole human beings' and this necessitated an investigation of their background, economic status, temperament, etc. A similar success, in *Gideon v Wainwright* (1963), was achieved by Lawlor, a practising lawyer and computer specialist. Schubert stressed that scientific prediction would result in the theoretical enrichment of the work of the realist movement in jurisprudence, but, to date, there is little evidence of this having occurred.

19.9 Jurimetrics

Loevinger (see *Jurimetrics, the Methodology of Legal Inquiry* (1963)), coined the term 'jurimetrics' to cover the application of communication theory and the use of mathematical logic in law in relation to jurisprudential enquiry. Use of quantitative techniques might enable lawyers to move *beyond* jurisprudence to a truly scientific investigation of the law. Thus, for example, confusion created by syntactic ambiguity in legal discourse might be minimised by the use of symbolic logic in, say, the interpretation of statutes.

19.9.1 Systems analysis

Loevinger believed that jurists could learn much from an analysis of legal structure and its procedures by analysing them in systems terms. A 'system' is described by Parsons as 'a complex of interdependencies between parts, components and processes that involve discernible regularities of relationship.' Any organisation, natural or artificial - a court, a university, a factory, a brain, a flower, a human being - is viewed as a unified and purposeful system, the quality of which may be determined largely by the pattern of its internal relationships.

A court may be visualised as an 'open system', interacting with its environment, and consisting of interrelated elements - judge, counsel, defendant, jury, rules and procedures, etc. Any activity involving any part of the court as system, will affect in some way the activity of *every other part*. Consider, for example, the effect upon the trial of the defendant and upon the various parts of the court system, of a failure of the prosecution to adduce appropriate evidence, or of the introduction by legislation of new procedural rules relating to trials of that nature.

Systems analysts point out that, almost invariably, *structure reflects strategy*. What might result from an application of the essence of this principle to an analysis of, say, the Court of Appeal or the rules of evidence?

19.9.2 Cybernetics

Wiener, founder of the science of cybernetics, defined it, in 1964, as the study of control and communication in man and machine. In order to study a system scientifically, it is necessary to analyse the ways in which communication flows around a system and affects the nature of relationships between the elements of that system. D'Amato, an American practising lawyer and jurist, has used the techniques of cybernetic modelling in his text, *Jurisprudence* (1984), to illustrate in the form of two-dimensional diagrams the arrangement of relationships within the positivist theories of Hobbes, Austin and Hart. He emphasises that cybernetics teaches jurists that they should no longer assume that a legal system is an entity that can be isolated and analysed without relation to those participating in it.

19.9.3 Computerisation of judicial decision-making

Advances in computer techniques led to suggestions by some jurists of the American realist movement that the less complicated aspects of adjudication, which could be modelled through the use of algorithms (a technique illustrated in *How To Do Things With Rules*, by Twining and Miers (1982)) might be performed by a computer which would produce a swift and totally disinterested decision. Cases turning upon the interpretation of quantitative data (some road traffic offences, income tax assessments, for example) lend themselves to techniques of this nature. Yet, in the event, little of substance has emerged from this extension of realist thinking: the relatively slow progress in the task of creating artificial intelligence, and the apparent limitations upon the capacity of machines 'to speculate in the bright light of wisdom', seem, for the time being, unlikely to affect legal practice and the features of jurisprudential thought.

19.9.4 Lawyers and science

Loevinger has suggested, in *Law and Science as Rival Systems* (1967), that the traditional hostility of the legal profession (including its teachers) to a study of science – its subject-matter and methods – is too pervasive to be explicable on historical or practical grounds. He considers that lawyers view science as a rival system which could displace legal dialectic methods with other and alien techniques. Lawyers must be made aware that their dialectical skills and science's empiric systems are merely different systems for dealing with problems in differing circumstances. A link between lawyers, their teachers and scientists has become essential if law is to utilise fully the scientific modes of enquiry which now characterise information gathering and interpretation.

Summary of Chapter 19

American Realism (2): Llewellyn, Scientific Prediction

Llewellyn

Llewellyn (1893-1962) claimed to have introduced the term 'realistic jurisprudence' into modern American legal literature. Realism was, for him, a method, and no more. It excluded discussion about 'whither to go'. The intrusion of 'ought-spectacles' into the process of investigation of law is to be rejected.

Legal rules are simply 'what they do'. It is, therefore, their operational significance which is important.

The law is to be found in *what officials do about disputes*. Standards which minimise arbitrariness are of particular importance.

Law jobs

The true measure of the success of an institution, such as the law, is its results in life. The effective functioning of law demands that certain 'law jobs' be carried out effectively.

Law jobs are enumerated as follows:

- the disposition of trouble cases;
- the preventive channelling of conduct and expectations in areas of actual or potential conflict;
- the allocation and exercise of authority or jurisdiction within society;
- the provision of directive and incentive through the organisation of society as a whole;
- the provision of an appropriate juristic method.

Around the performance of 'clusters of law jobs' will emerge those activities from which the 'stuff of the law' will become apparent. Specialisation will create a demand for lawyers.

The predictability of law

The 'predictability of the law' is emerging from the growth of 'reckonability' and a change in the style of judicial reasoning.

'Reckonability' is determined by three laws which can be deduced from the actual workings of the courts:

- a law of compatibility (under which applications of rules are compatible with good sense);
- a law of incompatibility (allowing the court to reject non-workable or just-workable, rules);
- a law of regularity and reason.

Styles of judicial reasoning are characterised by Llewellyn as 'grand' or 'formal'. The *grand style* (which Llewellyn discerned in growing measure in the decisions of the American appellate courts) seeks to minimise uncertainty and to give weight to relevant decisions of the past. The *formal style* seems concerned more with attention to the rules of law rather than the demands of social policy.

Scientific prediction of the law

Schubert has attempted to apply scientific methods of prediction to the work of the American appellate courts. Some few attempts were successful, but no general principles of prediction have emerged.

Loevinger has outlined a discipline of 'jurimetrics' which is concerned with the application of quantitative techniques to jurisprudential enquiry:

- *Systems analysis* has been employed so as to interpret the law in terms of systems - combinations of interrelated elements.
- *Cybernetics* - the study of control and communication - has been applied to visualisation of the legal process so as to highlight flows of information and control elements within court procedures.
- *Computerisation of judicial decision-making* has been studied, but little of substance has emerged from experimental work.

Chapter 20

American Jurisprudence Today (1): Rawls and Nozick

20.1 The jurisprudence of social justice

Most of the works considered in this chapter appeared during an era of political and social turmoil in the USA. Involvement in an unpopular war and an intensification of domestic unrest produced much 'soul-searching', a questioning of the quality of life, the distribution of wealth, and the role of law in American society. *Rawls* (b 1921), holder of the chair in philosophy at Harvard, produced, in 1971, *A Theory of Justice*, which called for a new look at the principles of social justice. *Nozick* (b 1938), who had studied under Rawls, and who also held a chair in philosophy at Harvard, produced, in 1974, *Anarchy, State and Utopia*, a plea for social libertarianism, based upon an entirely different approach to that taken by Rawls. Both works aroused considerable interest; both exemplify important facets of the continuing concerns of contemporary American jurisprudence.

20.2 Rawls: the public conception of justice

Rawls' theory is based upon three elements: a vision of society as it ought to be; a view of moral theory and its significance; and the derivation of principles which will enable an expression of that vision to be enunciated so as to reflect moral theory. He assumes a society whose members wish to decide a set of principles from which to construct a pattern of social justice. Their principal objective is the building of a well-ordered society which will advance the 'good' of its members in accordance with 'a public conception of justice'.

20.2.1 The original position

Rawls suggests the initiation of a hypothetical congress of persons who are to choose, as the result of discussion and agreement, the fundamental principles which will guide their society. In this 'original position', persons will select principles which will not take into account any particular interest; they are to define principles which are objectively just.

20.2.2 The veil of ignorance

It will be necessary, in the original position, to 'nullify the effects of specific contingencies which put men at odds and tempt them to exploit social and natural circumstances to their own advantage'.

The persons involved in the selection of principles will hold their discussions 'behind a veil of ignorance', so as to achieve objectivity. They will not know how the choice of various alternatives will affect their own particular lives; hence they will have to evaluate principles solely on the basis of 'general considerations'. No member of the group will know his place in society, his class position, social status, his conception of what is 'good', the generation to which he belongs, society's economic or political situation. 'They must choose principles the consequences of which they are prepared to live with, whatever generation they turn out to belong to.'

As far as possible, 'the only particular facts which the parties know is that their society is subject to the circumstances of justice and whatever this implies. It is taken for granted, however, that they know the general facts about human society. They understand political affairs and the principles of economic theory; they know the basis of social organisation and the laws of human psychology. Indeed the parties are presumed to know whatever general facts affect the choice of the principles of justice'.

20.2.3 Primary goods

The rational distribution of 'social primary goods' will be an important matter for discussion and decision. These 'goods' are the things every rational person is presumed to want in relation to his minimally tolerable life-plan, ie, rights, liberties, opportunities and powers. (At a later stage, Rawls suggested that the most important primary good is 'self-respect'.) For every person, 'the good' is the satisfaction of his rational desires; 'primary goods' are the necessary means to that end. Rawls suggests that the decision of those in 'the original position' would be that all social primary goods should be distributed *equally* unless an unequal distribution of any or all of them is to the advantage of the least-favoured members of society.

20.3 The principles of 'justice as fairness'

Rawls enunciates two fundamental principles of 'justice as fairness'. They will be compatible with different kinds of democratic regime; the decision as to which system is best for a given people will reflect their circumstances, historical traditions and institutions. Two vital principles will emerge, according to Rawls, from the discussions of those 'in the original position':

- 'Each person is to have an equal right to the most extensive total system of equal basic liberties compatible with a similar system of liberty for all.' 'Basic liberties' include political liberty, freedom of speech and assembly, liberty of conscience, freedom of thought, freedom from arbitrary arrest and seizure as defined by the concept of the rule of law. (Duties will be assigned equally.)
- The second principle:

  'Social and economic equalities are to be arranged so that they are both to the greatest benefit of the least advantaged, consistent with the just savings principle, and attached to offices and positions open to all under conditions of fair equality of opportunity.'

The 'just savings principle' is necessary for the securing of justice between the generations: each generation is expected to 'put aside in each period of time a suitable amount of real capital accumulation.'

20.4 The priority rules

Rawls suggests, further, that people in 'the original position' will enunciate 'priority rules' in order to resolve possible conflicts where the principles of justice might run against each other, ie 'those principles a person would choose for the design of a society in which his enemy is to assign him his place'.

20.4.1 The first priority rule: the priority of liberty

The principles of justice should be ranked 'in lexical order'; as a result 'liberty can be restricted only for the sake of liberty'; it always has priority. There are two cases:

- 'a less extensive liberty must strengthen the total system of liberty shared by all';
- 'a less than equal liberty must be acceptable to those with the lesser liberty'.

Thus, allowing the police to arrest a suspected offender amounts to his being deprived of some liberty, with the result that the community as a whole enjoys a greater liberty (eg, freedom from the effects of crime).

20.4.2 The second priority rule: the priority of justice over efficiency and welfare

This principle is 'lexically prior to the principle of efficiency and to that of maximising the sum of advantages'. Fair opportunity is to be considered prior to 'the difference principle' (ie, the principle that people ought to be treated differently only where this will be advantageous to those treated in this manner). There are two cases:

- 'an inequality of opportunity must enhance the opportunities of those with the lesser opportunity';
- 'an excessive rate of saving must on balance mitigate the burden of those bearing the hardship'.

An example of the first case might be the specific immunities granted to a judge in the course of judicial proceedings, with the result that the overall opportunities of parties to the proceedings are increased.

20.5 Supremacy of the basic liberties

In Rawls' scheme, basic liberties are supreme. Justice is fairness, but, fundamentally, *liberty is all-important*. The liberty referred to is that 'defined by the public rules of the basic structure of society'. Liberty may be interpreted as a certain pattern of social forms. The rules and laws defining basic liberties apply to all persons equally; they may not be circumscribed save where equal rights 'as institutionally defined' would interfere with one another. It should also be noted that a departure from the institutions of equal liberty required by the first principle 'cannot be justified, or compensated for, by greater social and economic advantages'.

20.6 The attainment of a just society

In *Political Liberalism* (1993), a partial revision of some aspects of *A Theory of Justice*, Rawls suggests a four-stage model of the transition to 'the just society' which would embody within its constitution and political and legal structures the principles of justice which he favours. The first stage would comprise 'the original position' (see 20.2.1 above) from where an articulation of the principles of justice will emerge. This will be followed by the creation of a constitution embodying an appropriate structure of government and citizens' rights. In the third stage legislation incorporating the second principle of justice (see 20.4 above) will appear. The fourth, 'the judicial stage' will be marked by the role of the judges, courts and administrators in applying and protecting the community's laws and rules.

20.7 Credibility of Rawls' theory

Rawls has been criticised on a variety of grounds. The 'original position' is so highly-artificial that it is very difficult to accept it as the basis of a credible hypothesis: it is almost impossible to imagine persons in the state of ignorance presumed by 'the veil'. If persons know virtually nothing of background, experiences, etc, how can they arrive at meaningful conclusions about their world and social arrangements within it? Further, what is the guarantee that people in 'the original position' will choose the 'social primary goods' as enumerated by Rawls? Why might they not choose, say, an authoritarian system of efficiency-for-its-own-sake in contrast to liberty? Suppose they arrived at an order of goods based upon strict restraint 'in the name of a greater freedom'? Some critics detect a bias within the theory towards the questionable values of the egalitarian society favoured by American liberals in the 1970s. Other more specific objections include the following.

20.7.1 Dworkin's criticism

Dworkin notes, in his *Taking Rights Seriously* (1977), that the very structure of the 'original position' produces false arguments in favour of the participants' views. Because a person might have consented to certain principles if asked when he was 'behind the veil', is it fair to attribute continued adherence to those principles after the veil has been removed and he has become aware of advantages and disadvantages pertaining to his social position and other interests?

20.7.2 Inherent conflict between the principles of justice

Is there not an inherent conflict between the two principles of justice, in that inequalities in wealth and the power which this confers may produce inequalities in liberty? How real is 'liberty' to those existing on the margins of society? What is the quality, and worth, of some of Rawls' social goods to persons whose everyday activities are concerned solely with economic survival? Is there confusion here of 'liberty' (which may be considered as indivisible) and specific 'liberties'?

20.7.3 A note on Rawls' concept of human rights

Writing in 1993, Rawls outlined a system of human rights based on law as imposing moral obligations and duties on all of its members. Basic rights would include the right to life, security, personal property, enjoyment of the rule of law, liberty of conscience, freedom of association and the right to emigrate. Human rights of this nature are seen by Rawls as having three roles:

- They are essential to a regime's legitimacy and 'the decency of its legal order'.
- They suffice to exclude any intervention by force of other peoples.
- They provide a limit on pluralism among communities comprising different peoples.

20.8 An excursus: Rawls on the question of rights and civil disobedience

Rawls' *A Theory of Justice* contains a remarkable account of the problems of rights inherent in the practice of civil disobedience. It should be remembered that the *Theory* was published one year after the intervention of the American National Guard in student anti-war demonstrations, an event which led to attempts at a fundamental re-consideration of the right to demonstrate in a democracy. Rawls stressed that his solution to the problem was appropriate only for the special case of a 'near-just society', ie, a democracy characterised by legitimacy and a constitution recognised by its citizens as valid.

Civil disobedience, ie, the right to participate in activities which indicate deep disagreement with aspects of government policies, is considered by Rawls as a 'political, public act', comprising events which are visible 'in the public forum'. It must be, essentially, non-violent because one individual's violence may constitute an interference with the civil liberties of others. It must warn and admonish; it ought not to be perceived by non-participants as a threat to their well-being. Rawls suggests that the right to civil disobedience is to be construed, and perceived, as an expression in non-violent terms of a disagreement *expressed within the limits of an overall fidelity to the law of the community and as a bond of the sincerity of participants*. Civil disobedience is *not* mere militant action: it should preclude organised forcible resistance to government policy and, therefore, should threaten no one.

It is important, says Rawls, to distinguish civil disobedience from so-called 'conscientious refusal'. Conscientious refusal does not take place in the public forum, it may not necessarily be based upon a desire to change the law, and it may not always reflect political principle (thus, it may stem from an interpretation of rights involving religious beliefs).

In order to justify participation in civil disobedience, it is necessary to consider the nature of the wrongs which have created disaffection. Rawls views attacks upon the principle of 'equal liberty' as justifying action of this type. Where liberties continue to be violated deliberately over a significant period, and where an 'immovable majority' backs its government (even by acquiescence) in that violation, then civil disobedience emerges as a *right* to be exercised. But participants must be clear in their minds that their acts have become necessary *as a last resort*, that the wider community will understand them, and that allowance has been made for the disturbing possibility that the particular form of civil disobedience which is in contemplation may escalate and result in a breakdown of the community's respect for law.

Civil disobedience may act, paradoxically, as a stabilising device within a democratic system, 'serving notice' on a complacent or hostile majority and informing them that the rights which constitute the conditions of freedom are in danger of unacceptable violation. The majority is put on notice that the accepted doctrine of 'a community based on a free contract of equals' is ceasing to operate effectively. In these circumstances, civil disobedience acts to expose contractual breaches and to restore constitutional liberties which may be in danger of disappearing. Rawls believes that, in democratic societies, the communal sense of justice can be invoked in appropriate measure when citizens are confronted by the expression of deeply-held anxieties.

20.9 Nozick's 'individual libertarianism'

Nozick is concerned to emphasise individual rights within society and to show how political obligation is derived, ultimately, from consent. Individuals have rights (in property, for example) which exist independently of social and legal institutions within society. These rights must not be interfered with by the State: indeed, where the State enforces such rights it is merely doing for individuals what they were already entitled to do on their own behalf. Concepts of liberty and equality are incompatible with each other, so that any attempt by the State through its legal and administrative organs to interfere with the pattern of resource distribution within society is to be construed as a violation of rights, in that it necessitates interference with individual liberty. The implications of Rawls' views, which suggest the importance of a redistribution of wealth in favour of the weak and deprived, appear to be anathema to Nozick. (It has been said – see *Modern Philosophy* by Scruton (1994) – that in Rawls liberty is absorbed into justice, whereas in Nozick justice is absorbed into liberty.)

20.10 The 'state of freedom'

Nozick draws upon Locke's hypothetical 'state of freedom' which is presumed to have existed under the 'state of nature' (see Chapter 3). A person living in that state was a 'distinct entity' and could not act so as to harm the life, liberty or possessions of others. Hence man enjoys specific natural rights - freedom from violence against the person, freedom to hold and alienate property, freedom to enforce one's rights against the violators and would-be violators of these freedoms.

20.10.1 Just entitlements to property

The right to hold property is based upon certain 'just entitlements':

- *Just acquisition*. One who acquires a holding in accordance with principles of justice is 'entitled' to that holding.
- *Just transfer*. One who acquires a holding in accordance with principles of justice by transfer from some other who is entitled to the holding, is fully 'entitled' to his holding. (Nozick appears to favour the implications of the maxim: 'From each as they choose, to each as they are chosen'.)
- *Rectification of breach*. Rectification of breach of the proposition that no person is entitled to a holding save by application of the above entitlements. Such a rectification will provide a ground of 'entitlement'.

20.10.2 Persons are not means to ends

Interference with justice in holdings (ie, the individual's natural right to possession) without the individual's consent is unjust and insupportable. No one person may justifiably claim rights in another; a person may not be treated as a means to an end. Hence there is no justice where society's goals involve one person's property or his natural abilities being made available, without that person's consent, for exploitation in the service of others who lack some advantage.

20.10.3 The 'truly just' society

The principle to be favoured in the search for justice is that of 'historical method'. If a society has grown in a just fashion; if property is held by citizens in accordance with justice in holdings (ie, if each person's holdings are just, then the totality of holdings may be considered just); if there is total respect for rights and the forbidding of rights, then that society is truly 'just'.

20.11 The minimal State

An appropriate political and legal background for the society in which Nozick's favoured type of justice would flourish is 'the minimal State', protecting life, liberty and possessions. In practice, the minimal State would carry out 'night watchman functions' only. It would act to protect against force, fraud, theft, and would enforce contracts.

20.11.1 Unacceptability of the supra-minimal State

Essentially, the minimal State, argues Nozick, is designed to protect the right of individuals to hold what they possess. To act so as to redistribute resources, eg, through compulsory taxation, is unacceptable and immoral. The 'difference principle', enunciated by Rawls, which would allow a patterned redistribution of wealth to the advantage of the poorer members of society, is a violation of individual liberties. Indeed, suggests Nozick, some aspects of taxation of the earnings of labour are akin to forced labour. The creators of wealth have inviolable rights over its possession and use.

Any growth of the State so that it takes on a supra-minimal character is, generally, unacceptable.

20.12 The 'protecting agency' parable

Nozick is concerned to show that the State has developed spontaneously, reflecting the self-interest of individuals. He hypothesises the early existence of 'mutual protection associations' which acted so as to defend members of society. Conflicts among these associations were ended when one association was able to exert its dominance and take over control of all individuals within the area of its operations. Thus was the State born; its activities assist in the workings of an 'invisible hand' process by which, in Adam Smith's words: 'self-seeking men are led by an invisible hand ... without knowing it, [to] advance the interest of society'.

20.13 Objections to Nozick's theses

Objection has been taken to the lack of historical evidence produced by Nozick in relation to his 'growth of the State' theory. Additionally, the implications of his views as they relate to the distribution of social resources have been questioned. There are suggestions that Nozick is providing a justification for a society without compassion or philanthropy. There must be few persons who, while objecting to the level of taxation, would not accept the necessity for those who possess wealth to contribute to the welfare of the poor.

20.13.1 Based on inadequate evidence

The fable of the State's emergence from conflict among 'protective agencies' has been dismissed as mere fantasy. Little historical evidence has been produced in support of his picture of the origins of the State.

20.13.2 Derivation of fundamental rights ignored

There is no explanation given by Nozick of the actual derivation of the so-called 'fundamental rights'. How, why and where they originated is not made clear. Nor is there any explanation of the absence from Nozick's list of fundamental rights of, say, the right to shelter, to education. Additionally, a list of fundamental duties, which would reflect the reciprocal relationships which bind together our type of society, would have drawn attention to the close links between rights and duties.

20.13.3 The minimal State is impracticable

The concept of 'the minimal State' gives rise to problems of interpretation. Is it possible, or desirable, to prevent growth in the activities of such an organisation? How, in an era of growing insecurity, of rapid increase in the scale of production and growth in internal and external trade of communities, is it possible for the legal organs of the State to engage only in 'night watchman activities' without a collapse of the very standards which the law seeks to uphold and protect?

20.12.4 A simplistic approach to reality

The comparison of forced labour and taxation, often cited so as to epitomise Nozick's 'libertarianism' has been dismissed by some jurists as mere hyperbole. The essence of taxation is that it can be avoided legitimately by the exercise of free choice in not accepting taxed employment, whereas forced labour cannot be avoided. Forced labour is a denial of human dignity and basic rights; it arises from no free choice. Some jurists see in this perception of an equivalence a simplistic approach to the concept of rights within society which is based upon a misunderstanding - common to Nozick's theories - of the nature of the relationship of those rights and duties which most societies have found essential for their continued existence and growth.

- The second rule is the priority of justice over efficiency and welfare. Any inequality of opportunity must enhance the opportunities of those with the lesser opportunity.

  Liberty is all-important in all circumstances.

Nozick: individual libertarianism

Nozick (b 1938) enunciated, in his *Anarchy, State and Utopia* (1974), principles which would emphasise individual rights within society.

The right to hold property is vital and is based upon certain 'entitlements': just acquisition; just transfer; rectification of the breach of either of the previous principles.

Interference with just holdings without the consent of the individual involved is unjust and insupportable. There can be no redistribution of individual wealth without individual consent. Indeed, some aspects of taxation designed to benefit poorer citizens violate individual rights over the possession and use of wealth.

The legal background for Nozick's libertarian community would be 'the minimal State', which would carry out 'night watchman functions' only. Life, liberty and possessions would be protected. Any growth of the State so that it takes on a supra-minimal character is generally unacceptable.

Chapter 21

American Jurisprudence Today (2): Dworkin, Critical Legal Studies

21.1 A radical approach to jurisprudence

Dworkin (b 1931), who has occupied the chairs of jurisprudence at Yale, New York, and Oxford, typifies a strand of American legal thought which favours a radical approach to an examination of law and its place in society. In his texts, *Taking Rights Seriously* (1978) and *Law's Empire* (1986), he rejects both natural law and the type of legal positivism associated, in particular, with Hart. He argues that *one cannot reduce the concept of a legal system solely to patterns of rules.*

The Critical Legal Studies Movement (CLS) founded in the Harvard Law Faculty in the 1970s, represents a very radical wing of American jurisprudence today. Its language is often that of the ultra-left, and its thought appears to be characterised by the belief that law should be interpreted as 'politics under another guise' and that, therefore, law does not stand above or beyond political ideologies. Although the movement's writers favour patterns of interpretation expressed in a linguistic form which is heavy with Marxist overtones, they are, nevertheless, highly critical of the now-defunct State-socialist systems and their legal ideologies. CLS calls for a radical, dramatic transformation of society and of the jurisprudence which CLS adherents perceive as an elaborate attempt to justify, where it cannot hide, the unpleasant reality at the heart of existing society.

21.2 Dworkin and the natural law

Dworkin interprets the doctrines of natural law as suggesting: that lawyers tend to follow criteria that are not totally factual when they question which propositions of law are true; or that law and justice are identical, in a sense which makes it impossible for an unjust proposition of law to be 'true'. This outlook is to be rejected: the examination of a legal structure and a consideration of its validity require an analysis based *solely* upon the system of which it is a part. Jurisprudence requires empirical study, so that the *a priori* reasoning associated with natural law concepts becomes unacceptable.

21.3 The attack on positivism and the concept of 'law as rules'

Dworkin sees positivism as an argument for the concept of law as a mere system of rules. 'Rules are applicable in an all-or-nothing fashion.' A legal rule is applied automatically once the appropriate conditions are met. There is a 'rule', for example, that the penalty for murder is life imprisonment. There is a 'rule' that it is an offence to possess a firearm or imitation firearm with intent to cause fear of violence: Firearms Act 1968, s 16A, Firearms (Amendment) Act 1994, s 1. The Social Security Contributions and Benefits Act 1992, s 79(1), sets out a 'rule' (in the full sense of that term) concerning an 'age addition' to a retirement pension. If, in an application for that addition, the requisite conditions of s 79(1) are shown to exist, the rule will be followed. The rules of the statute dictate particular results. But Dworkin rejects the concept of law as consisting *exclusively* of rules.

> 'I want to make a general attack on positivism ... Positivism, I shall argue, is a model of ... a system of rules, and its central notion of a single fundamental test for law forces us to miss the important roles of those standards that are not rules.' (*Taking Rights Seriously* (1978)).

21.3.1 Standards

There are important *standards* that are not rules, which have to be taken into account in constructing a model of the legal system as it is.

> 'The law of a community consists not simply in the discrete statutes and rules that its officials enact, but in the general principles of justice and fairness that these statutes and rules taken together presuppose by way of implicit justification.'

- 'Policy' must be considered as an element in the law.

  'I will call a "policy" that kind of standard that sets out a goal to be reached, generally an improvement in some economic, political or social feature of the community.'

  An example may be found in the social goal of effecting a reduction in drug dependence, as exemplified by the Misuse of Drugs Act 1971, and an improvement in road safety, as seen in the various Road Traffic Acts of recent years.

- 'Principle' is also of significance.

  'I will call a "principle" a standard that is to be observed, not because it will advance or secure an economic, political or social situation deemed desirable, but because it is a requirement of justice or fairness or some other dimension of morality.'

  An example is the type of maxim at the basis of a standard which guides, but which does not in every circumstance determine, a result. Dworkin examines the maxim stating that a person shall not profit from his own wrong, in relation to the American case, *Riggs v Palmer* (1899), in which the court balanced that maxim against the formal rule that a person may inherit under a valid will (in considering the actions of a legatee who killed a testator so as to prevent a revocation of the will). Similarly, in *Reading v A-G* (1951), the House of Lords considered the principles relating to unjust enrichment in the case of an appellant who had brought a petition of right so as to recover money seized by the Crown. *Per* Lord Porter:

> '"You have earned", the master can say, "money by the use of your position as my servant. It is not for you, who have gained this advantage, to set up your own wrong as a defence to my claim".'

21.3.2 Weights

Principles have a *dimension of weight*. It may be that legal principles will conflict with one another in a consideration of a case. This does not invalidate them, for within the particular circumstances their relative 'weights' (ie, their significance for the facts in dispute) may be balanced by the court. Thus the general principle that there shall be no fetters upon the right to use one's property as one wishes, may have to be weighed against the principle that one may not use one's property so as to inflict injury upon others.

It has to be noted, however (see, eg, *How To Do Things With Rules*, by Twining and Miers (1982)) that few legal positivists accept a concept of law as consisting *entirely* of categorised precepts. Thus a positivist would surely find room for the principles of statutory interpretation in outlining his view of what the law *is*.

21.4 Law and morality

Dworkin will not accept a dividing line between law and morality, which characterises positivist interpretations of the law. A judge engaged in the process of adjudication may have to make moral judgments. He may have to balance principles and policies, and his decision is unlikely to be divorced from the community's general perceptions of 'right' and 'wrong' which constitute morality. The variety of abstract rights which, at any given time, epitomise communal morality are unlikely to be disregarded by a judge. There ought to be no judgment which runs contrary to social standards. *Law's Empire* (1986) states:

> 'Law as integrity asks judges to assume so far as this is possible, that the law is structured by a coherent set of principles about justice and fairness and procedural due process, and it asks them to enforce these in the fresh cases that come before them.'

Integrity requires a judge 'to construct, for each statute he is asked to enforce, some justification that fits and flows through that statute and is, if possible, consistent with other legislation in force'. In this way a 'community of principles' within the law will be established.

21.5 Judge-made law

Dworkin rejects the positivist contention that law is, in considerable part, judge-made. Judges, he declares, do not make law. In advanced legal systems, such as those of the UK and USA, there is always a 'right answer' to a dispute, which can be 'hunted by reason and imagination' and which the judge has a *duty* to discover. In 'hard cases' (in which the application by the court of a precise and unmodified legal rule would almost certainly produce injustice) the judge must not apply standards in mechanical fashion; he has a *duty* to decide a case one way or another, and has *no discretion* to refuse to decide either for the plaintiff or defendant.

21.5.1 The judge's 'balancing function'

In reality, says Dworkin, the judge is never in a position in which he needs to act (even in surreptitious fashion) as a legislator. He may have to balance carefully any existing, competing legal principles and policies so as to discover the correct solution; but he will have no occasion to utilise legal reasoning so as to produce new law (which is a task for the community's legislature).

21.5.2 The application of rules and principles

Judges must recognise, argues Dworkin, that mere *rules* may be modified or even repealed by the legislature. But *principles* may not be altered deliberately in this fashion. The decision in a case will take this into account. The judge applies rules and principles which complement them; he is not 'making law', in any sense of that phrase.

21.6 Rights

Dworkin seeks to show that the law is an embodiment of rights and responsibilities. Rights do not flow from any source outside man. 'What an individual is entitled to have, in civil society, depends upon both the practice and the justice of its political institutions.' Judicial decisions have the effect of enforcing existing political rights. Jurisprudence can do no more than provide a guide to the discovery of which rights a specific political theory assumes men and women to possess.

21.6.1 Abstract and concrete rights

Abstract rights tend to result from abstract principles. Rights such as 'freedom of speech' stem from the great abstract principle of respect for human dignity. Concrete rights are defined more precisely, often in a manner which indicates their weight in relation to general principles. The right to print fair and accurate reports of Parliamentary proceedings (see *Cook v Alexander* (1973)) is a concrete right to be seen in the context of the general right to free speech and the protection against defamation afforded to individuals.

21.6.2 Finding new rights

The courts will not 'make' new rights; they will merely 'find them' within the existing law - a tapestry of principles, the inspection and interpretation of which will indicate an individual's legal entitlement under given circumstances.

21.6.3 Trump rights

Rights must be protected, according to Dworkin, as a reflection of society's deep concern for the dignity of its members. In general, such rights ought to be inviolable. (In Rawls' words: 'Each person possesses an individuality founded on justice that even the welfare of society cannot override'.) Dworkin is emphatic:

> 'If rights make sense at all, then the invasion of a relatively important right must be a very serious matter. It means treating a man as less than a man, or as less worthy of concern than other men. The institution of "men's rights" rests on the conviction that this is a grave injustice ... and that it is worth paying the incremental cost in social policy or efficiency that is necessary so as to prevent it.'

'Trump rights' should override government policy arguments, as where, for example, the right to free speech is in conflict with policy issues propounded by the government. (Note *R v Secretary of State for the Home Department ex p Brind* (1991) and the European Convention on Human Rights, Article 10.)

Basic rights could be overridden justifiably, according to Dworkin's argument, in three cases:

- Where the government can show that the values protected by the right in question 'are not really at stake in the marginal case'.
- Where the government can show that if the right is defined to include the marginal case, then some significant competing right would be affected.
- Where the government can show that 'if the right were so defined, then the cost to society would not be simply incremental, but would be of a degree far beyond the cost paid to grant the original right, a degree great enough to justify whatever assault on dignity or equality might be involved.'

21.6.4 Extending 'law's empire'

The extension of 'the empire of the law' involves the recognition, maintenance and interpretation of individual rights as determined in the light of authorised principle:

> 'Law's attitude is constructive: it aims, in the interpretive spirit, to lay principle over practice to show the best route to a better future, keeping the right faith with the past.'

21.7 Critical Legal Studies: the background

The CLS movement in the US grew from a Harvard conference in 1976 of a group:

> 'composed primarily of law teachers, lawyers, law students and social scientists who are developing a critique of the legal system and legal education.'

21.7.1 A radical movement

From its meetings, discussions and the literature produced by jurists such as Unger, Kennedy, Gabel, Horwitz and Kairys, there has emerged an identifiable jurisprudence characterised by a radical criticism of American society, its legal ideologies and scholarship. The movement seems committed to a more egalitarian society and rejects the concept of law as separate from politics. *Law is politics* and it is a task of CLS jurists to show, in particular, how the existing legal system operates so as to shape popular consciousness towards an acceptance of the political legitimacy of the *status quo*.

21.7.2 The influence of radical philosophy

Three radical philosophers seem to have exerted considerable influence upon the writings constituting CLS. Gramsci (1891-1937), an Italian Marxist, who sought to transform aspects of early Marxist ideology is cited widely in CLS literature. He saw all ideological struggle, including controversy surrounding the nature of jurisprudence, as a struggle for the hearts and minds of society. Jurisprudence was to be interpreted in terms of a 'social activity' which contributed to the creation and development of cultural norms and values. Althusser (b.1918), a French neo-Marxist philosopher, argued that in order to understand social manifestations such as law, the analysis of a society's culture becomes essential. Derrida (b.1930), a French philosopher, taught the technique of 'deconstruction', involving a fundamental analysis of the significance of conceptual opposites ('contradictions') in systems of thought. (Gabel, a prominent CLS theoretician, considers that legal disputes are founded 'ultimately upon conflicts and contradictions within the social system as a whole'.)

21.8 The stance against liberalism

The term 'liberal' was used in a positive sense by the early American realists: it referred to a political and legal system characterised by humanitarian values, as exemplified by freedom of speech, tolerance and social equality. CLS views 'liberalism' in a different light: the very term is given a pejorative, reactionary overtone. Indeed, 'liberal scholarship' in law has become a target for a 'frontal ideological assault'.

21.8.1 Law and fetishism

CLS rejects the 'fetishism' associated with the concentration of liberalism upon civil rights and the struggle for their extension. To work merely for the securing of rights is to paralyse the will to radical action which is necessary for society's transformation. Kennedy suggests, somewhat cynically, that:

> 'it may be necessary to use the "rights argument" in the course of the political struggle to make gains. But the thing to be understood is the extent to which it is enervating to use it.'

In similar vein, the liberal preoccupation with the rule of law is criticised as a legitimation of an 'adversarial and atomistic conception of human relations'. CLS:

> 'celebrates the position [of the rule] as a human accomplishment of enormous importance, yet also exposing its limitations and pointing out the ways in which it can be used to defend or obscure existing injustice.'

21.8.2 Objections to the 'consensus model'

The liberal 'consensus model' of society is rejected as based on ignorance of social life which is dominated by exploitation and repression. The very social arrangements which seem natural and neutral in the 'consensus society' must be investigated so as to expose their contingency.

21.8.3 Social sciences as sources of false values

The reliance of liberal jurisprudence upon the support of the social sciences is condemned. Social science is viewed as an elaborate justification of the *status quo*, and the support which it gives to jurisprudence results in the sanctification of false values and 'contextless', abstract theories unrelated to the true functions of law.

21.8.4 Legal theory as 'reification'

Liberal jurists have failed to recognise the insidious nature of 'reification' in much current legal theory. 'Reification' is defined by Gabel as: 'the attribution of a thing-like or fixed character to socially constructed phenomena'. It is seen by CLS jurists as:

> 'an essential aspect of an individual's alienated consciousness, leading people to accept existing social orders as the "inevitable facts of life".'

Thus, the law of contract, when it involves the relationship of parties to a contract of employment 'presents as an accomplished fact an "equality" which is completely spurious'. See *Contract Law as Ideology* by Gabel (1990).

21.9 CLS and Marxism

Critics have noted in CLS literature what appears to be a heavy reliance upon mid-twentieth century neo-Marxist categories of social and jurisprudential thought. Gabel, in *Building Power and Breaking Images* (1983), writes of the work of the CLS conference as closely allied with neo-Marxist social theory:

> 'a central feature of which is a shift of focus away from the tendency of classical Marxism to explain all aspects of social life as resulting from underlying economic factors.'

Gabel suggests that classical Marxism is false because it misunderstands the significance of 'the relationship between the elaboration of legal ideas and the maintenance of social hierarchies'. In this context, CLS stresses the 'social conditioning', in which jurisprudence plays an important role, which results in the 'legitimising' of the existing order. Rules are enunciated which appear to be based upon 'rights and obligations'; they are reinforced by being applied in a more-or-less even-handed way, with the result that State power, reflecting a hierarchy, is legitimised. Gabel states:

> 'The legal system is an important public arena through which the State attempts – through manipulation of symbols, images and ideas – to legitimise a social order that most people find alienating and inhumane.'

'Dominant groups maintain their social position through the creation of ideologies that have sufficient appeal to win over important segments of the lower and middle classes': Gabel, in a comment on the contribution of Gramsci to jurisprudence.

Kairys, in *Politics of Law* (1990), notes that the task of exposing the perceptions of legitimacy of the law is complicated by 'the reality that the law is, on some occasions, just and sometimes serves to restrain the exercise of power.'

It should be noted that CLS writers do not accept fully the Marxist theory of law as mere superstructure (see 14.5.1); law, they argue, must be understood as an aspect of social totality.

21.10 Opposition to formalism

CLS spokesmen are highly critical of the role of contemporary jurisprudence in broadcasting the view that law stands above political and social struggle.

21.10.1 Politics and law are virtually conterminous

Politics and law are virtually conterminous, say CLS writers. 'Conceptual formalism', which rejects this assertion, makes impossible a correct analysis of the form and content of law. Law is non-neutral and concepts such as 'the sovereignty of communal needs' are masks for highly-partisan views, cloaking support for the *status quo*.

21.10.2 Criticism of legal education

The sedulously-cultivated myth of 'law-above-politics' means that law students are rarely allowed the opportunity of engaging in a fundamental analysis of the role of law in society. (Examples: the conspicuous absence from the typical criminal law syllabus of the social context of crime; the failure to teach torts in their economic setting.) (See Kennedy's *The Ideological Content of Legal Education* (1983).)

So-called 'comprehensive systems of legal doctrine', aiming to enunciate principles which will cover *all* types of legal situation, are denounced by CLS writers as empty formalism based on the 'mere manipulation of categories'.

21.11 CLS and legal reasoning

CLS theoreticians are opposed, in general, to the type of legal reasoning which underpins much contemporary liberal jurisprudence. Kairys, in *Politics of Law* (1990), uses the principle of precedent embodied in *stare decisis* to suggest that much of currently accepted legal reasoning is faulty, but is used because 'it is essential to the fundamental legitimising claim of government by law, not people'. *Stare decisis* applied by skilled and fair legal minds should lead to and require particular results in specific cases; but this does not emerge in practice. Kairys cites a line of Supreme Court contradictory decisions as illustrating confusion in the US concerning the use of precedent. (Compare the string of confusing decisions in the English courts following the decision of the House of Lords, relating to leases and licences, in *Street v Mountford* (1985).)

To understand the implications of *stare decisis* requires, according to Kairys, 'a separation of the social role from the functional impact of the decision-making process'; liberal jurisprudence fails to comprehend this matter. The socially and legally important focus of judicial law-making, which is concealed by *stare decisis* and the notion of legal reasoning, 'should be on the content, origins, and development' of values and priorities inherent in decisions of the courts.

'In sum,' writes Kairys, '*stare decisis* serves a primarily ideological rather than functional role'. Its ultimate basis is a social and political judgment. 'Law is simply politics by other means.'

21.12 Dworkin and CLS

Dworkin devotes no more than a few pages of *Law's Empire* to comments on CLS. He is, not unexpectedly, dismissive:

> 'Save in its self-conscious leftist posture and its particular choice of other disciplines to celebrate, critical legal studies resembles the older movement of American legal realism.'

21.12.1 Criticism of exploration of contradictions

He refers elsewhere, in scathing terms, to the attempts of CLS writers to understand a culture and its legal traditions through 'the infertile metric of contradiction'.

21.12.2 CLS and earlier American realism

Dworkin's suggestion of a connection between CLS and earlier American realism is of particular interest. Both movements attempted a deliberate 'demystification' of law; both were concerned to reveal the law as it really is; both sought to place law firmly within its social context.

However, CLS has moved away at a rapid rate from its early realist progenitors. The concentration on the work of the legislature and the judiciary, which characterised early realist studies is of relatively restricted interest to CLS. 'What the courts do in practice' is not to be understood merely by observation of the judicial process; an appropriate analysis demands awareness of the class interests and the political ideologies reflected in the formalities of adjudication. The 'neutrality of the law', favoured by early realists, is rejected as a myth by CLS. The CLS polemic against liberalism would have been incomprehensible to the early realists for whom any advance in the sphere of human rights provided occasion for a reaffirmation of the liberal-democratic ideology and its jurisprudence.

21.12.3 Altman's reply to Dworkin

Altman criticises Dworkin's dismissal of CLS. He has missed, Altman argues, in *Legal Realism, CLS and Dworkin* (1986), the significance of CLS revelations of inconsistencies in modern jurisprudence, and has paid insufficient attention to the CLS demonstration of how 'debates in the political arena are replicated in unsuspected corners of private law doctrine'.

The following specific points are made by Altman; they may be read also as an apologia for some of the central tenets of CLS.

- Dworkin, says Altman, has followed the contemporary trend of downgrading the legal realist movement. He devotes no more than one page out of three hundred in his *Taking Rights Seriously* (1977) to commenting upon the doctrines of the movement, of which CLS is an important contemporary component. (It should be noted, too, that in *Law's Empire* (1986), Dworkin's treatment of realism is of meagre measure: there is for example, a short reference to CLS as possibly an anachronistic attempt 'to make that dated movement [legal realism] reflower'. Another brief passage suggests that realists express their ideas 'in dramatically sceptical language. They say that there is no such thing as law, or that law is only a matter of what the judge had for breakfast'.) Referring to Dworkin (and Hart), Altman suggests that realism is regarded 'as having had its insights' which have been recognised long ago and are absorbed into mainstream legal philosophy, 'while the deficiencies have been presumably identified and repudiated.'

- Altman argues that Dworkin speaks of judges searching for the most cogent principles and theories which can be thought of as 'embodied in the relevant authoritative materials' and deciding cases according to those principles and theories. But even if judges do take decisions in such a fashion, and even if (according to Dworkin) there is 'a theory' which dictates correct legal outcomes in problematic situations, 'the existence of such a theory makes no practical differences' because a judge will interpret his favourite ideology as essentially constituting that theory.
- Dworkin has failed to take seriously the conflicting ethical visions and principles which are to be discovered in legal doctrine. Further, he has not given sufficient attention to the work of CLS jurists resulting in their exposing the doctrinal incoherencies in much of contemporary legal theory.
- For some CLS theoreticians, such as Gabel, Dworkin's jurisprudential analysis is merely the latest in a series of theoretical efforts to justify the capitalist system. See Gabel's review of *Taking Rights Seriously* in Harvard Law Review 91 (1977).
- Dworkin has paid insufficient attention to what lies behind the legal forms of which he writes. CLS writers have demonstrated that behind those forms may be discerned 'all of the significant ideological controversies of the political culture'. Legal form cannot screen out the intensity of ideological conflict which exists within that culture.
- There is no recognition by Dworkin of the achievement of CLS theoreticians in effectively elaborating and extending the view of the early realists that the law often fails largely in the task of determining the outcome of cases brought to litigation. This work and other investigations by CLS jurists suggest, according to Altman, that 'it is well past the time when legal philosophers can justifiably ignore the body of work associated with the CLS movement'.

Summary of Chapter 21

American Jurisprudence Today (2): Dworkin, Critical Legal Studies

Dworkin's opposition to positivism and 'law as rules'

Dworkin (b 1931) rejects the positivist interpretation of law as a mere system of rules. Law does not consist exclusively of rules.

Other matters must be taken into account in constructing a model of the legal system:

- *Standards* are of importance. Justice and fairness should be taken into account.
- *Policy* is significant. Policy is 'that kind of standard that sets out a goal to be reached, generally an improvement in some feature of the community.'
- *Principle* is also of significance. A principle is a standard that is observed because it is a requirement of 'justice or fairness or some other dimension of morality'.

Dworkin will not accept the positivist division of law and morality. There should be no judgment of the courts which runs contrary to social standards.

Judges, Dworkin declares, do not make law. There is always a 'right answer' to a dispute which can be 'hunted by reason and imagination'. A judge is never in a position where he is obliged to use legal reasoning so as to produce new law.

Dworkin's view of 'rights'

The law embodies rights and responsibilities. Rights do not flow from any source outside man.

The courts do not 'make' new rights; they discover them within the existing law.

Once a right has been identified and established it ought not to be disregarded save in very special circumstances. In 'hard cases' (in which the application by the court of a precise rule would almost certainly affect rights adversely) the judge must not apply standards in a mechanical fashion. He must so act as to preserve rights.

Critical Legal Studies

The background to CLS is a series of conferences held in the United States in the 1970s, which brought together radical law teachers, lawyers and students who were developing a critique of the legal system and legal education.

CLS writers have made a specific target of 'liberalism'; its concentration on issues such as civil rights is seen as a diversion from the main task for jurists and lawyers, which is the radical transformation of society. The consensus model of liberalism is said to be based upon a misreading of social reality and, in particular, a failure to understand the class nature of the modern State.

Jurists who rely upon the intellectual support of the social sciences are condemned for their failure to realise that these sciences are based essentially upon support for the *status quo*.

Opposition to 'classical Marxism' and formalism

CLS scholars are highly critical of the legal systems and the supporting jurisprudence associated with the now-defunct Marxist regimes. State socialism is viewed by CLS writers as a tyranny and its jurists as little more than apologists for oppression. Some CLS writers, however, claim to find the 'new Marxism' a source of useful material for jurisprudential theory.

Law is politics, and those who reject this are espousing a 'conceptual formalism' which is based upon a fiction. Contemporary jurisprudence does not stand above the political struggle. In fact, CLS scholars claim that they have demonstrated the non-objectivity of much current jurisprudence and have shown 'how debates in the political arena are replicated in unsuspected corners of private law doctrine'.

Chapter 22

Law and Morality: The Hart-Devlin Debate

22.1 Background to the debate

The links between law and morality constitute the subject-matter of an age-old jurisprudential debate. Ought the law to concern itself with morality? Ought the law to reflect shifts in public opinion concerning moral questions? What significance ought to be attached to Lord Simonds' assertion in *Shaw v DPP* (1962) that the courts retain a residual power, where no statute has intervened to supersede the common law, to superintend those offences which are prejudicial to the public welfare? Ought the law to intervene in order to prevent an individual's chosen course of action which moves him along 'the primrose way to the everlasting bonfire'? (See, more recently, the decision of the House of Lords in *R v Brown* (1993) – consent is no defence to sado-masochistic assault.)

22.1.1 Korkunov on law and morality

Korkunov, in his *Theory of Law* (1900), states:

> 'The distinction between morals and law can be formulated very simply. Morality furnishes the criterion for the proper evaluation of our interests; law marks out the limits within which they ought to be confined. To analyse out a criterion for the evaluation of our interests is the function of morality; to settle the principles of the reciprocal delineation of one's own and other people's interests is the function of the law.'

22.1.2 JS Mill on law and morality

JS Mill (see Chapter 7) argued, in terms which were to be used repeatedly as a reference point during the Hart-Devlin debate, that the only purpose for which power can be rightly exercised over any member of a civilised community, against his will, is to prevent harm to others. (Subsequent commentaries questioned the precise meaning of 'harm' - did it refer exclusively to physical injury? Ought it to include mental, emotional injury? What is meant by 'others'? Does it include, for example, a foetus? How should Mill's doctrine be applied to, say, adultery, or the use of cannabis?)

22.1.3 Post-war concerns

The problem of morality and the law emerged in Britain in acute form in the era following the Second World War. There was an upsurge of concern, prompted by highly-publicised criminal trials of homosexual offenders, and the appearance and sale of literature of a sexually-explicit nature. It was suggested in some quarters that the restraints imposed by the law in the name of morality were no longer effective and that the disintegration of the social fabric was not far off. Public concern hastened the appointment of a Royal Commission to investigate patterns of homosexual offences and prostitution. Unhappily for subsequent debate and jurisprudential enquiry, the phrase 'morality and the law' seems to have been narrowed down to 'sexual morality and the criminal law'.

22.2 Occasion for the debate

The *Report of the Committee on Homosexual Offences and Prostitution* (known as 'the Wolfenden Report') appeared in 1957, and recommended changes in the law; some of the recommendations became the basis of the Sexual Offences Act 1967, decriminalising certain homosexual practices in specified circumstances. Intense debate followed, producing points of view which tended to polarise around the arguments stated by Professor HLA Hart (1907-1992), and Sir Patrick (later Lord) Devlin (1905-1992), a former Lord Justice of Appeal and Lord of Appeal in Ordinary.

22.2.1 Philosophy of the Wolfenden Report

The 'philosophy' of the Wolfenden Report was based upon the following theses:

- The function of the criminal law (in relation to the subject area of the enquiry) was 'to preserve public order and decency, to protect the citizen from what is offensive or injurious, and to provide sufficient safeguards against exploitation and corruption of others ...'
- 'Unless a deliberate attempt is to be made by society, acting through the agency of the law, to equate the sphere of crime with that of sin, there must remain a realm of private morality and immorality which is, in brief and crude terms, not the law's business.'

22.2.2 Devlin's rejection of the philosophy of Wolfenden

Devlin, who had shown himself to be in favour of easing the penalties for some homosexual crimes, rejected the basic philosophy of the Wolfenden Report. 'The criminal law of England has from the very first concerned itself with moral principles.' 'The smooth functioning of society and the preservation of order require that a number of activities should be regulated.' (See *Knuller Publishing v DPP* (1973).)

22.2.3 Hart's reaction

Hart, who in subsequent debate tended to focus on the individual, rather than on society, rejected Devlin's approach and argued that it is not morally permissible to enforce the tenets of morality. He drew particular attention to the fallacies which he detected in Devlin's argument that those who deviate from conventional sexual morality might be in other ways hostile to society.

22.3 Devlin's questions

Devlin states that, hitherto, the criminal law has been based upon certain standards of behaviour or moral principles which society requires to be observed, and that their breach is an offence not merely against the person who is injured, but against society as a whole. He poses three questions:

- First question

  'Has society the right to pass judgment at all on matters of morals? Ought there, in other words, to be a public morality, or are morals always a matter for private judgment?'

- Second question

  'If society has the right to pass judgment, has it also the right to use the weapon of the law to enforce it?'

- Third question

  If so, ought it to use that weapon in all cases or only in some; and if only in some, on what principles should it distinguish?'

22.4 Devlin's answers

The answers given by Devlin to his own interrogatories constitute the essence of his stance against the philosophy of the Wolfenden Report.

- Answer to the first question

  The answer to the first interrogatory must be a resounding 'Yes'. Wolfenden takes for granted the existence of a public morality (which condemns, *inter alia*, homosexuality and prostitution). Each member of a community has ideas about good and evil; these ideas cannot be kept private from the society in which he or she lives.

  If persons attempt to create a society in which there is no fundamental agreement about good and evil, they will fail. Society is held together 'by the invisible bonds of common thought'.

  If the bonds of common thought are too far relaxed, members of the community will drift apart.

  A common morality is part of the bondage. That bondage is 'a part of the price of society'. Mankind needs society and it must pay its price.

- Answer to the second question

  The answer to the second question is also 'Yes'. Society may use the law to preserve morality 'in the same way as it uses it to safeguard anything else that is essential to its existence'.

  It is not possible to set theoretical limits to the State's power to legislate against immorality. Society has the right to use its laws to protect itself from internal or external dangers, as evidenced by the law of treason, for example. (See *Jones v Randall* (1744).)

An established morality is as necessary to the welfare of society as is good government. If no common morality is observed, society will disintegrate; indeed, the loosening of moral bonds is a prelude to such disintegration.

Society is justified in taking steps to preserve its moral code, and there can be no theoretical limits to this process.

- Answer to the third question

  In answer to the third interrogatory, it is necessary to discuss how society's moral judgments ought to be ascertained.

  Reference should be made to the judgment of 'the right-minded man' (not necessarily 'the reasonable man'); he can be thought of, perhaps, as 'the man in the jury box'. Let immorality be considered as what every 'right-minded man' considers to be immoral.

  But certain 'elastic principles' must be kept in mind by a legislature anxious to protect morality and the State. *First*: there should be 'toleration of the maximum individual freedom that is consistent with the integrity of society'. *Second*: punishment should be reserved for that which lies beyond the limits of tolerance. These limits will be reached when an activity creates disgust among 'right-minded persons'. 'No society can do without intolerance, indignation and disgust; they are the forces behind the moral law.' Further, society cannot be denied the right to eradicate 'a vice so abominable that its mere presence is an offence'. (It has to be stressed, however, that the limits of tolerance will change from one generation to another.) *Third*: the need to enforce the law must be balanced against respect for privacy. *Fourth*: the law should be concerned with minima, not maxima, so that society's standards ought to be set *above* those of the law.

22.5 Hart's response

The reaction to Devlin's arguments was mixed: he was supported by those who thought that Wolfenden had moved beyond tolerable limits; he was opposed by those who considered that he was out of tune with the times, had forgotten Mill's 'harm-to-others' principle, and was providing jurisprudential justification for a firm-handed paternalism. Hart led the opposition to Devlin's stance.

22.5.1 Unsound basis of Devlin's axioms

The basis of Devlin's axioms was unsound, argued Hart. 'Legal moralism' – the justification for attempts to prevent conduct which is perceived as immoral even though no person is harmed – had to be questioned. In particular, Devlin's stress on 'intolerance, indignation and disgust' as marking the boundaries for tolerance, was difficult to accept. The popular limits of tolerance shift to a greater extent than Devlin seemed prepared to accept; 'social morality' is rarely static for long periods of time.

22.5.2 No seamless web of morality

Devlin's concept of morality as a single 'seamless web' which will be torn beyond repair unless communal vetoes on behaviour are enforced by law, is, according to Hart, an unacceptable viewpoint. Single breaches of morality do not necessarily affect the integrity of society in its entirety.

22.6 Sexual morality and subversive activities

Devlin's comparison of the suppression of subversive activity and the suppression of sexual immorality was used by Hart to illustrate the inadequacy of that approach to the problem.

22.6.1 A grotesque comparison

It is grotesque, says Hart, to think of the homosexual behaviour of two adults in private as resembling in any way whatsoever treason or sedition either in intention or effect. Behaviour of this nature might be considered alongside treason only if the very wide assumption is made that a deviation from a general moral code will lead to its utter destruction.

22.6.2 Exaggeration in Devlin's claims

There is little plausibility in the suggestion that an offence against one item of morality is likely to jeopardise a community's total state of morality. There is evidence, says Hart, for believing that members of a community 'will not think any better of murder, cruelty and dishonesty' simply because private sexual practices, which may be abominated by most in the community, are not within the ambit of the criminal law.

The analogy with treason is absurd. Common sense and logic tell us that 'though there could not logically be a sphere of private treason, there is a sphere of private morality and immorality'.

22.7 Punishment for sexual misdemeanour

Hart argues that the legal punishment which followed on sexual misdemeanour could, and often did, result in disproportionate personal misery. (It is not always easy in our day to comprehend the severity of the condemnation which was reserved by the courts and many organs of public opinion for those who had committed the *crimen innominatum.*) This ought not to be forgotten. Blackmail and other evil consequences of a finding of guilt may often outweigh any harm said to have been caused directly by homosexual offences.

22.8 Hart's caution to legislators

Hart warns legislators against the implications of Devlin's arguments.

22.8.1 What is 'general morality'?

Devlin puts forward as the criterion for the 'immorality' of a deviant sexual practice, the disgust it will produce in the mind of 'the right-thinking man'. But, says Hart, legislators must pause and ask what is the precise nature of the so-called 'general morality' which the 'right-thinking man' is held to embrace. Is it, in reality, a rational reaction to behaviour which is disliked, or is it based on sheer ignorance, superstition or misunderstanding? Does that morality foster the falsehood that those who deviate from the moral code are dangerous to society in some other way? Does 'the right-thinking man' understand the intensity of the misery which can follow on a conviction for sexual misdemeanour?

22.8.2 Dangers of populism

Hart is warning against the dangers which can result from the 'populism' which Devlin appears to advocate. There is a special risk in a democracy, argues Hart, 'that the majority may dictate how all should live'. This is a risk we should gladly run since it is a price for the many good features of democratic rule; but we ought not to maximise the risk. Yet this is exactly what will occur if we tell the man on top of the Clapham omnibus 'that if only he feels sick enough about what other people do in private to demand its suppression by law, no theoretical criticism can be made of his demand'.

22.9 The debate continues

The deep-seated concerns of supporters of Devlin and Hart have not been put to rest, and reminders of the intensity of attitude which surrounds perceptions of sexual morality and its significance appear whenever legislation in this area is contemplated.

Devlin's supporters insist that the suppression of vice remains as much the law's business as the suppression of subversive activities. They are conscious, too, of the practical significance of Devlin's point of view: 'Philosophers may philosophise under the shadow of perpetual doubt, but the rulers of a society must act on what their society believes to be right'. They are urged by their opponents to consider the significance of Spinoza's observation (in 1670):

> 'He alone knows what the law can do who sees clearly what it cannot do ... He who tries to determine everything by law will foment crime rather than lessen it.'

Hart's supporters emphasise that 'to use coercion to maintain the moral *status quo* at any given point in society's history would be artificially to arrest the process which gives social institutions their value'. Argument, exhortation and advice are important and people must not be forced to choose 'between deliberate coercion or indifference'. Those who agree with Hart's general approach are reminded to contemplate the significance of Holmes' words that if a body of law is to be sound, it must correspond with the community's actual feelings and aspirations, and that people learn what is moral by observing what others tend to enforce.

22.10 A footnote by Dworkin

In his preface to *The Philosophy of Law* (1986) (which contains reprints of Devlin's *Morals and the Criminal Law* and Hart's *Immorality and Treason*), Dworkin suggests an extension to the debate. Let the attempt to distinguish between acts that cause harm and those that do not be abandoned. Let there be, rather, a concentration on a distinction between 'basic liberties' which should never be curtailed except to prevent serious, direct harm to persons, and 'liberty in general' which may be constrained so as to secure an overall gain in welfare. It will be necessary, too, argues Dworkin, to demonstrate why a person's freedom 'to choose sexual partners, and to read what he likes' is considered to be a basic liberty, while that person's liberty to conduct his business as he wishes is not. In effect, Dworkin is urging that the debate be broadened so as to embrace consideration of 'morality' in a much wider sense.

Summary of Chapter 22

Law and Morality: The Hart-Devlin Debate

Background to the debate

The question of the links between law and morality constitutes a matter of abiding interest for jurisprudence. Interest in the question was aroused during the period following the Second World War with the growth of public concern for what was perceived as a decline in sexual morality.

The government responded by setting up a Commission to examine offences connected with homosexuality and prostitution. The Wolfenden Report 1957 polarised juristic opinion.

The Report noted that there must remain a realm of private morality and immorality which is not the law's business.

Devlin (1905-1992) opposed the philosophy of the Report. Hart (1907-1992) attacked Devlin's approach and its implications.

Devlin's interrogatories and replies

Devlin asked, and answered, three questions.

- The *first* question: has society the right to pass judgment on moral matters?

  Devlin's answer was in the affirmative. There is a public morality reflecting shared opinions.

  If the bonds of common thought are too far relaxed, society will suffer. There is, therefore, a right to judge breaches of morality.

- The *second* question: if society has the right to pass judgment, has it the right to use the law to enforce it?

  Devlin's answer is again in the affirmative. Society may take steps to protect itself from disintegration.

  There can be no theoretical limit to the exercise of this right.

- The *third* question: ought society to use the weapon of the law in all cases, or only in some, and on what principles?

  Devlin urges that the judgment of 'the right-minded man' be taken into account.

  There should be toleration, however, of the maximum individual freedom that is consistent with society's integrity.

Hart's response

The basis of Devlin's axioms is unsound. There is no seamless web of morality which will be torn beyond repair by individual sexual deviancy. Single breaches of morality do not necessarily affect the integrity of society in its entirety.

Devlin's attempt to equate the need to suppress subversion with the need to suppress sexual immorality is, according to Hart, grotesque. There is no proof that deviation from a moral code will lead to its utter destruction with harmful effects on society in general.

Hart urges that consideration be given to the disproportionate misery which results for the individual convicted for sexual misdemeanour.

Hart warns legislators of the dangers of using as a criterion for legislative action the disgust produced by deviant behaviour in the mind of the 'right-thinking man'. This can lead to the condoning of intolerance.

There is a special risk in a democracy, argues Hart, that the majority may dictate how all should live. We ought not to maximise the risk of this happening by adopting the populist approach inherent in Devlin's observations.

The debate continues

Devlin's supporters continue to stress the need for the law to assist in the suppression of intolerable vice. Critics remind them of the assertion that he who tries to determine everything by law will foment crime rather than lessen it.

Hart's supporters urge that argument on these matters must continue. Critics remind them of the need for the law to correspond with the community's declared feelings and aspirations.

Chapter 23

Problems of Rights (1): Essential Features

23.1 Rights as the essence of law

For some jurists, the essence of law is to be discovered in the enunciation, interpretation and protection of rights. They view jurisprudence as 'the science of rights', involving a search for a unified theory of the nature and significance of rights within legal systems. 'Law' is considered from this point of view as involving little more than recognition by the courts of rights and correlative duties, together with procedural systems aimed at the resolution of disputes stemming largely from the consequences of failing to acknowledge rights, that is to say, failing to carry out duties. Jurists of this persuasion would view the separate sections of the substantive law - contract, torts, succession, etc - as, fundamentally, sets of rights related to particular types of social activity and grouped solely for purposes of convenience.

23.1.1 Rights as claims

Ginsberg, in *On Justice in Society* (1965), draws attention to the wide significance of rights within society. Broadly, a person's rights are constituted by the *claims* he may make on his fellows in relation to the conditions of his well-being. (Ginsberg has in mind 'moral' *and* 'legal' rights.) A person's rights to liberty, property, etc, presuppose his capacity and ability to claim the initiation of activities which will recognise and protect those rights in the event of their being challenged, ignored or invaded. His moral and legal rights become manifest in society's reactions to those who reject his claims. (Ginsberg views a person's 'duties' as constituted by what society expects him to contribute to its well-being.)

23.1.2 Becker's comments

Becker comments in *Individual Rights* (1987):

> 'Rights are more than just norms, or expectations, or standards of conduct. They are rules which define the boundaries of what is "owed" to a specified group of people (the right holders) by another group (the right respecters) ... Rights may be demanded and enforced: they are therefore part of our system of permissions and requirements.'

23.1.3 Rights as interests

Legal rights, however, are not necessarily claims based upon what society *ought* to bestow upon its members; rather are they claims which the law *will* recognise, uphold and enforce - 'legally guaranteed powers to realise an interest' (an 'interest' is considered as being to a person's advantage, eg, his liberty).

Salmond (see *Jurisprudence* (1986)) defines 'right' as an interest recognised and protected by law, respect for which is a legal duty, disregard of which is a legal wrong (defined more specifically as 'a violation of justice according to law').

23.2 Rights formally defined

The following definitions are typical of juristic approaches to the nature of rights.

- Allen

  'The legally guaranteed power to realise an interest.' A right is interpreted here as a *'power'* to modify a state of affairs; the exercise of that power is recognised by the law, and presupposes a guarantee as to the acceptability of consequences related to the interest (ie, advantage) of the owner of the right.

- Holland

  'The capacity residing in one man of controlling, with the assent and assistance of the State, the actions of others.' A right emerges from this definition as a *'power'*, underwritten by the State, to affect another's circumstances.

- Holmes

  'Nothing but permission to exercise certain natural powers and upon certain conditions to obtain protection, restitution, or compensation by the aid of public force.' This definition stresses the individual's reliance for the exercise of his powers upon the possible threat of sanctions applied to those who ignore or invade the rights. (Holmes defined a legal duty as 'nothing but a prediction that if a man does or omits certain things he will be made to suffer in this or that way'.)

23.3 The characteristics of a right

Salmond's analysis of a right is applied in relation to the purchase of Blackacre in fee simple by P from V.

A right involves a *party of inherence* (ie, P, following the purchase) in whom the rights relating to Blackacre are now vested, eg, his rights *in rem* concerning the exclusive use of Blackacre.

A right in P's favour is now available against any person upon whom rests a correlative duty - a *party of incidence*, eg, V, who, in accordance with the terms of the conveyance, must transfer title in Blackacre to P. The transfer of title is the content of this particular right.

A right must have an *object* or 'subject-matter' - the ownership of Blackacre in this case.

A right involves *title*, that is, all those events leading to the vesting of the right of possession and ownership in P, as set out in the conveyance to P.

(It would be instructive to apply Salmond's analysis to a consideration of the rights which emerge, say, from the Access to Neighbouring Land Act 1992, s 1:

> 'A person who, for the purpose of carrying out works to any land (the "dominant land"), desires to enter upon any adjoining or adjacent land (the "servient land"), and who needs, but does not have, the consent of some other person to that entry, may make an application to the court for an order under this section (an "access order") against that other person'.)

23.4 Rights as equivalent to duties

Some jurists argue that rights and duties are neither separate nor even capable of being interpreted as different aspects of the same theory. The maxim, 'No right, no duty; no duty, no right' suggests that 'right' and 'duty' are correlatives. Radin, in his essay *A Restatement of Hohfeld* (1938), suggests that 'right' and 'duty' are 'absolutely equivalent statements of the same thing'; they are not correlatives but are one and the same thing to which different terms are applied. Thus, X and Y make a contract for sale of goods by which Y agrees to transfer the property in those goods to X for a price. Radin would argue that, under the Sale of Goods Act 1979, Y's 'duty' to deliver the goods to X does not follow from X's right, nor is it 'caused' by that right. Y's duty *is* X's right.

23.5 Types of right

The following categories of right are of significance:

- Perfect and imperfect rights

  Perfect rights will be fully enforceable by law, imperfect rights are those recognised by the law but not always enforceable by the courts, eg, claims barred by lapse of time under the Limitation Act 1980.

- Primary and secondary rights

  Primary rights are those created without reference to rights already existing, eg, the right to life. Secondary (or 'accessory') rights are created, or arise, solely for the purpose of enforcing a primary right.

- Public and private rights

  Public rights are those vested in the community at large, ie, the State. Private rights are those vested in individuals (eg, the right of a person to enjoy possession of his property).

- Positive and negative rights

  Positive rights call forth positive acts from those on whom the correlative duties rest. Negative rights are related to negative duties of refraining from specified acts.

- Proprietary and personal rights

  Proprietary rights involve a person's property, and are generally transferable. Personal rights relate to an individual's status and are not transferable.

- Rights *in rem* and rights *in personam*

  The right *in rem* (a 'real' right) is available against the world at large. The right *in personam* (a 'personal' right) is available against determinate persons only. (These rights are of particular significance in relation to possession and ownership.)

23.6 Hohfeld's analysis of rights

The American jurist, Hohfeld (1879-1917) (*Fundamental Legal Conceptions as applied in Judicial Reasoning* (1917)), was concerned with the ambiguities resulting from the traditional vocabulary associated with the conceptual analysis of rights:

> 'In any closely-reasoned problem, whether legal or non-legal, chameleon-hued words are a peril both to clear thought and lucid expression.'

23.6.1 'Right' in context

Thus, the term 'right' takes on a colour (like a chameleon) related to its context, as exemplified by the following statements. 'I have a *right* to my opinion.' 'The owner of a *profit à prendre* has the *right* to enter, and take something off, another's land.' 'The Cheques Act 1992 protects the *right* of a banker and drawer in relation to a crossed cheque.'

23.6.2 Definitions

Hohfeld produced a new set of definitions in relation to rights. He isolated basic legal concepts and analysed them in terms of functions and relationships: there emerged 'the lowest common denominators of the law', as follows:

- *Right*. 'An enforceable claim to performance, action or forbearance, by another.'
- *Duty*. 'The legal relation of a person who is commanded by society to act or to forbear for the benefit of another person either immediately or in the future, and who will be penalised by society for disobedience.'
- *Privilege*. 'The legal relation of A to B when A (with respect to B) is free or at liberty to conduct himself in a certain manner as he pleases; when his conduct is not regulated for the benefit of B by the command of society; and when he is not threatened with any penalty for disobedience.'

- *No-right*. 'The legal relationship of a person in whose behalf society is not commanding some particular conduct of another.'
- *Power*. 'The legal relation of A to B when A's own voluntary act will cause new legal relations either between B and A or between A and a third person.'
- *Liability*. 'The relation of A to B when A may be brought into new legal relations by the voluntary act of B.'
- *Immunity*. 'The relation of A to B when B has no legal power to affect one or more of the existing legal relations of A.'
- *Disability*. 'The relation of A to B when by no voluntary act of his own can A extinguish one or more of the existing legal relations of B.'

23.6.3 Jural relations

Hohfeld also conceived a scheme of 'jural relations' based on 'opposites' and 'correlatives'.

- Jural opposites

  An example is 'right' and 'no-right'. No pair of opposites can exist in the same person; thus, if A has a 'privilege' in relation to the sale of Blackacre, he cannot have a 'duty' in relation to the sale of Blackacre at the same time.

- Jural correlatives

  An example is 'right' and 'duty'. Each pair of correlatives must be a related 'unity'; thus, if A has one of the pair, some other person (B) must have the other. Thus, A has a right against B, whereby B shall not enter Blackacre, so that the correlative of A's right is B's duty not to enter.

- Summary of opposites and correlatives

Opposites	right	privilege	power	immunity
	no-right	duty	disability	liability
Correlatives	right	privilege	power	immunity
	duty	no-right	liability	disability

- Diagrammatic representation

  In this diagram *jural correlatives* are shown connected by *vertical* arrows; *opposites* by *diagonal* arrows. (*Jural contradictories* are shown connected by *horizontal* arrows.) The diagram may be interpreted as showing, in the case of correlatives that a privilege in A implies the presence in B of a no-right; in the case of opposites, that a duty in A implies the absence in himself (A) of a privilege.

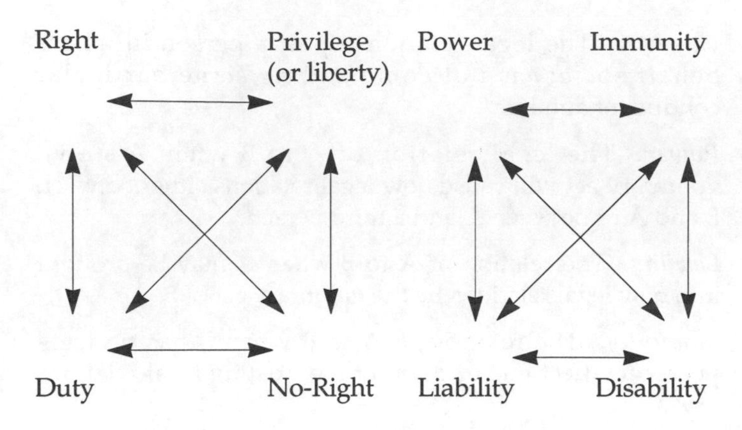

23.6.4 Hohfeld criticised

In Pound's *Fifty Years of Jurisprudence* (1937), Hohfeld's analysis was subjected to criticism, particularly because of the derivation of his methodology from Hegelian thought, which was considered by many philosophers and jurists to be based upon questionable assumptions. Hegel's so-called 'opposites', which are central to his analysis of phenomena as reflecting 'unities of opposites', are often not 'opposites', but merely 'contrasts', as explified by Hohfeld's 'powers' and 'disabilities', 'rights' and 'no-rights'. Pound notes: 'All we have here is a contrast of a right in the narrow sense with the absence of such a right, and a power with the absence of a power.' Hohfeld seems to suggest that there is but one opposite and one correlative, and that 'there must be an opposite and a correlative'. In reality, however, there may be many contrasts and, in some cases, more than one correlative.

Pound warns that the search for opposites and correlatives may produce concepts which have no real meaning. A 'no-right', for example, has little significance. Pound cites as an example of futility in this area, a jurist's contention that where a court finds that a plaintiff has not proved his case on the facts, it decides that he has a 'no-right': see *Affirmative and Negative Legal Relations*, by E Goble.

Hohfeld remains for many jurists and legal practitioners a scholar who provided a fresh impetus for jurisprudence in the continuing search for precision in the use of the terminology of the law. Hobbes (see 3.4) writes in *Leviathan* in terms which are applicable to the task to which Hohfeld set his hand:

> 'A man that seeketh precise truth had need to remember what every name he uses stands for and to place it accordingly, or else he will find himself entangled in words as a bird in lime-twigs; the more he struggles, the more belimed.'

23.7 The concept of fundamental human rights

'Human rights' have been the subject of much jurisprudential discussion which centres upon the idea of the entitlement of human beings to a range of legal rights, some of a fundamental and inviolable nature. 'Absolute human rights', it is argued, may not be abridged, according to jurists such as Finnis, in any circumstances whatsoever. Proponents of some types of natural law theory argue that, because man is made in the image of his Creator, he possesses an intrinsic dignity which must be translated into legal rights. Other jurists, such as Gewirth (*Epistemology of Human Rights* (1984)), describe human rights as 'rights which all persons equally have simply insofar as they are human'. Feinberg, in *Social Philosophy* (1983), defines human rights as 'generically moral rights of a fundamentally important kind held equally by all human beings, unconditionally and unalterably.' A problem arises immediately in attempting to enumerate the 'fundamental rights' necessary to recognise and preserve man's dignity. Few would argue as to the primacy of the right to life and the protection of that right under the law. Thus, Finnis, in *Natural Law and Natural Rights* (1980), classifies as an absolute human right 'not to have one's life taken directly as a means to any further end'. What of other rights, such as the rights to food, shelter, work, or Finnis' enunciated 'right not to be positively lied to in any situation in which factual communication ... is reasonably expected'? See, also, Rawls' views at 20.7.3.

Note the comments of Garvin, in *A Modern Introduction to Ethics* (1953) 'There is one right which is to all intents and purposes an absolute right. That is the right to equal consideration – the right to be treated as the formula for justice provides. For this right is one which is the most basic of all, one which is under no conditions to be violated.'

23.7.1 Universal Declaration of Human Rights

The Charter of the United Nations (1945) affirmed faith in 'fundamental human rights, in the dignity and worth of the human person, in the equality of men and women and of nations large and small'. *The Universal Declaration of Human Rights* (1948) stated that the fundamental rights necessary for a civilised society comprise equality before the law, freedom of thought and religion, freedom of peaceful assembly, protection from arbitrary arrest.

23.7.2 European Convention on Human Rights

The European Convention on Human Rights (1950) (ECHR) is of considerable significance in recent moves towards a general recognition of fundamental human rights. ECHR (to which the UK is a party, although the Convention is not yet a part of English law (see *R v Secretary of State for the Home Department ex p Brind* (1991)) protects the right to life; liberty and individual security are also protected; torture and slavery are outlawed;

Summary of Chapter 20

American Jurisprudence Today (1): Rawls and Nozick

Rawls: a public conception of justice

Rawls (b 1921) set out, in his *A Theory of Justice* (1971), the principles upon which a 'just society' might be constructed. A complex hypothetical situation is envisaged from which the principles emerge.

Members of society will meet to discuss and choose principles which will guide the well-ordered society they wish to establish.

In their *original position* they will select principles which will be objectively just and will not reflect sectional interests.

The persons involved in the discussions will be behind a *veil of ignorance* so as to achieve total objectivity. They will not know how their choices will affect their individual lives. They will evaluate principles solely on the basis of general considerations.

From the discussions will emerge a call for the rational distribution of 'social primary goods', ie, those things every rational person is presumed to want in relation to his life-plan. An equal distribution will be suggested, unless an unequal distribution is to the advantage of the least-favoured members of society.

The principles of justice

Two principles of justice will emerge from the deliberations:

- The first principle:

  'Each person is to have an equal right to the most extensive total system of equal basic liberties compatible with a similar system of liberty for all.' Basic liberties include political liberty, freedom of speech, etc.

- The second principle:

  'Social and economic equalities are to be arranged so that they are both to the greatest benefit of the least advantaged, consistent with the just savings principle, and attached to offices and positions open to all under conditions of fair equality of opportunity.' (The 'just savings principle' involves the putting aside of wealth for the use of future generations.)

The priority rules

There will be two priority rules:

- The first rule is the priority of liberty. Liberty can be restricted only for the sake of liberty.

freedom of religion and conscience is assured; discrimination related to gender, race, colour and religion, is banned. There was general agreement among the signatories to the Convention on the need to enunciate and recognise certain rights as constituting the essential basis for a civilised society. (See *Teare v O'Callaghan* (1982); *Reid v UK* (1984); *Open Door Counselling Ltd v Ireland* (1993) (freedom to receive and impart information).)

23.8 The overriding of rights

Against the theory of 'inviolable human rights' is ranged a variety of arguments.

23.8.1 Cancellation by the State

Rights, it is argued, are bestowed, recognised and protected by the State; they can be cancelled by legislation, eg, the Clean Air Act 1993, which limited severely the rights of some individuals in relation to the environment. There cannot be, it is urged, any area of rights outside the purview of the State and its legal organs, because no right can be recognised as 'absolute'. *Liversidge v Anderson* (1942) stressed that the liberty of the subject is 'a regulated freedom ... It is not an abstract or absolute freedom ... In the constitution of this country there are no guaranteed or absolute rights'. (See also *IRC v Rossminster Ltd* (1980).)

23.8.2 Need for security

Society's need for security often overrides individual rights. The Official Secrets Acts 1911-89 remove from some categories of persons their right to free expression of their opinions, in the interests of national security. (See *R v Bingham* (1973).) Those same interests may override the right of an individual to join an association (eg, a trade union) of his choice (in accordance with ECHR, Article 11, 'everyone has the right to ... freedom of association with others, including the right to form and join trade unions for the protection of his interests'): see *Council of Civil Service Unions v Minister for the Civil Service* (1985); *Sigurjonsson v Iceland* (1993). The Northern Ireland (Emergency Provisions) Act 1991 removed a number of rights in the interests of the preservation of peace and the maintenance of order. (See *R v Killen* (1974).)

Council of Civil Service Unions v Minister for the Civil Service (1985) provides a clear illustration of the approach of the courts (and many jurists) to the need for the overriding of rights under certain very important and closely-defined circumstances. A union of workers at the Government Communications Headquarters (GCHQ) had taken industrial action, thus disrupting work vital to the nation's security. The Minister for the Civil Service, without consulting the appellate union, issued an instruction preventing employees of GCHQ from exercising their right to join an appropriate union of their choice. The House of Lords held that the union had a 'legitimate expectation of consultation', which founded a claim for judicial review of the Minister's action, *but*, on the facts, the competing interests of national security served to outweigh the union's right in this area.

Per Lord Scarman:

> 'I would dismiss this appeal for one reason only. I am satisfied that the respondent has made out a case on the ground of national security ... I have no doubt that the respondent refused to consult the unions before issuing her instruction because she feared that, if she did, union-organised disruption of the GCHQ monitoring services could well result ... I am satisfied that a reasonable minister could reasonably consider such disruption to constitute a threat to national security...
>
> I conclude that where a question as to the interest of national security arises in judicial proceedings the court has to act on evidence ... Once the factual basis is established by evidence so that the court is satisfied that the interest of national security is a relevant factor to be considered in the determination of the case, the court will accept the opinion of the Crown of its responsible officer as to what is required to meet it, unless it is possible to show that the opinion was one which no reasonable minister advising the Crown could in the circumstances reasonably have held...'

(For a criticism of the GCHQ case from the standpoint of individual rights, see 'End this affront to individual freedom', by David Pannick QC, in *The Times* (18 January 1994).)

23.8.3 Restrictions on free speech

The right to freedom of speech, held by many Western jurists to be a touchstone of a free, civilised society, is restricted in the UK by common law and statute. The tort of defamation (see, eg, *Hulton v Jones* (1910); *Telnikoff v Matusevitch* (1991)) is a reminder of limitations on the expression of certain types of statement. Exercise of the right of publication is held in check by the Obscene Publications Acts 1959 and 1964. *R v Lemon* (1979) is a warning that freedom of speech may not be exercised when the result is an insult or vilification of Christianity, ie blasphemy. See also *R v Bow Street Magistrates ex p Choudhury* (1990)).

23.8.4 Restrictions in ECHR

The ECHR (1950) illustrates the difficulties in the enunciation of 'inviolable human rights'. Thus, deprivation of life is not to be regarded as having been inflicted in contravention of Article 2 ('everyone's right to life shall be protected by law') when it results from the use of force which is no more than absolutely necessary, eg, 'in action lawfully taken for the purpose of quelling a riot or insurrection'. The prohibition of forced labour (Article 4) is subject to the exception of service 'exacted in the case of an emergency or calamity threatening the life or well-being of the community'. Freedom to manifest one's religion or beliefs (Article 9) is subject 'to such limitations as are prescribed by law and are necessary in a democratic society in the interests of public safety, for the protection of public order, health, morals'.

23.9 Human rights and 'the common good'

Dworkin (*Taking Rights Seriously* (1978)) (see 21.6.3 above) insists that rights ought not to be violated by the State even though it can be shown on policy grounds that the community as a whole would be better off in such a circumstance, eg, as in the case of the right to publish some kinds of pornography. An appeal to the common good would not, in itself, provide the justification for the removal of an individual freedom. (Finnis reminds us that we ought not to say that the exercise of human rights is subject to the common good, 'for the maintenance of human rights *is* a fundamental component of the common good'.) The problem may be in the definition of 'common good' - essentially a highly-subjective and emotive concept. Finnis sees a deep significance, therefore, in the right of individuals 'to be taken into respectful consideration of what the common good requires'. Here is a restatement of the concern for human dignity which is at the basis of much jurisprudential discussion of 'fundamental human rights'.

Summary of Chapter 23

Problems of Rights (1): Essential Features

Rights as the essence of law

Some jurists view the essence of law as the enunciation, interpretation and protection of rights.

Jurisprudence becomes, on this reading, 'the science of rights'.

Examples of definitions of rights include:

- Allen: 'The legally guaranteed power to realise an interest.'
- Salmond: 'An interest which the law will recognise and protect, respect for which is a legal duty, disregard of which is a legal wrong.'
- Holland: 'The capacity residing in one man of controlling, with the assent and assistance of the State, the actions of others.'

Rights as equivalent to duties

Radin argues that 'right' and 'duty' are absolutely equivalent statements of the same thing.

Hence, Y's duty to pay X for goods received from him, is X's right to receive payment from Y.

Rights classified

Rights have been classified as: perfect and imperfect; primary and secondary; public and private; positive and negative; proprietary and personal.

Rights *in rem* and rights *in personam* are of particular significance in matters affecting possession and ownership.

Hohfeld's analysis

Hohfeld (1879-1917) was concerned to eradicate the misunderstanding caused by the use in law of 'chameleon-hued words'.

He produced a new set of definitions for the basic legal concepts which he isolated and analysed in terms of functions and relationships. These 'lowest common denominators of the law' were: right, duty, privilege, no-right, power, liability, immunity, disability.

He also conceived a scheme of 'jural relations' based on jural opposites and correlatives.

Fundamental human rights

Some jurists argue for the enunciation of fundamental human rights which may not be abridged. Man's dignity requires their recognition and protection.

The Charter of the United Nations (1945) and the Universal Declaration of Human Rights (1948) call for the recognition and protection by States of certain rights necessary for a civilised society, eg, the rights to life and security.

The European Convention on Human Rights (1950) calls for protection to be given to certain fundamental rights.

The overriding of rights

There are circumstances in which the overriding of rights is justified by some jurists.

Rights bestowed by the State may be removed, it is argued, by the State when national security is threatened or when the exercise of those rights may harm some members of society.

The European Convention on Human Rights recognises that freedoms may be restricted when, eg, the life or well-being of the community is threatened.

Whether there can be any category of human freedoms which comprises 'absolutely inviolable rights' is arguable, given the duty of the State to guard the interests of citizens at all times.

Chapter 24

Problems of Rights (2): Children's Rights, Abortion, etc

24.1 Recent concerns

In recent years there has been a significant growth of interest in the question of rights relating specifically to children: international Conventions concerning the rights of the child have been agreed, and the intensification of support for a Bill of Rights for the UK, which would seek to entrench some children's rights now taken for granted, has led to renewed jurisprudential speculation (see, eg, the writings of Bainham, Dewar and Eekelaar) on the basis of these rights and the desirability of their extension as a matter of policy. An upsurge of feeling in the UK and the US in relation to the vexed questions of the right to abortion and the rights urged concerning euthanasia have resulted in jurisprudential argument (see, eg, the writings of Dworkin) intended, in some cases, to change the shape of debate on these topics so that the 'pro-life' and the 'pro-choice' lobbies might consider their shared concern for life's sanctity and might examine whether that concern can burgeon into some kind of unity.

24.1.1 Contemporary legal thinking on the nature of children's rights

Earlier jurisprudential concerns with 'the problem of the correlative', which sought to question the very existence of a child's rights because he was incapable of duties, and which, presumably, would have effectively denied rights to neonates, have almost disappeared. Jurists, legislators and the courts have given increased attention to arguments in favour of an extension and deepening of children's rights. The Children Act 1989 (described by the Lord Chancellor as 'the most comprehensive and far-reaching reform of child law which has come before Parliament in living memory') gave expression to a wide-spread belief among the community that parenthood is the primary legal status in relation to the child, and that the rights of the child demand a consideration of his welfare as the paramount consideration where upbringing is in question.

- Problems of the rights of the child in relation to the age of criminal responsibility were considered recently by the House of Lords in *C v DPP* (1995), in which the House restated, as good law, the presumption that children in the 10-under 14 age group are *doli incapax* and that the burden of rebutting the presumption rests on the prosecution.
- The House of Lords examined afresh the fundamental question of children's rights and parental responsibilities in the *Gillick* case (see 24.3.2 below).

24.1.2 Recent examination of juristic thinking in relation to 'the edges of life'

The perennial questions of the rights of the foetus, the right to have an abortion, the right to carry out so-called 'mercy killings' have been considered by Dworkin in *Life's Dominion* (1993) (see 24.4 below), in which principles of liberal jurisprudence are applied to an examination of the concept of the sanctity of life in the light of declarations such as that of the Vatican Congregation (1987), that every human being has 'a right to life and physical integrity from the moment of conception until death'. Euthanasia has been considered and rejected by the House of Lords in the *Airedale NHS Trust Case* (1993) (see 24.11 below), raising wide questions which Dworkin seeks to clarify.

24.2 International recognition of children's rights

Recognition by the international community of children's rights *as moral claims* to be accepted by States and underwritten in the form of legislation, was upheld in part by the Geneva Declaration of the Rights of the Child 1924, which set out general principles concerning child welfare. The 1950 European Convention on Human Rights included in its Protocol the right of children to receive an education.

The United Nations Convention on the Rights of the Child 1989 was ratified by the UK in 1991. It applies 'to every human being below the age of 18, unless, under the law applicable to the child, a majority is attained earlier'. The 'best interests of the child' are to be a primary consideration in all actions relating to children: Article 3(1). The child's inherent right to life, its right to survival and development, to freedom of thought, conscience and religion, to protection from certain forms of exploitation and from cruel, inhuman or degrading treatment or punishment, are recognised in the Convention. Earlier juristic argument suggesting that rights of this nature were applicable only to adult members of the community are rarely advanced today in discussions on children's rights as *claims* on the community.

24.3 A new look at children's rights and parental responsibility: the *Gillick* case (1986)

In *Gillick v West Norfolk and Wisbech Health Authority* (1986), plaintiff, a Roman Catholic mother of five under-16 daughters, asked the court for a declaration that DHSS advice given to family doctors which stated that in exceptional circumstances they might give advice and treatment concerning contraception to girls under 16, *without consent of the mother*, was unlawful.

The application for a declaration failed at first instance. The patient's age (under 16) did not mean in itself that she could not give consent to treatment. The patient must be capable of making a reasonable assessment of the advantages and disadvantages of the proposed medical treatment.

The Court of Appeal *allowed* Mrs Gillick's subsequent appeal. A girl under 16 was not able to give a valid consent to the treatment under consideration. Except in an emergency, the doctor ought to seek parental consent or apply to the court.

24.3.1 House of Lords

The House considered the question involving the child's rights and parental responsibility. The decision of the Court of Appeal was *reversed*. *Per* Lord Fraser: 'Provided the patient, whether a boy or girl, is capable of understanding what is proposed, and of expressing his or her wishes, I see no good reason for holding that he or she lacks the capacity to express them validly and effectively and to authorise the medical man to make the examination or give the treatment which he advises.'

24.3.2 Lord Scarman's speech

In his speech in *Gillick*, Lord Scarman analysed the concept of *parental rights in relation to the child.* He stressed the law's perception of the child as *a person possessing recognised rights in this area.*

> 'Parental rights clearly do exist, and they do not wholly disappear until the age of majority. Parental rights relate to both the person and the property of the child. But the common law has never treated such rights as sovereign or beyond review and control. Nor has our law ever treated the child as other than a person with capacities and rights recognised by law. The principle of law ... is that parental rights are derived from parental duty and exist only so long as they are needed for the protection of the person and property of the child. The principle has been subjected to certain age limits set by statute for certain purposes; and in some cases the courts have declared an age of discretion at which a child acquires before the age of majority the right to make his (or her) own decision. But these limitations in no way undermine the principle of the law, and should not be allowed to obscure it ...
>
> ... The underlying principle of the law was exposed by Blackstone and can be seen to have been acknowledged in the case law. It is that parental right yields to the child's right to make his own decisions when he reaches a sufficient understanding and intelligence to be capable of making up his own mind on the matter requiring decision ...
>
> ... I would hold that as a matter of law the parental right to determine whether or not their minor child below the age of 16 will have medical treatment terminates if and when the child achieves a sufficient understanding and intelligence to enable him or her to understand fully what is proposed. It will be a question of fact whether a child seeking advice has sufficient understanding of what is involved to give a consent valid in law. Until the child

> achieves the capacity to consent, the parental right to make the decision continues save only in exceptional circumstances. Emergency, parental neglect, abandonment of the child or inability to find the parent are examples of exceptional situations justifying the doctor proceeding to treat the child without parental knowledge and consent; but there will arise, no doubt, other exceptional situations in which it will be reasonable for the doctor to proceed without the parent's consent.'

24.4 Dworkin's *Life's Dominion* (1993)

In Dworkin's recent exploration of current social and legal thinking on questions of abortion and euthanasia (*Life's Dominion* (1993)), an attempt is made to apply juristic principles in an argument designed to show that competing views in these areas of concern are not necessarily irreconcilable, provided that both sides accept certain basic views relating to the sanctity of life. Dworkin is guided in his approach by his belief that law and morality are indivisible and, therefore, that legal discussion must not divorce itself from moral thought. The book's central thesis draws attention to the sanctity or inviolability of *every stage* of every human life, and emphasises the difficulties inherent in taking a position on either side of the current debate. The greatest insult to the sanctity of human life is to be indifferent or merely lazy when faced with the complexity of the issues raised in current arguments.

24.4.1 *Roe v Wade* (1973)

Dworkin makes many references in his argument to the famous decision of the United States Supreme Court in *Roe v Wade* (1973), a judgment which has been criticised incessantly and vehemently by those who say that, in effect, it has licensed murder. The Supreme Court decided (7-2) that the abortion law of Texas which considered abortion as a crime, save where carried out in order to save the life of the mother, was *unconstitutional*, and that any State law which forbids abortion so as to protect a foetus within the first two trimesters is unconstitutional. A State could prohibit abortion so as to protect the life of a foetus only in the third trimester, ie, when the foetus is *a viable being*. A pregnant woman's constitutional right of 'procreative autonomy' is affirmed. Dworkin expresses anxiety that the case might be overturned in the future as the result of changes in the composition of the panel of judges who constitute the Supreme Court.

24.4.2 The paradigm liberal position concerning abortion

Dworkin perceives four components of the typical American liberal position on abortion and the rights surrounding it. First, there is a rejection of the view that abortion holds no moral problems. On the contrary, abortion invariably involves a moral decision and ought not to be permissible, therefore, for a trivial reason. It can never be justified except to prevent some form of serious damage. Secondly, abortion can be morally justified in some serious cases, eg, to save a mother's life, or where a severe foetal abnormality has been discovered. Thirdly, abortion should be allowed where the consequence of the birth of the child would be permanent and grave damage to the mother or her family. Fourthly, until late in pregnancy, the question of justifying an abortion is, ultimately, for the woman to decide: the moral convictions of others must not be forced upon her.

These views, argues Dworkin, represent the moral convictions of at least a substantial minority in the US and other western countries.

24.4.3 The situation in the UK

Abortion in English law is covered largely by the Abortion Act 1967, as amended by the Human Fertilisation and Embryology Act 1990, s 37. Abortion is allowed where two medical practitioners agree that the pregnancy has not exceeded its 24th week and that the continuance of the pregnancy would involve risk, greater than if the pregnancy were terminated, of injury to the physical or mental health of the pregnant woman (W) or any existing children of her family; *or* the termination is necessary to prevent grave permanent physical or mental health of W; *or* the continuation of the pregnancy would involve risk to W's life, greater than if the pregnancy were terminated; *or* there is a substantial risk that if the child were born it would suffer from such physical or mental abnormalities as to be seriously handicapped.

24.5 Opposition to abortion

Opposition in the US to abortion has intensified in remarkable fashion, often assuming violent forms, and based largely, according to Dworkin, upon a widespread perception of the destruction of a foetus as murder. Jurisprudential argument used in opposition to abortion, both in the UK and the US, has been characterised by the neo-Thomist interpretation of the process of abortion as a direct interruption of the generative processes already begun, and a waste of God's gift of human life. (Note *The Rights and Wrongs of Abortion* by Finnis (1973).)

The view of the Roman Catholic Church on abortion is uncompromising, and has been restated in the Papal Encyclical, *The Gospel of Life* (1995). 'I [Pope John Paul] confirm that the direct and voluntary killing of an innocent human being is always gravely immoral.' The foetus is seen as a person with a right to life, such right having existed from the very moment of conception. Abortion is characterised as an insult to the sanctity of human life and, therefore, is to be condemned absolutely. (It should be noted that many non-Catholic Christians accept this view of the rights of the unborn child and the consequent interpretation of abortion as unwarranted homicide.)

24.6 Opposition of feminists to *Roe v Wade*

Dworkin notes unexpected opposition to the decision in *Roe v Wade* from many proponents and supporters of the views expressed in Chapter 25 ('Feminist Jurisprudence'). That opposition is derived from belief by feminists in the need for the law to recognise the 'special connection' between the pregnant woman and the foetus. *Roe v Wade* is seen as embodying a correct result reached for the wrong reasons: thus, it included an opinion by Justice Blackmun that women have a general 'constitutional right to privacy', from which it follows that they have a right to abortion (before the end of the second trimester of their period of pregnancy). The concept of a 'right to privacy' has been attacked by some feminist jurists as a dangerous illusion: freedom of choice concerning abortion in a male-dominated society ought to rest not on principles of 'privacy', but on a wider concept of sexual equality. Further, the privacy argument is said to ignore the uniquely creative role of the woman in pregnancy. Her right to abortion ought not to derive from the insubstantial rhetoric of 'privacy'; it should arise from 'her responsibility to make a complex decision she is best placed to make'.

24.7 What is sacred ?

Dworkin argues against the absolutist view that the foetus is ensouled at the moment it is conceived. He suggests that Augustine (see 4.3.1) was not certain on this point, that St Jerome stated that destruction of a foetus is not homicide until the elements within the uterus receive their appearance and members, and that Aquinas taught that the foetus acquires a rational soul *after* the time of conception. Modern research suggests that sentience of the foetus requires a neural substrate which is not formed until later than the initial stages of growth. Dworkin urges that those who consider human life to be sacred should, without abandoning their basic belief, consider the implications of applying the term 'person' (and the concept of rights) to the foetus in its initial stage of existence.

24.8 Dworkin's plea for a measure of agreement

Dworkin argues that, fundamentally, the beliefs by liberals and their opponents as to the sacred nature of life might make for a general, if limited, agreement on the acceptability of abortion in some circumstances. First, he argues, the foetus is not to be considered absolutely as a 'person' from the moment of conception; it becomes a 'person' only when development of the brain and other organs allows it the capacity to live as a human being. Secondly, many individuals share the view that life is 'sacred' and should never be destroyed without good reason; such individuals are to be found on both sides of the abortion divide. Thirdly, 'life' may be thought of in its strict biological sense *and* in a wider sense as embracing our capacities to experience existence as fully-developed human beings: a foetus which lacks a cerebral cortex, for example, and is unable, therefore, to live as a distinctively human being cannot enjoy that human autonomy which is a significant constituent of 'the sacredness of life'. It ought to be possible for individuals who respect that quality of sacredness to agree, even partially, upon the need to consider the actions which might be appropriate in the case of an unborn child doomed to an existence in which human autonomy is impossible to attain.

24.9 The right to an easy death

Euthanasia (from a Greek phrase meaning 'easy death'), ie, so-called 'mercy-killing', in which one person intentionally brings about a gentle pain-free death for another suffering from an incurable and painful disease, is considered in the UK and the US as a criminal offence.

- *Per* Lord Goff in *Airedale NHS Trust v Bland* (1993) (see 24.11 below): 'It is not lawful for a doctor to administer a drug to his patient to bring about his death, even though that course is prompted by a humanitarian desire to end his suffering, however great that suffering may be... So to act is to cross the Rubicon which runs between on the one hand the care of the living patient and on the other hand euthanasia – actively causing his death to avoid or to end his suffering. *Euthanasia is not lawful at common law.*'
- The House of Lords Select Committee on Medical Ethics, reporting in 1994, rejected arguments put forward in support of voluntary euthanasia as being 'not sufficient reason to weaken society's prohibition of intentional killing', a prohibition considered as 'the cornerstone of law and social relationships'. 'We believe that the issue of euthanasia is one in which the interest of the individual cannot be separated from the interests of society as a whole.'

(It should be noted that States in the US recognise 'living wills', allowing persons to sign documents stipulating that certain identified medical procedures are not to be used to keep the named persons alive in certain circumstances. See also the Law Commission Report 1995: *Mental Incapacity*.)

24.10 Deciding about dying

Dworkin suggests that there are three principal types of situation in which persons may have to make decisions about their own death, or that of someone else. First, when the person whose death is contemplated is conscious or competent, eg, when he is merely sick or handicapped. Secondly, when the person is unconscious and dying. Thirdly, when the person is conscious but incompetent, eg, a sufferer from the severe dementia associated with Alzheimer's disease. Dworkin argues that, in all cases, one should take into account the autonomy of the sufferer, his best interests, and the sanctity of life (a concept which has for many persons a secular dimension). Thus, in considering the case of the third type of person, we should ask what the proper respect for the *intrinsic value* of his life necessitates by way of action. We must respect human autonomy and must not deny the consequences of our belief in the sacredness of life by imposing on persons, in spite of their obvious distress, a continued existence which deprives them of that autonomy. Dworkin's argument is fundamentally that associated with his views on abortion. Further, people have *a right* not to suffer indignity, and we should insist that nothing be done to deny their dignity, particularly in circumstances where, say, serious dementia has deprived them of the self-respect which should be characteristic of the human condition.

24.11 The deliberate withdrawal of medical aid leading to death

Jurisprudential discussion on the problem of liability in cases where medical care was withdrawn from a patient in a vegetative state was deepened after *Airedale NHS Trust v Bland* (1993). X, aged 21, remained in a permanent vegetative state for three and a half years, following hypoxic brain damage which had destroyed the higher functions of his brain. The health authority responsible for X's care applied to the court for a declaration that all life-sustaining treatment be withdrawn from X allowing him to end his life and die peacefully 'with the greatest dignity and the least pain, suffering and distress'. A declaration was granted by the President of the Family Division. Here were the elements of a situation which had been the subject of hypothesis in many discussions by jurists and others.

24.11.1 Court of Appeal

The President's decision was *affirmed* and the Official Solicitor *appealed* to the House of Lords. *Per* Mustill LJ:

> 'The decision of the Court should carry conviction with the ordinary person as being based merely on legal precedent but also upon acceptable ethical values ... I have tried to examine the underlying moral principles which have led me to the conclusion at which I have

> arrived. In doing so, I must acknowledge the assistance I have received from reading the manuscript of Professor Dworkin's forthcoming book, *Life's Dominion*.'

24.11.2 House of Lords

The appeal of the Official Solicitor was *dismissed*. *Per* Lord Goff:

> '... We are concerned with circumstances in which it may be lawful to withhold from a patient medical treatment or care by means of which his life may be prolonged. But here too there is no absolute rule that the patient's life must be prolonged by such treatment or care, if available, regardless of the circumstances ...
>
> 'I am of the opinion that there is no absolute obligation upon the doctor who has the patient in his care to prolong his life, regardless of the circumstances. Indeed, it would be most startling, and could lead to the most adverse and cruel effects upon the patient if any such absolute rule were held to exist ...
>
> 'In the end, in a case such as the present, it is the futility of the treatment which justifies its termination. I do not consider that in circumstances such as these a doctor is required to initiate or to continue life-prolonging treatment or care in the best interests of his patient. It follows that no such duty rests upon the respondents or upon Dr Howe, in the case of X, whose condition is in reality no more than a living death, and for whom such treatment or care would, in medical terms, be futile ...'

Medical treatment was withdrawn from X, following the affirmation of the original declaration, as a result of which he died.

24.11.3 The broader issues

Per Lord Browne-Wilkinson:

> '...The ability to sustain life artificially is of relatively recent origin. Existing law may not provide an acceptable answer to the new legal questions which it raises. Should judges seek to develop new law to meet a wholly new situation? Or is this a matter which lies outside the area of legitimate development of the law by judges, and requires society, through the democratic expression of its views in Parliament to reach its decisions on the underlying moral and practical problems and then reflect those decisions in legislation? I have no doubt that it is for Parliament, not the courts, to decide the broader issues which this case raises ...'

24.12 The continuing opposition to legalised euthanasia

Opposition to the legalisation of euthanasia remains strong in the US and the UK. Religious opposition was repeated in the 1995 Papal Encyclical: 'I confirm that euthanasia is a grave violation of the law of God, since it is the deliberate and morally unacceptable killing of a human person'. The Archbishop of York has spoken in Parliament of 'the danger of changing the whole ethos of medicine and law if the absolute prohibition on intentional killing were removed'. A number of jurists and lawyers have argued that the 'slippery slope' from legalised killing may lead ineluctably to a denial of fundamental rights to the sick and aged who are a severe burden on others.

24.13 The desirability of agreement

Dworkin urges, as on the question of abortion, that consideration be given by those on either side of the debate to the possibility of reaching some agreement on the desirability of legislation which will allow persons to die with all possible dignity when pain or dementia have become intolerable. He stresses the *rights* of human beings in these circumstances and argues that the shared concept of the sanctity of life should bring together, rather than continue to divide, supporters and opponents of legalised euthanasia.

Divided opinions among jurists and legislators concerning the legalisation of euthanasia remain. The belief that a person should be allowed to die with dignity and self-respect when he is no longer able to live in a dignified manner is countered by the argument that the prohibition of intentional killing is, and must remain, essential to our society, and that to allow it in any circumstances would involve a serious denial of human dignity. Dworkin is arguing for a smoothing of life's uncertain edges and for life's dominion to be perceived in terms of sanctity and humanity's intrinsic values. Moves toward acceptance of this point of view would necessitate a reappraisal of fundamental human rights and duties.

Summary of Chapter 24

Problems of Rights (2): Children's Rights, Abortion, etc

Rights in relation to children

In recent years much attention has been paid by jurists, legislators and the courts to the problem of extending children's rights. Rights of this nature are now considered by many to be in the nature of 'claims' on society which must be met.

The Children Act 1989 is an example of the legislative widening of the area of children's rights. It seeks to establish rules relating to the legal status of parents, and places emphasis on the consideration of the child's welfare as a paramount consideration where upbringing is in question.

International Conventions

The Geneva Declaration on the Rights of the Child (1924) set out some general principles concerning child welfare. The European Convention on Human Rights (1950) included an affirmation of the child's right to receive education. The important United Nations Convention on the Rights of the Child (1989) set out the importance of legislation concerning the child's 'best interests'.

The *Gillick* case (1986)

In *Gillick v West Norfolk and Wisbech Health Authority* (1986), the House of Lords declared that parental rights yield to the child's right to make his own decisions when he reaches a sufficient understanding and intelligence to be capable of making up his own mind on the matter requiring decision (in this case the acceptance or rejection of medical advice).

Life's Dominion (1993)

Dworkin's recently-published book attempts to explore the common ground which he sees as existing between 'pro-life' and 'pro-choice' arguments in relation to abortion and euthanasia.

Opposition to abortion tends to stem from the deeply-held conviction that the destruction of a foetus is equivalent to murder of a human being. Advocates of the right to abortion reject the view that the foetus in its early stages of existence is a 'human being'. Dworkin argues that there are considerable doubts as to the veracity of the belief that a foetus is a 'human being' from the very moment of its conception.

Both sides in the debate accept the concept of the sanctity of life and it ought to be possible to arrive at some general consensus, accepting that each side views abortion primarily in relation to that concept.

Dworkin applies a similar pattern of reasoning to the arguments concerning proposals to introduce legalised euthanasia (ie, 'easy death' for those suffering from an incurable disease or a condition involving extreme pain). He suggests that where a person is unable to maintain the self-respect, dignity and autonomy which characterise human life, the question of the continued survival of that person becomes a matter to be considered in earnest. A loss of the characteristics of the human condition brings into question the desirability of the termination of life.

In *Airedale NHS Trust v Bland* (1993), the House of Lords considered, and allowed, the deliberate withdrawal of medical aid, leading to the death of a person who had been in a persistent vegetative state following serious injury. The House stated categorically, however, that euthanasia is not lawful at common law.

Respect for the sanctity of human life and the dignity of the person might provide a ground for drawing together those with differing views on euthanasia.

Dworkin notes the continued opposition to the very idea of euthanasia, which stems largely from religious conviction. Any moves toward acceptance of the voluntary termination of the lives of those experiencing intense suffering would necessitate a reappraisal of fundamental human rights and duties.

Chapter 25

Problems of Rights (3): Natural Justice

25.1 The general concept

The term 'natural justice' is used in contemporary jurisprudence to refer to the body of general principles and acceptable minimum standards of fairness now required in the overall processes of adjudication. Natural justice is often equated with fairness, and there is no such thing as a *technical breach* of it: *R v Chief Constable of Thames Valley Police ex p Cotton* (1990). (In *John v Rees* (1970), the court referred to natural justice as 'justice that is simple and elementary, as distinct from justice that is complex, sophisticated and technical'.)

Usage suggests that for some commentators the concept has overtones of the notion of natural law – natural justice is to be viewed as linked inextricably with metaphysical and religious thought. Thus, Lord Denning, in *The Changing Law* (1953), wrote that 'our conception of justice is only the Christian teaching of love':

> 'Some people speak of "natural justice" as though it was a thing well recognisable by anyone, whatever his training or upbringing. But I am quite sure that our conception of it is due entirely to our habits of thought through many generations... The precepts of religion, consciously or unconsciously have been [the judges'] guide in the administration of justice.'

This is 'natural justice' from the standpoint of those who seek to place the law within a setting of 'true religion and virtue'.

A more prosaic view of the general concept of natural justice partly emerges from the following selection of recent decisions of the courts.

- Where an appellant was unable to attend a public inquiry owing to a lack of communication of the date of the hearing, the inquiry should have been adjourned. The holding of the inquiry was effectively a breach of natural justice: *Majorpier v Secretary of State for the Environment* (1990).
- Where applicants sought political asylum and were not directed to the considerations which would have defeated their applications and were not reminded of their previous answers, there was a breach of natural justice: *R v Secretary of State for the Home Department ex p Thirukumar* (1989).

- There was a clear breach of the rules of natural justice in failing to give an applicant for planning permission an opportunity to make representations on the nature of the application of a local plan to the proposed development: *Second City v Secretary of State for the Environment* (1990).
- Failure to enquire into a person's means before binding him over to keep the peace in a substantial sum was held to be a breach of natural justice: *R v Nottingham Crown Court ex p Brace* (1990).
- Where a fine (for driving a vehicle on the road with an excess load) was imposed without consideration of past record, capacity to pay, and by the application of a rigid formula, there was a breach of natural justice: *R v Chelmsford Court ex p Birchall* (1990).

25.1.1 A long-established jurisprudential concept

The term 'natural justice' may be found in the literature of the law, including treatises on jurisprudence, and case reports, over the centuries. In *Thornborough v Baker* (1675), Lord Nottingham's judgment concerned a mortgagee's interest in relation to the demands 'of natural justice and equity'. *Fowler v Padget* (1798) involved the court's declaration that the concept of *actus non facit reum* could be considered as one of the principles of natural justice. The right of mortgagees to tack was considered in *Union Bank of Scotland v National Bank of Scotland* (1886) and held to rest upon the principles of natural justice. A violation of natural justice was avoided, according to the decision in *Valentini v Canali* (1889), by the rejection of a minor's claim.

25.1.2 An empty phrase?

Some jurists and judges have condemned the concept of 'natural justice' as 'mere verbiage', 'an unhelpful jurisprudential fiction', 'a popular misnomer for proper dealing between parties', and 'yet another synonym for natural law'. Lord Shaw, in *Local Government Board v Arlidge* (1915) characterised the concept as 'high-sounding but harmless'. In *Holt v Markham* (1923), Scrutton LJ suggested that use of the phrase was an indication of 'well-meaning sloppiness of thought'. *Per* Ormrod LJ, in *Norwest Holt Ltd v Department of Trade* (1978):

> 'The phrase "the requirements of natural justice" seems to be mesmerising people at the moment. This must, I think, be due to the apposition of the words "natural" and "justice". It has been pointed out many times that the word "natural" adds nothing except perhaps a hint of nostalgia for the good old days when nasty things did not happen'.

In *CCSU v Minister for the Civil Service* (1985) (see 23.8.2), Lord Roskill suggested that the phrase 'natural justice' ought to be allowed to find a permanent resting place and be replaced by speaking of a duty to act fairly. Several legal writers have argued that the phrase is so ambiguous as to resist any precise meaning being attached to it and that its use serves only to induce error in jurisprudential thought and legal procedure.

25.1.3 Problems concerning the adjective 'natural'

Some contemporary jurists have claimed that the adjective 'natural', when applied to nouns such as 'law', 'rights', 'justice', results in phrases which seem to label legal categories as 'manifestations' of nature itself – as in early legal thought which held out nature as 'the great exemplar'. This is often not what is in the minds of those who hold 'natural justice' to be synonymous with fairness or even-handed dealing.

Note the comments of Megarry VC in *McInnes v Onslow-Fane* (1978) (and see also *R v Gaming Board ex p Benaim* (1970)):

> 'I do not think much help is to be obtained from discussing whether "natural justice" or"'fairness" is the more appropriate term. If one accepts that 'natural justice' is a flexible term which imposes different requirements in different cases, it is capable of applying appropriately to the whole range of situations indicated by terms such as "judicial", "quasi-judicial" and "administrative". Nevertheless, the further the situation is away from anything that resembles a judicial or quasi-judicial situation, and the further the question is removed from what may reasonably be called a justiciable question, the more appropriate it is to reject an expression which includes the word "justice" and to use instead terms such as "fairness" or "the duty to act fairly": see *Re HK (An Infant)* (1967), *Re Pergamon Press* (1971)... The suitability of the term "fairness" in such cases is increased by the curiosities of the expression "natural justice". Justice is far from being a "natura"' concept. The closer one goes to a state of nature, the less justice does one find...'

Support for the final observation in the above extract comes from anthropologists who have queried the view of early jurisprudential writers suggesting that nature provides a pattern to be followed in our legal structures and procedures. 'Nature in the raw' provides a negation of the very ideas associated with the concept of 'justice'. Maugham J noted, in *Green v Blake* (1948) that use of the phrase 'natural justice' should not be taken to mean that there is some state of justice, some rights, which are 'natural' among men. The fantasy of 'the just savage' recognising and upholding the rights of his neighbours is not underpinned by modern research.

The publication in 1902 of *Mutual Aid* by Kropotkin, the Russian scientist and theoretician of anarchism (1842-1921), provided some support for the idea of a 'justice' existing in a 'natural mode' among men and not based upon formal laws. Mutual aid among human beings, said Kropotkin, is a dominant rule rather than the exception; co-operation rather than conflict is evident in a study of the evolution of our species. Man's innate 'sociability' reflects his close links with 'the natural world' and produces a type of informal justice – a 'natural justice' which assists in ensuring the survival of the species. Anarchism, he wrote, was correct in rejecting any other type of justice, which served only to enslave mankind.

The use of the word 'natural' in relation to justice has been defended by jurists who claim that it draws attention to the place of human society within the natural order by emphasising the 'basic, natural virtues' of co-operation, tolerance and mutual respect, so that where a legal ideology and structures are built upon the absence of these features, collapse will be inevitable. 'Natural justice' marks out the vital minimum standards, rules and regulations – and patterns of behaviour – which are necessary for survival and progress.

25.1.4 Growing precision in the meaning of 'natural justice'

During this century the phrase 'natural justice' has been invested with much more precision than was evident in earlier times. Its usage now reflects the concern of the courts with problems of 'right' and 'fairness'. The law reports provide many examples of reference to natural justice in cases turning on failures to recognise individual rights and duties. The courts seem to interpret the phrase with particular reference to minimum standards of rational and fair decision-making which the community has a right to expect from those who have been entrusted with the duties inherent in acting judicially. The formerly-held view of natural justice as relating only to the decisions of the superior courts has disappeared; the growth of the doctrine that even-handedness is to be demanded from *all* persons and bodies involved in the making of decisions which affect the rights of others, reflects an increased awareness of what is now implied in the concept of natural justice.

25.1.5 Natural justice and 'fairness'

Administrative law has so developed that the courts now have a general duty to ensure that when administrative powers are exercised, the principles of 'fairness in procedure' shall not be disregarded. In *Ridge v Baldwin* (1964) (see 25.5.2 below), Lord Reid rejected the suggestion that natural justice was a concept which was so vague as to be without meaning: he stressed the significance of the relationship of the concept to 'the fair procedure' which might be expected by reasonable people in certain circumstances. Even where a body of persons is not obliged to conduct adversarial proceedings of a judicial nature before arriving at a decision, those persons are obliged to show fairness in the proceedings *Pearlberg v Varty* (1972).

Lord Bridge summed up the situation in relation to natural justice, rights and the requirement of fairness in *Lloyd v McMahon* (1987) (in which a district auditor issued a certificate against councillors for wilful misconduct in not fixing a rate; his failure to offer them an oral hearing, which they had not requested, did not render his decision open to challenge at law):

> 'The so-called rules of natural justice are not engraved on tablets of stone. To use the phrase which better expresses the underlying concept, what the requirements of fairness demand when any body, domestic, administrative or judicial, has to make a decision which will affect the rights of individuals depends on the character of the decision-making body, the kind of decision it has to make and the statutory or other framework in which it operates. In particular, it is well established that when a statute has conferred on any body the power to make decisions affecting individuals, the courts will not only require the procedure prescribed by statute to be followed, but will readily imply so much and no more to be introduced by way of additional procedural safeguards as will ensure *the attainment of fairness.*'

25.2 ECHR 1950

The European Convention on Human Rights, signed at Rome in 1950 and ratified by the UK in 1951, is concerned with *the protection of human rights*. Many commentators see it as a translation into law of some of the basic principles of natural justice. Article 6, which, in the event, has proved to be the most frequently violated of the Articles comprising the Convention, contains a number of clauses which relate directly to the quality of 'fairness' inherent in many interpretations of natural justice.

> Article 6: Right to a fair and public hearing
>
> 1 In the determination of his civil rights and obligations or of any criminal charge against him, everyone is entitled to a fair and public hearing within a reasonable time by an independent and impartial tribunal established by law. Judgment shall be pronounced publicly...
>
> 2 Everyone charged with a criminal offence shall be presumed innocent until proved guilty according to law.

3 Everyone charged with a criminal offence has the following minimum rights:

a to be informed promptly, in a language he understands and in detail, of the nature and cause of the accusation against him;

b to have adequate time and facilities for the preparation of his defence;

c to defend himself in person or through legal assistance of his own choosing, or, if he has not sufficient means to pay for legal assistance, to be given it free when the interests of justice so require;

d to examine or have examined witnesses against him and to obtain the attendance and examination of witnesses on his behalf under the same conditions as witnesses against him;

e to have the free assistance of an interpreter if he cannot understand or speak the language used in court.

Here are many of the rights which jurists and others have in mind when the essence of natural justice, as it relates to legal procedure, is under discussion.

25.3 The significance of natural justice in procedures for application for judicial review

The recent growth in the number of applications for judicial review has heightened interest in natural justice and procedural fairness. The following matters should be noted in relation to questions of rights, natural justice and applications for judicial review.

- For the procedural regulations concerning applications for judicial review, see the Supreme Court Act 1981, s 31, and RSCO 53 (as revised).
- An application for judicial review may involve a challenge to public law actions of public bodies by those persons who are able to establish an appropriate *locus standi* by demonstrating a 'sufficiency of interest' in the subject matter of the application.
- Potentially, the scope of judicial review extends to *all* matters of public law.
- A successful application generates a right to avail oneself of a number of remedies including the prerogative orders of *certiorari*, prohibition, *mandamus*, and declarations and injunctions. (It should be remembered that remedies of this nature are essentially discretionary; a remedy might be refused although a breach of natural justice has been proved, where the court feels that the applicant's case lacks merit.)

- An application for judicial review involves the court's deciding whether or not the decision of a body is *legally valid*. The court is *not* concerned with the question of whether or not the body had made a decision which could be held to be 'good' on the specific merits of the case in question.
- A long series of cases has established that in the area of administrative law, observance of the principles of natural justice in relation to the exercise of individual rights involves reference to recognised standards of behaviour which are based largely upon the fundamental principles involving the 'rule against bias' and the 'rule against condemning a person unheard'.

25.4 The rule against bias

Jurisprudential thought has taken for granted the absolute importance of the presence of 'the disinterested adjudicator'. It is of the essence of natural justice that a fair judicial decision involves the presence of *a judge who is totally impartial*. Thus, a judge is disqualified from acting in a case where, for example, he has a direct interest (of a pecuniary nature) in the subject matter of that case. Additionally, he must not have any bias whatsoever in favour of a party. Justice must be done and manifestly seen to be done: *R v Sussex Justices ex p McCarthy* (1924). The rule, which is considered essential if the right to a fair hearing is not to be vitiated, is summarised in the maxim, *nemo judex in causa sua potest* – no person should be a judge in his own cause.

25.4.1 *Metropolitan Properties v Lennon* (1969)

In *Metropolitan Properties*, the court quashed the decision of a Rent Assessment Committee because its chairman was connected, albeit indirectly, with a party to the proceedings.

> *Per* Lord Denning MR:
>
> 'In considering whether there was a real likelihood of bias, the court does not look at the mind of the justice himself or at the mind of the chairman of the tribunal, or whoever it may be, who sits in a judicial capacity. It does not look to see if there is a real likelihood that he would, or did in fact, favour one side at the expense of the other. *The court looks at the impression which would be given to other people.* Even if he was as impartial as could be, nevertheless if right-minded people would think that in the circumstances there was a real likelihood of bias on his part then he should not sit. And if he does sit, his decision cannot stand. Nevertheless there must be a real likelihood of bias. Surmise or conjecture is not enough. There must be circumstances from which a reasonable man would think it likely or probable that the justice, or chairman would or

did favour one side unfairly at the expense of the other. Suffice it that reasonable people might think that he did.'

25.4.2 *R v Barnsley MDC ex p Hook* (1976)

In the case of *Hook* (1976), he was dismissed as a stallholder in Barnsley market following a disciplinary action against him which was initiated by the market manager who sat on the committee which decided on the dismissal.

Per Lord Denning MR:

'I do not think that the right of a stallholder arises merely under a contract or licence determinable at will. It is a right conferred on him by the common law under which, so long as he pays the stallage, he is entitled to have his stall there; and that right cannot be determined without just cause ... *and then only in accordance with the principles of natural justice* ... I will assume that Mr Hook was given sufficient notice of the charge to be able to deal with it. But nevertheless each of the hearings was vitiated by the fact that the market manager was there all the time. He was the only one who gave evidence ... When the committee discussed the case and came to their decision, the market manager was there all the time ... *It is contrary to natural justice that one who is in the position of a prosecutor should be present at the deliberations of the adjudicating committee.*'

25.4.3 *R v Altrincham Justices ex p Pennington* (1975)

In the case of *Pennington* (1975), informations laid by a county council weights and measures inspector, alleging short weight deliveries to county council schools, were tried by a bench which included a justice co-opted by the education committee. This situation was held to be contrary to natural justice: it was held that the justice should have disqualified herself.

25.5 The rule against condemning a person unheard

Natural justice demands respect for the right of an accused person to be heard. 'If the right to be heard is a real right which is worth anything, it must carry with it a right in the accused man to know the case which is made against him': *Kanda v Government of Malaya* (1962). Rights are vitiated, or destroyed, where a party to a hearing is prevented from being made aware of the essence of the charge he is required to answer or is not allowed to present his case. The displeasure voiced by generations of legal theorists at the existence of rules or practices which kept prisoners in ignorance of the nature of their alleged offences, and the weight of popular opinion against such practices is responsible in large measure for the generation of the rule – *audi alteram partem* (hear the other side). An example of the rule in operation is evident in *Malloch v Aberdeen Corporation* (1971), in which it was held that a teacher who was 'dismissible at pleasure' had to be given a full opportunity to present his case before being formally dismissed.

25.5.1 *Ridge v Baldwin* (1964)

In *Ridge v Baldwin* (1964), the appellant, a chief constable, had been dismissed by the Watch Committee in pursuance of its statutory powers, but he had not been allowed a full opportunity to present his case before formal dismissal. The House of Lords held that the Watch Committee had acted in breach of the principles of natural justice.

> *Per* Lord Reid :
>
> 'I find in the cases [concerning dismissal from office where there must be something against a man to warrant his dismissal] an unbroken line of authority to the effect that an officer cannot be lawfully dismissed without first telling him what is alleged against him and hearing his difference or explanation'.

25.5.2 *B v W* (1979)

In *B v W* (1979),the House of Lords held that the Court of Appeal had acted in breach of natural justice when, in considering an order committing two wards of court to the care of the local authority, the Court had refused to allow the children's grandparent to see a document which had been regarded as important.

25.5.3 *R v Thames Magistrates ex p Polemis* (1974)

Polemis (1974) concerned a ship's master, summonsed at 10.30 am, returnable at 2 pm the same day, charging him with the discharge of oil into navigable waters. His request for an adjournment which would allow him to prepare his defence was refused, and this was held to amount to a breach of natural justice.

25.5.4 *R v Secretary of State ex p Hosenball* (1977)

Hosenball, an American journalist working in Britain was notified that he was to be deported in the interests of national security, having obtained for publication information harmful to the security of the UK. He requested further particulars of the allegations against him but these were refused and he was deported. The principles of natural justice could be modified in circumstances involving the protection of the realm, and Hosenball's inability to present his case adequately because of lack of knowledge of the case against him could not justify the overriding of the interests of national security.

> *Per* Cumming Bruce LJ:
>
> 'The field of judicial scrutiny by reference to the enforcement of the rules of common fairness is an extremely restricted field in the sphere of operations necessary to protect the security of the State.'

25.6 Natural justice, rights and legitimate expectations

An important extension of rights has resulted in recent years from the expansion of the rules of natural justice designed to embrace the *legitimate expectations* of individuals affected by express promises made by persons and bodies charged with the making of decisions, or by the existence of a regularly-continuing and established practice which might be reasonably expected to persist.

25.6.1 Early statement of the doctrine

In *Schmidt v Secretary of State for Home Affairs* (1969), two American citizens who had been admitted to the UK for a fixed period were refused an extension of time and appealed against a decision taken without their being given a hearing. Their appeal was dismissed.

Per Lord Denning MR:

> 'Speeches in *Ridge v Baldwin* (1964) show that an administrative body may, in a proper case, be bound to give a person who is affected by their decision an opportunity of making representations. It all depends on whether he has some right or interest, or, I would add, *some legitimate expectation*, of which it would not be fair to deprive him without hearing what he has to say.'

25. 6.2 *A-G of Hong Kong v Ng Yuen Shiu* (1983)

In the case of *Ng Yuen Shiu* (1983) an undertaking had been given to a specified group of illegal immigrants in Hong Kong that before decisions were taken to repatriate members of the group to China each case would be examined on its own particular merits. The Privy Council held that the undertaking had given rise to the expectation of a fair hearing, and on the facts of the case it had not been met. The Privy Council gave support to the concept of a public body being bound by its undertakings concerning procedures.

> 'The justification [for the principle] is primarily that, when a public authority has promised to follow a certain procedure, it is in the interests of good administration that it should act fairly and implement its promise, so long as implementation does not interfere with its statutory duty. The principle is also justified by the further consideration that, when the promise was made, the authority must have considered that it would be assisted in discharging its duty fairly by any representations from interested parties and as a general rule that is correct.'

25.6.3 *R v Secretary of State ex p Khan* (1984)

The nature of the rights arising from so-called 'legitimate expectations' was considered in *Khan* (1984). The Secretary of State had issued a circular setting out the criteria to be applied by the Home Department in considering the admission of children into the UK for the purposes of adoption. The applicant sought judicial review of a refusal to admit a relative's child whom he wished to adopt; his ground was that the criteria had not been followed. The applicant was suggesting *a breach of a right*. The Court of Appeal held that

Khan had a legitimate expectation that decisions concerning entry of children to the UK would be based upon the criteria set out in the circular. The expectation had been disappointed; the decision rejecting entry was quashed.

25.6.4 *CCSU v Minister for the Civil Service* (1985)

For the facts of the *CCSU* case (1985), see 23.8.2 above. Lord Diplock's speech in the House of Lords considered judicial review and legitimate expectations.

> 'To qualify as a subject for judicial review, the decision must have consequences which affect some person (or body of persons) other than the decision maker, although it may affect him too. It must affect such other person either: (a) by altering rights or obligations of that person which are enforceable by or against him in private law; or (b) by depriving him of some benefit or advantage which either he had in the past been permitted by the decision maker to enjoy and which he can legitimately expect to be permitted to continue to do so until there has been communicated to him some rational grounds for withdrawing it on which he has been given an opportunity to comment, or he has received assurance from the decision maker will not be withdrawn without giving him first an opportunity of advancing reasons for contending that they should not be withdrawn.'

25.6.5 *R v Secretary of State ex p Ruddock* (1987)

The Home Secretary had published details of the criteria to be used by his Department in authorising 'phone tapping. Ruddock claimed that his 'phone calls had been intercepted by security officials. He applied for judicial review so as to quash the warrant for interception, claiming that it was unlawful because it failed to comply with the published criteria concerning interception. He had been deprived of his legitimate expectation that the Home Secretary would follow the published criteria. The Home Secretary contended that the court ought to decline jurisdiction on grounds of national security requirements; further, the doctrine of legitimate expectations did not apply.

It was held that the court would not decline to exercise its supervisory jurisdiction over the Home Office merely because a claim of national security had been raised. Publication of the criteria governing 'phone interception warrants did establish a legitimate expectation that the criteria would be followed.

25.7 Natural justice and the extension of rights

The development of the doctrine of natural justice would seem to have extended the area of individual rights and to have provided procedures enabling citizens to assert some newly-formulated rights against the pretensions of administrative bodies. The concerns expressed by jurists such as Finnis, Hart and Dworkin, that the recognition and implementation of basic rights must be seen as essential to the maintenance of liberty, the disquiet of Rawls confronted by the growth in the powers of the modern State, must now be viewed within the context of the growth of a doctrine which limits deliberately the overall powers of decision making bodies. The significance of a *right* to be heard in the resolution of a dispute, a right to insist that an adjudicator be without bias, a *right* arising from one's legitimate expectations as to the persistence of a course of conduct – and the corresponding duties emerging from the exercise of these rights – rests in the growing recognition of their *fundamental nature.*

Any person possessing legal authority to adjudicate on disputes affecting individual rights is now obliged to observe the principles of natural justice: *A-G v Ryan* (1980). Here may be discerned a new basic factor to be taken into account in any jurisprudential analysis of contemporary rights.

Summary of Chapter 25

Problems of Rights (3): Natural Justice

General concept

The term 'natural justice' has a long history in jurisprudential literature and in the cases. It is now used to refer specifically to the general principles and acceptable minimum standards of fairness expected in adjudicational processes.

Examples of the concept may be seen in *Majorpier v Secretary of State for the Environment* (1990); *R v Nottingham Crown Court ex p Brace* (1990).

An empty phrase?

Some commentators condemn the phrase as little more than mere verbiage, as unhelpful, or 'high-sounding but harmless'.

Exception is taken to the pretentious nature of the phrase and – more significantly – to the problems which arise through use of the adjective 'natural'. It is suggested that confusion is inevitable because of the overtones of the phrase 'natural law' and the implicit suggestion that there is a type of justice linked directly with 'great Nature itself'.

Natural justice and fairness

The attainment of fairness in decision making has become an important objective.

The concept of natural justice underpins the nature of fairness. See *Lloyd v McMahon* (1987).

ECHR 1950

Article 6 of the European Convention on Human Rights is seen by some jurists as exemplifying the spirit of natural justice principles. Article 6, which is concerned with the right to a public and fair hearing, sets out desirable features of legal procedure which appear to take into account the objectives of natural justice.

Natural justice and the growth of applications for judicial review

In recent years there has been an upsurge in the use of applications for judicial review. The Supreme Court Act 1981, s 31, and RSCO 53 constitute the technical basis of applications for judicial review which may result in the courts deciding whether or not decisions are legally valid.

Two important rules of natural justice are central to the process of judicial review: the rule against bias and the rule against condemning a person unheard.

Nemo judex in causa sua potest

No person may be a judge in his own cause: total impartiality is expected from a judge. Justice must be done and must be seen to be done.

For illustrations of the rule against bias, see, eg, *Metropolitan Properties v Lennon* (1969), *Ex p Pennington* (1975).

Audi alteram partem

A person should not be condemned unheard. 'The other side' must be heard before a dispute is determined.

For illustrations of this rule, see, eg, *Ridge v Baldwin* (1964), *Ex p Hosenball* (1977).

Legitimate expectations

A party's legitimate expectations, eg, that an established course of conduct will continue, may not be ignored in the process of adjudication.

For illustrations of this rule, which is now closely associated with natural justice, see *Ex p Khan* (1984), *Ex p Ruddock* (1987).

Natural justice and the extension of rights

Individual rights, some of a fundamental nature, have been generated and extended as the result of a deepening of the concept of natural justice and a growth in the use of applications for judicial review. The principles of natural justice must be taken into account in an analysis of the nature of contemporary rights.

Chapter 26

Problems of Rights (4): Bill of Rights

26.1 Essence of the problem

The phrase 'Bill of Rights' is now used widely to refer to a document setting out 'the liberties of the people'. It is characteristic of this type of document that it is couched in very broad terms ('painted with a flat brush rather than etched with a jeweller's pin'); it may list liberties to be preserved (eg, freedom of speech, religion, association) and it may provide guarantees of a general nature, but rarely outlines the mechanisms for enforcing those guarantees. The Bill may form part of a wider document which enshrines a nation's constitution; it may stand on its own, externalising a community's *Grundnorm* (see 12.7) or setting out declarations of belief which have characterised a nation's social and legal development.

An example of a generalised statement of rights (and duties) is to be found in Chapter III of the Constitution of Japan, imposed by the victorious Allies, and drawn up with the assistance of American and British jurists in 1946. The Chapter is headed 'Rights and Duties of the People'. The following extracts give an indication of the nature and purpose of the document.

> 'Article 11. The people shall not be prevented from enjoying any of the fundamental human rights. These fundamental human rights guaranteed to the people by this Constitution shall be conferred upon the people of this and future generations as eternal and inviolate rights.
>
> Article 12. The freedoms and rights guaranteed to the people by this Constitution shall be maintained by the constant endeavour of the people, who shall refrain from any abuse of these freedoms and rights and shall always be responsible for utilising them for the public welfare.
>
> Article 13. All of the people shall be respected as individuals. Their right to life, liberty, and the pursuit of happiness shall, to the extent that it does not interfere with the public welfare, be the supreme consideration in legislation and other governmental affairs.
>
> Article 14. All of the people are equal under the law and there shall be no discrimination in political, economic or social relations because of race, creed, sex, social status or family origin. '

(Note also the Canadian Charter of Rights and Freedoms 1982, which is mentioned at 26.7.2 below.)

The problems surrounding the introduction of a Bill of Rights are extensive and complex. What is to be seen as the precise purpose of the Bill? Does it demand the existence of a written constitution? What would be the mechanisms and canons of interpretation of the Bill's content? Would it increase further the powers of unaccountable judges? How would it affect existing legal structures? Would it rest upon the maintenance of a political consensus? How would it affect the common law, seen by generations of legal theoreticians and judges as providing a flexibility which keeps the law up-to-date? Would the Bill necessitate entrenchment against any subsequent attempts to introduce legislation incompatible with its spirit? Would it introduce, in practice, a rejection of 'rolling constitutional change', of dealing with problems as they occur, in favour of a constitutional and legal upheaval? Would the tenets expressed in a Bill of Rights have the effect of discouraging -movements in jurisprudential (and political) thinking in relation to a community's rights and duties ?

The debate in Britain concerning the desirability of the introduction of a Bill of Rights continues apace. Support for a Bill has been voiced by the Lord Chief Justice and the Master of the Rolls, The Liberal Democratic and Labour Parties have indicated their general support. Professor Zander has spoken of the case for the introduction of a Bill of Rights into the UK as resting on the belief that it would make a valuable contribution to 'the better protection of human rights'. Lord Lester QC has argued in the House of Lords for a Human Rights Bill which would incorporate into English law the rights declared by the European Convention for Human Rights (and by the First Protocol to the Convention). In his speech in the Lords (during the Second Reading on 25th June 1995), Lord Lester said that the Convention was 'the jewel in the crown of the Council of Europe', that it reflected universal human rights and freedoms, as well as duties and responsibilities, that it owed much to British legal drafting 'and much to the philosophy and values of British thinkers of the past three centuries'.

Opposition to the introduction of a Bill of Rights and to the very idea of such a Bill is reflected in the refusal of the Government to lend support and in the views of senior judges, such as Lord Denning and Lord Donaldson, who have voiced fears of a politicisation of the judiciary which they view as an inevitable outcome of the type of Bill which has been advocated.

For many jurists, lawyers , political activists and other members of the community, the major problem is whether the introduction of a Bill of Rights will heighten or diminish the *quality* of existing rights and will it strengthen or weaken the protection afforded to citizens against abuses of power.

26.1.1 Recent background

The movement in favour of a Bill of Rights for the UK received fresh impetus in the 1970s with the publication of texts which questioned the general effectiveness of the safeguards of civil liberties in the UK. Scarman's *English Law – The New Dimension* (1974) exemplified a strand of jurisprudential thought which favoured the introduction of safeguards based upon a Bill of Rights. The Standing Advisory Commission on Human Rights in Northern Ireland reported in 1977 in favour of a Bill of Rights for the UK as a whole (see Cmnd 7009).

The 1980s brought intensive criticism of aspects of the role of the UK in relation to the maintenance of rights – the *CCSU* case (see 23.8.2) generated much criticism – and to what was perceived as an unnecessarily heavy-handed approach by the government to public and State security in the Public Order Act 1986 and the Official Secrets Act 1989. Concern was expressed also at the implication of *R v Ponting* (1985). Some writers and groups, such as *Charter 88* argued that a restatement of the basis of civil liberties was essential and that this might be accomplished best through an entrenched Bill of Rights based upon the European Convention. Lord McCluskey's *Reith Lectures*, delivered in 1986, fuelled the debate by the enunciation of reasons for opposing such a Bill.

The 1990s brought endorsement by the Leader of the Labour Party of the campaign aimed at incorporating the Convention into the mainstream of our law. Britain's membership of the European Community (which was to become the European Union), and the highly-publicised decisions of the European Court of Justice and the European Court of Human Rights intensified the strength of calls for a Bill of Rights which would be, in the words of Lord Scarman, 'a constitutional law which it would be the duty of the courts to protect even against the powers of Parliament'. Lord Lester's Bill (see 26.9 below) is a reminder of the continuing arguments aimed at the creation of a Charter or Bill of Rights.

26.1.2 The form of a Bill of Rights

Advocates of the concept of entrenched rights argue that the *form* of a Bill of Rights is not of overriding importance: Charter, Bill, Convention, Declaration – each can provide a model for the form of document require within the context of the UK's political and legal structures in the 1990s. The following models are among those which have emerged in political and jurisprudential writing.

- A Bill of Rights which would be drafted in a manner which would ensure that its intentions prevailed over earlier statutes and decisions of the courts. Additionally, the Bill would entrench certain rights specifically stated in its text so that they would stand against the opposition of any future parliamentary assembly.
- A Bill which would incorporate the European Convention into the general law of the UK (see, for example, Lord Lester's Bill).
- A Bill which would enunciate certain specified rights which appear not to be covered by the common law, such as an individual's right to privacy.
- A written constitution for the UK which would state unequivocally that certain rights (which would be expressed as unambiguously as possible), are guaranteed and may not be destroyed by any judicial decision or act of the legislature now or at any time in the future.

There appears to be growing support for the *second* of these models as indicating a path which could be followed without the need for a radical transformation of political or legal practices.

26.2 Rights are too important to be left to oral tradition

The law of our country, its principles and procedures, stem from the community's acceptance of duties and rights. Successive governments have chosen to define in statutory form a very extensive group of those duties and rights. Why, then, would it be a retrograde step to set out in statutory form the intention that all persons who are resident within Her Majesty's domains shall enjoy freedom of conscience, religion, etc? Would not a declaration of this nature remove the lingering doubts and fears of those who remain unsure of the fundamental attitudes of the legislature and the judiciary to particular forms of the invasion of personal rights? It is argued that to reduce rights to the written form is to strengthen and secure them.

Among arguments to the contrary are ranged the following.

- There is no historical evidence which suggests that rights invariable flourish or are respected – where they are set down in documentary form. The complex guarantees of workers' rights given by the Soviet Constitution proved empty in the face of authoritarian repression (see Berman's *Justice in the USSR* (1963)). The publication of written guarantees by government organs in the People's Republic of China, which placed emphasis on 'a new quality of rights for the people' had little effect on programmes of political repression.

- It is one thing to set down a right, but quite another to interpret its precise meaning, its implications and purpose. How is the statement, 'Freedom of thought and conscience shall not be violated' to be interpreted in practice? What rights, if any, ought to be granted to those whose conscience leads them to indulge in activities which are repugnant to a large majority within the community?
- What is to be gained by reducing to writing beliefs which are embedded in a nation's history, culture and beliefs? The American judge and jurist, Learned Hand (1872-1961), argues thus:

  'I often wonder whether we do not rest our hopes too much on constitutions, upon laws and upon courts. These are false hopes ... Liberty lies in the hearts of men and women; when it dies there is no constitution, no law, no court can save it; no constitution, no law, no court can even do much to help it. While it lies there it needs no constitution, no law, no court to save it.'

26.3 The shield of the common law has become less effective

It is argued that a Bill of Rights has become necessary because of changed social patterns which could not have been within the contemplation of those who have nurtured the common law. As the UK moves along the path leading to a multicultural society, as old legal structures appear to be unable to withstand 'the winds of change', so, it is urged, a Bill of Rights is needed in order to reconstruct and transform rights within the context of new communal aspirations. Lord Scarman, writing in support of such a Bill, stated:

> 'When times are normal and fear is not stalking the land, English law sturdily protects the freedom of the individual and respects human personality. But when times are abnormally alive with fear and prejudice, the common law is at a disadvantage: it cannot resist the will, however frightened and prejudiced it may be, of Parliament.'

Arguments of this nature are countered by those who make the following points.

- The flexibility of the common law has given it a responsiveness and strength which allow it to serve the community well. Rights under the common law have been extended and statutory development (particularly in relation to public order) has followed a path marked out clearly by common law principles.
- The common law is seen at its best, it is argued, when fundamental freedoms are threatened. Incitement to racial

hatred, certain types of harassment, other manifestations of unacceptable levels of intolerance, have elicited effective responses from the legislature and the courts, reflecting continued awareness of the significance of ancient common law rights. It is not easy to envisage how a Bill of Rights would have proved more effective in these areas than existing law and procedures.

26.4 Judges would receive much support from a Bill of Rights

The judiciary, it is claimed by some commentators, lacks a unified approach to the task of protecting the community's civil liberties: judges are confronted with a dense pattern of precedents and statutes, many of which inevitably overlap and occasionally contradict one another. The provisions of a Bill of Rights, it is suggested, would provide a *touchstone,* supporting the judges in their attempts to balance apparently conflicting rights and duties which emerge in some allegations of crime, for example. The very precision which ought to be expected from a Bill of Rights would strengthen judges who might have to face the demands of a legislature and executive which appeared to be intent on reducing the area of individual rights.

Jurists have argued against these assertions as follows.

- A Bill of Rights would necessitate problems of interpretation, the weight of which would fall inevitably on the judges and might lead to conflict between legislature and judiciary. There is no guarantee of agreement on the interpretation of fundamental phrases, such as 'freedom of thought', 'right to privacy', 'right to education'.
- There is, according to Lord Denning and other judges, a danger of the politicising of the judiciary. Lord Denning has observed that the existence of a Bill of Rights might involve a judge in the process of overthrowing a statute which appeared to be incompatible with the spirit of the Bill. 'If judges were given power to overthrow sections or Acts of Parliament, they would become political, their appointments would be based on political grounds, and the reputation of our judges would suffer accordingly.'
- Ultimately, it is maintained, a Bill of Rights would assist in destroying the separation of powers which is essential for the successful working of our constitutional practices. Judges who considered that their duties involved the protection of the principles of a Bill of Rights would be seen as an arm of the legislature, giving aid to the political principles upon which the Bill was based.
- Attention has been drawn to the difficulties which might follow on the interpretation of a Bill by a judiciary whose

values, culture and outlook are those of a small minority. See, on this matter, *The Politics of the Judiciary* by Professor J Griffith. Lord Milford, speaking in a debate in the House of Lords concerning a Bill of Rights, expressed concern with the 'class bias' which he detected in the judiciary. 'Why should [the judges] be made the custodians of the liberties of the ordinary people, rather than Parliament ?'

26.5 A Bill of Rights is essential if the UK is to fulfil its growing international obligations

The American jurist, Brennan, (see 26.8 below), argues, in the *Hart Lecture in Jurisprudence and Moral Philosophy*, delivered in Oxford in 1989, that a Bill of Rights is necessary if Britain is to carry out its full obligations as a member of the European Community and a party to the European Convention. 'Although the European Convention has not been incorporated into Community law, the European Court of Justice has issued its decisions in the light of it. Because Community law is perforce domestic law in Britain, a Bill of Rights is already part of British law, albeit indirectly and only in a limited economic sphere.' Further, Britain is committed to abide by the decisions of the European Court of Human Rights. On both these counts, therefore, the existence of a Bill of Rights becomes vital if Britain's links with bodies which appear to work within a basis of written, codified laws are to be fully productive.

Brennan concludes by stating that both 'coherence and efficiency' argue for incorporating the European Convention into English law, and that a Bill of Rights is the obvious way to achieve this.

Brennan's arguments have not been accepted in their entirety in the UK.

- Differences in legal systems have not prevented the UK's fulfilling its role as a member of international committees other than the European Community. The UK has been able to work very effectively in international organisations demanding close links in economic matters, for example, without adopting charters and declarations built upon principles which are contrary to our traditions.
- The decisions of the European Court of Human Rights and the European Court of Justice are accepted fully by the UK even though there is no UK Bill of Rights.

26.6 A Bill of Rights will provide an assurance of fundamental rights for future generations

Just as Magna Carta 1215 (and the re-issues of 1217 and 1225) embodied the liberties of the realm as they existed at that time, and have since endured in their essentials (as statements of liberties rather than an assertion of general liberty), so, it is contended, a Bill of Rights, enacted in the final years of the twentieth century, will transmit to future generations a guarantee of rights rooted firmly in the fertile ground of the common law , and acting as a bridge between existing and new legal traditions in Britain.

It is argued, however, that there can be no real guarantee of the attainment of an objective of this nature.

- History is replete with examples of constitutions and declarations of rights which have crumbled under the onslaught of time and the growth of new patterns of thinking and political upheaval. Where now, for example, is the celebrated Weimar Constitution of Germany, written by Germany's greatest jurists immediately following the defeat in Word War I and intended to stand as 'an exemplar for the future', or the much-vaunted 1963 constitution of Yugoslavia which enshrined 'for the future' the novel doctrine that popular rights are delegated from the people to its representative bodies, but not conferred on the people from any institution above?
- Given the existing principle of Parliamentary sovereignty in the UK, it is difficult to see how a Bill of Rights could be fully entrenched (particularly in the absence of a written constitution). Would not the 'permanent nature' of a Bill of Rights constitute an implied contradiction of the nature of the rights of a future Parliament built on twentieth-century lines?

26.7 An example from Canada

An interesting example of a Bill of Rights is *the Canadian Charter of Rights and Freedoms,* embodied in the Constitution Act 1982 which emerged from the Canada Act 1982.

26.7.1 Background

The Canada Act 1982 gave effect to a request by the Senate and House of Commons of Canada. Under s 52(1), the Constitution of Canada is the supreme law of Canada 'and any law that is inconsistent with the provisions of the Constitution is, to the extent of the inconsistency, of no force or effect'. Amendments to the Constitution are to be made only in accordance with the authority contained in the Constitution of Canada.

26.7.2 Extracts from the Charter of Rights and Freedoms

The following extracts from the Canadian Charter of Rights and Freedoms provide an indication of the essential matters covered in a number of Charters and Bills of Rights.

> 'Whereas Canada is founded upon principles that recognise the supremacy of God and the rule of law:
>
> 1. The Canadian Charter of Rights and Freedoms guarantees the rights and freedoms set out in it subject only to such reasonable limits prescribed by law as can be demonstrably justified in a free and democratic society.
>
> 2. Everyone has the following fundamental freedoms: freedom of conscience and religion; freedom of thought, belief, opinion and expression, including freedom of the press and other media of communication; freedom of peaceful assembly; and freedom of association. ...
>
> 7. Everyone has the right to life, liberty and security of the person and the right not to be deprived thereof except in accordance with the principles of fundamental justice.
>
> 8. Everyone has the right to be secure against unreasonable search or seizure §12. Everyone has the right not to be subjected to any cruel and unusual treatment or punishment. ...
>
> 15. Every individual is equal before and under the law and has the right to the equal protection and equal benefit of the law without discrimination and, in particular, without discrimination based on race, national or ethnic origin, colour, religion, sex, age or mental or physical disability.'

An important question for jurists is: would it be possible to transpose a document of this nature to fit into the constitutional and legal setting of the UK, and, if so, what would be the likely effects, if any, upon the nature and significance of existing fundamental rights under common law and statute?

26.8 A comment from an American jurist

In his *Hart Lecture* (1989) (see 26.5 above), Judge William J Brennan, Associate Justice, Supreme Court of the United States, writer on jurisprudence and observer of the legal scene in the UK, argued the case for a Bill of Rights for Britain. His general thesis was built upon his belief that the case for adopting a Bill is perhaps stronger for Britain than it is for the USA. Britain's need of a Bill so as to fulfil international obligations is noted at 26.5 above; yet a stronger need rests upon a perception of a general lacks of checks on the majority party in Parliament.

Brennan believes that there is now little possibility of the exercise of restraint on the Commons majority by the Lords or Crown. 'The House of Lords now has mainly an advising and revising function: the Crown has, in practice, virtually no control over legislation. ...the party in power faces no legal or intragovernmental obstacle to the effectuation of whatever measures it wishes to introduce.' A Bill of Rights would protect the people against the possible abuse of powers stemming from the prime minister's parliamentary majority.

Brennan finds Britain's claim that its law already protects civil liberties adequately 'hard to square with Britain's comparatively poor showing before the Court of European Rights'. (An article in *The Times*, 20 June 1995, notes that only Turkey has been found guilty by the Court of more abuses of human rights than has Britain.) He is unable to accept the argument that judges in the UK are too legalistic in their approach to problems involving statutory interpretation to be able to deal successfully with an open-ended Bill of Rights. The claim that judges in the UK would become overly political seems to Brennan to be exaggerated, 'especially when civil rights cases would for most constitute a small fraction of their docket'.

26.9 A question of timing

The *inevitability* of a Bill of Rights for the UK has been proclaimed by a growing number of jurists who note the demands of membership of the European Union (formerly the Community)which appears to presuppose a common approach to the legal basis of human rights. There can be, it is argued, no turning back: sooner, rather than later, Britain's Parliament will have to legislate for a Bill of Rights, not necessarily in terms suggesting a sharp break with the traditions of the common law, but in a form which will allow a utilisation of tradition so as to guarantee fundamental freedoms in new contexts. In short, adherence to tenets of the common law does not rule out the adoption of a Bill of Rights; the elasticity of common law is its real strength.

Per McCardie J in *Prager v Blatspiel* (1924) :

> 'The object of the common law is to solve difficulties and adjust relations in social and commercial life. It must meet, so far as it can, sets of facts abnormal as well as usual. It must grow with the development of the nation. It must face and deal with changing or novel circumstances. Unless it can do that it fails in its function and declines in its dignity and value. An expanding society demands an expanding common law.'

A Bill of Rights *now* – so runs the argument – can be set with ease within the common law as we know it.

Opponents of this line of argument see no need whatsoever for a Bill of Rights at the present time: there may well be a case for the introduction of such a Bill at some future date, but at the moment the liberties of British citizens are as secure as those of individuals elsewhere; deficiencies can be noted and repaired as and when they emerge through the normal Parliamentary procedures. The alleged crisis of human rights in the UK is, it is emphasised, purely illusory.

Lord Lester sums up the significance of a Bill of Rights *as a constitutional guarantee,* in terms which suggest that change may be needed without delay. He concluded his speech in the House of Lords on 25 January 1995 with the following points:

> '... A constitutional guarantee surely acts as a rallying point and a bulwark for all who cherish freedom. It strengthens the sinews of democracy and promotes good governance. It provides orderly legal redress for infringements of civil rights and liberties and it contributes to public education in winning hearts and minds. The power of government needs to be matched by the power of the law if the individual is to be secure. The law of the British constitution should encourage the spirit of liberty, and our courts should give redress where basic civil rights and freedoms are infringed.'

Summary of Chapter 26

Problems of Rights (4): Bill of Rights

Essence of a Bill of Rights

A Bill of Rights is usually a document which sets out in broad terms 'the liberties of a people'. Those liberties generally involve basic freedoms, such as, freedom of thought, speech, religion. Debate concerning the introduction of a Bill of Rights into the UK is widespread and turns largely on the effect of a document of this nature, in the absence of a written constitution, upon common law traditions and judicial decisions concerning so-called fundamental human rights. Although there is mounting support for such a Bill, opposition remains strong.

Form of a Bill of Rights

Four models have emerged from jurisprudential and political discussion: a Bill drafted so as to ensure that certain fundamental rights are entrenched; a Bill (such as Lord Lester's) incorporating the European Convention into the general law of the UK; a Bill enunciating certain specified rights which are apparently not covered by common law; a written constitution which would include a section guaranteeing the existence and continuation of certain specific rights. The second of these models has attracted much support.

Arguments concerning a Bill of Rights for the UK

'Rights are too important to be left to oral tradition; they would be strengthened and secured by being set in writing in a document with constitutional significance.' But, it is argued, there is no historical evidence suggesting that 'written rights' tend to endure.

'The common law is no longer as effective as it was in face of a challenge to certain types of right.' It is argued to the contrary that the strength of the common law is its flexibility which can provide a strong shield against new challenges.

'Judges would receive much support from a Bill of Rights.' But Lord Denning and others have warned against the politicisation of judges who may become involved in the protection of rights which are politically inspired.

'A Bill of Rights is now essential if the UK is to fulfil its growing international obligations (such as membership of the EC).' But other international organisations in which the UK has participated have not required the shedding of British basic traditions.

'A Bill of Rights would provide an assurance of fundamental rights for future generations.' In practice, there can be few guarantees of a continuation of laws passed in our era.

Judge Brennan's observations

The American judge, Walter Brennan, has argued that the most compelling reason for the introduction of a Bill of Rights into the UK is the powerful position held in Parliament by the prime minister and the majority party. There are few checks over legislation and a Bill of Rights could work effectively to minimise any abuse of powers.

A matter of timing

Much of the discussion in recent debates concerning a Bill of Rights has tended to concentrate upon the matter of timing. There is much support for the introduction of a Bill now, particularly from jurists and others who see this as a necessity in a fast-changing social order. Others prefer to accept the assurances given by those who are wedded to the concept of a common law which contains the principles enabling any breach of rights to be repaired as and when it occurs.

Chapter 27

Codification of the Law

27.1 The problem

Much attention has been given by jurists to the problems said to arise from the existing 'untidy and incoherent' shape of English law. Scarman J, in a lecture delivered in 1966 (*A Code of English Law?*) suggested that the shape of current law is neither simple nor modern and that it is accessible only to those with the training (and the stamina) 'to explore the jungle of case and statute law'. He advocated codification of the law in a manner which would allow the judges to retain a vital legislative function by continuing to interpret the law and, specifically, to deal with situations with which a code might have failed to deal: the judges would be, in effect, 'critics in continuous session'.

Jurists have, for centuries past, called for a codification of English law. Bentham (see 6.1) argued for a codification of English law *in its entirety*. He had objected strenuously to the 'highly excessive role' played by judges' decisions in the moulding of the common law and argued that laws ought to be known before they are enforced, a process which demanded a systematic code which would ensure that 'everyone may consult the law of which he stands in need, in the least possible time'. That which is not contained in the code should not have the force of law. A code was required which would be drafted with clarity and simplicity and would be revised in great detail every century.

Austin (see 10.1) agreed with Bentham in emphasising the duty of jurists to oppose the pretensions of 'judiciary laws' which had resulted in a vast increase in the bulk and complexities of English law. The law was difficult to discover, was unsystematic and less than comprehensive, Codification had become necessary in order to remove the uncertainties and difficulties of judge-made law. The code would include:

> 'a perpetual provision for its amendment, on suggestions from the judges who are engaged in applying it, and who are in the best of all situations for observing its defects. By this means the growth of judiciary law explanatory of, and supplementary to, the code, cannot indeed be prevented altogether, but it may be kept within a moderate bulk, being wrought into the code itself from time to time.'

Austin's views on the requisite talents of the codifiers are of particular interest in that they reveal the pattern of the *type* of code favoured by him and by other systematisers of his and our eras:

> 'It is pre-eminently necessary that they should possess clear and precise and ever-present conceptions of the fundamental principles and distinctions, and of the import of the leading expressions; that they should have constantly before their minds a map of the law as a whole; enabling it to subordinate the less general under the more general; to perceive the relations of the parts to one another; and thus to travel from general to particular and particular to general, and from a part to its relations to other parts, with readiness and ease; to subsume the particular under the general, and to analyse and translate the general into the particulars that it contains.'

27.1.1 Definitions

The following definitions should be noted

> *Code.* A code is a systematical collection in comprehensive, statutory form of the laws of a State. A general dictionary defines it thus: 'A written, complete, logical, systematic statement of the entire law which is in effect in a jurisdiction, with complete index and table of contents, and repealing all prior laws.'
>
> *Codification.* 'The reduction of the whole law of a country, or at least the great bulk of it, to a coherent body of enacted law': Jolowicz. 'The aim of a codifier is to put as much law as possible into compact and more or less scientific legislation': Wortley. 'The reduction of the whole *corpus juris*, so far as is practicable, to the form of enacted law': Salmond.

27.1.2 Codification and consolidation

The processes of *codification* and *consolidation* ought not to be confused. *Codification* has the effect of rewriting the law in its entirety. It is a process which is complete in itself, having the objective of fashioning a *total system* of written general principles from which precise deductions may be made, in the style of a geometrician solving problems by deducing solutions from the general principles set out systematically by Euclid or Riemann.

Consolidation is the process of enacting in one statute all the law, including case law, relating to *one topic,* Examples: the Bills of Exchange Act 1882, the Theft Act 1968.

27.2 Codes in history

Codes appeared and were developed during the early stages in the history of civilisation. Their growth depended, to a large extent, on the use of the written word within a community. Maine (see 13.9.3) suggests that when early societies experienced a need for the adequate preservation of legal rules, they preferred to indite those rules on stone, or other tablets, in a permanent form, rather than to rely on the memories of priests and other functionaries. Codes were used so as to collect and present in some kind of ordered form important customs which prevailed within communities. The use of codes resulted in the spreading and popularisation of general principles through which a simple type of justice was administered. Maine believed that the value of early codes was 'in their publicity and in the knowledge which they furnished to everybody as to what he was to do and what not to do.'

27.2.1 Two early codes

Two early codes, the Code of Hammurabi, and Justinian's codification are noted below.

The Code of Hammurabi (c 1758 BC) was issued in the name of the sixth ruler of the first Babylonian dynasty, who ruled 1792-1750 BC. A record of the codified laws was discovered on a stone monument in 1901. The code comprises a prologue, 282 paragraphs, and an epilogue. The paragraphs are made up of 'case laws' concerning the family, prices, trade, theft, slavery, debt. Penalties appear to vary according to the social status of the offender and the circumstances of the case. It is believed that the code was intended to have application beyond a single country, so that it is much more than a collection of tribal customs.

Justinian's codification of Roman law (c 529-565) is what Maine had in mind when he spoke of Roman law thus: 'The most celebrated system of jurisprudence known to the world begins, as it ends, with a code.' In the early days of Rome, *The Twelve Tables*, which declared existing customary law around 450 BC, recorded the law in the following codified form: Tables I-III, civil procedure; Table IV, paternal power; Tables V-VII, guardianship, inheritance and property; Table VIII, crimes; Table IX, public law; Table X, sacred law; Tables XI-XII, supplementary laws. Justinian began an extensive process of legal reform, built upon codes such as the *Codex Theodosianus* (c 435), which culminated in the great *Corpus Juris Civilis*, comprising the *Codex Vetus* (529), the *Digest* (533) (upon which no commentaries were allowed), the celebrated *Fifty Decisions* (532), *The Institutes* and the *Novellae* (Enactments) (565).

27.2.2 Beginnings of modern codification

One of the most interesting of the early codifications of the Age of Reason, and one which was the precursor of many modern legal codes, was the *General Land Law for the Prussian States* (1794) which was drawn up by order of Frederick II. Its concern for systematisation and the articulation in precise form of principles seems to reflect the search for methodical explanations of reality which characterised the end of the eighteenth century. Its structure owed much to the jurisprudential writings of Pufendorf (1632-94), who had argued that man has a double nature – as an individual and as a member of various groups within society. The first part of the code sets out rules relating to individual property, the second deals with the legal position of the individual as member of a family and a citizen of the Prussian State. By royal order, judges were not allowed to construe the code in independent fashion; doubts were to be resolved by reference to Frederick's Minister of Justice.

27.2.3 Savigny and codification

The Prussian jurist, Savigny (1799-1861) (see 13.2.1), was a vigorous opponent of codification on grounds reflecting his philosophy of jurisprudence, and succeeded in delaying the introduction of a unified German civil code for many years. In 1814, the jurist, Thibaut, suggested the replacement of the unwieldy, diverse German territorial laws by a unified code to be patterned on the French Code Civil. Savigny opposed this suggestion: the time was 'not ripe' for codification. Few jurists, he claimed, had the appropriate skills or 'vocation' for such a task and, further, codification would delay 'the natural development of the law' which could come about only through the workings of 'the spirit' of the German people. Codification would become a 'correct' objective for the German people only when jurists were able to discern the true roots of the people's 'folk-spirit'. Until that time codification was to be rejected as being an inorganic and unscientific development. See 27.2.5 below.

27.2. 4 The French *Code Civil*

The *Code Civil* (known also as the *Code Napoleon*) remains one of the most celebrated of all European codes of law, exemplifying, as has been said, the 'furious systematising drive' of Napoleon, who participated personally in several meetings of the codifying committees which had been charged with the swift completion of a 'national, uniform code'. The *Civil Code* (1804) was followed by the drafting of a *Code of Civil Procedure* (1806), *Commercial Code* (1808), and a *Penal Code* (1811), all of which remain at the basis of much contemporary French law. The style of the *Code Civil* has been held by French literary scholars to be masterly; it favours the epigram and the statement of legal principles in a precise form: 'Spouses owe each other the duty of fidelity', 'The child conceived in marriage takes the husband for its father'.

The *Code Civil* replaced almost sixty general systems of law in France. It was divided into three parts: the *First Book*, 'On Persons', deals with civil rights, divorce, domicile, legitimacy and illegitimacy, guardianship, etc; the *Second Book*, 'On Goods and Property', concerns moveables, immoveables, ownership, servitudes; the Third Book, 'The Acquisition of Property', deals with acquisition of ownership, general principles of contract, quasi-contract, matrimonial property law, partnerships, security rights.

The *Code Civil* was adopted for use in many parts of the world. Its 'egalitarian and centralising tendencies' gave it an appeal which enabled it 'to march victoriously through the world of the nineteenth century'.

27.2.5 The German Civil Code

The German Civil Code, which appeared in 1896 and was brought into force in 1900, was characterised by systematisation and an intensely conservative philosophy of law. Radbruch said that it was 'more a cadence of the nineteenth century than the upbeat to the twentieth century.' It was couched in rigid fashion, in which some scholars detect military overtones and had the logical exactitude associated with the German Pandectist School of jurists whose learning owed much to studies of classical Roman law.

The five books constituting the Code were arranged as follows: a 'general part' set out the law relating to institutions involved with private law; Book II dealt with the Law of Obligations and was built upon the concepts of *jura in rem* and *jura in personam*; Book III covered the Law of Property ('real rights', such as ownership, mortgages, pledges); Book IV covered Family Law; Book V set out the Law of Succession.

27.2.6 The Swiss Civil Code

A civil code was adopted by the Swiss Parliament in 1907, dealing with the Law of Persons, Family Law, Law of Succession, Law of Property and Law of Obligations. It was drafted on the basis of principles set out by the Minister of Justice, who stated his aim thus: 'The code must be comprehensible to all ... it ought to mean something to the educated layman although it will always have a deeper meaning for the specialist.' A number of the rules within the code are of an outline nature only, allowing 'judicial amplification': where it is not possible for a judge to find a relevant provision he is expected to decide in accordance with the customary law or, in the absence of such a law, in accordance with the rule which he would prefer to adopt if he were the legislator.

27.3 Arguments in favour of codification

Because the *aims* of codification of the law have been identified repeatedly as the provision of 'greater accessibility, comprehensibility, consistency and certainty', the arguments advanced in its favour tend to stress the rationality of the codifying procedure and the improvements which are expected to flow from its implementation. Among such arguments are the following.

- *The law will be more comprehensible, certain and clearer than it is today*. A codified law will allow the broad, abstract principles of the law to be set out and illustrated in detail and with precision. Because the code will be all-embracing it will become clear and unambiguous. The obfuscation of many years of judicial interpretation, often of a conflicting nature, will disappear and the search for relevant principles should be made easier than it is today.
- *It will be possible to express the law as a unity*. Codification, it is argued, will reduce complexity and untidiness and will allow the framework of law and judicial decisions to be perceived as one, systematic structure. In particular, a unified system will make it possible to *perceive relationships* among separated aspects and branches of the law.
- *Logical arrangement of the law will become possible.* Codification allows the presentation of information to be made in logical and schematic form. Principles and supporting material can be set out in the form of connected axioms, making deduction swift and relatively simple. This type of arrangement , it is argued, would make for ease of reference which would save time and result in accuracy. In recent years, jurists who have advocated the use of computers in the arrangement and retrieval of legal data have urged the importance of codes of law arranged in hierarchic, systematic form which lends itself to swift data processing.
- *Accessibility should be improved*. The existence of a code would be advantageous for those engaged in the important task of making the law accessible to all an important facet of rights within a democracy. Whereas case law might be seen as a 'sealed book to the masses', a code may make the law more accessible and widely-known. Further, a codified law might become more accessible for the legal profession. The advantages of working with a precisely-formulated code rather than a mass of statutes and reports would seem obvious.
- *Amendment of the law might become easier*. The very nature, design and structure of a code ought to allow amendments to be made with ease. Sections of a code may be modified, cancelled with a minimum of delay.
- *Law reform might be facilitated*. For some jurists (see, eg, Diamond's *Codification of the Law of Contract* (1968)) the

most attractive case for codification is the promise of facilitation of law reform: a code is unlikely to be created initially unless it has been subjected to a process of refinement and reform which will be repeated on each occasion the code is subsequently restated. The actual procedure of reform will be eased by the ordered structures which require alteration.

- *Flexibility of the law will not be lost and may be intensified.* The existence of a code does not render the law inflexible. Judges will be expected to continue to interpret the code so that the flexibility which is derived from the courts' moulding of principle to suit contemporary society remains. The judges will interpret the law; the code remains supreme and cannot be altered decisively under the guise of interpretation.

27.4 Arguments against codification

Strong arguments against codification of the law have come from jurists and others who fear that the common law tradition, its inherent power to 'move with the times', its reliance upon the judiciary's powers of interpretation, will disappear. Codification, it is argued, would involve a virtual revolution in legal patterns of thought and procedure, and the price for that would be very high. Specifically, the following arguments have been raised.

- *The law will become static.* Codes tend to make for a static law: principles, details are reduced to a structured form and become 'fixed'. There then emerges a powerful tendency for legislators and codifiers to become unresponsive to demands for changes in the law necessitated by changes in social conditions, for example.

- *The law may ossify.* The malleability and freedom of the common law is replaced by a rigidity imposed by the overall demands of adherence to the written code. The adaptation of general principle to particular, unusual circumstances is difficult and may become impossible. In the Law Commission's *A Criminal Code for England and Wales*, reference is made to a critic of codes in general, who argues that unless codes are stated 'in terms so general as to be unacceptable to the modern codifier', they must lead – inevitably – to ossification (and the perpetuation of error). Consistency and certainty, claimed as principal advantages of codification, may involve rigid, immutable frameworks, which do not favour development of the law.

- *The code is 'all-sufficient' in name only.* In reality, it is argued, the 'all-embracing' and 'all-sufficient' aspects of a code are rarely evident. No law-maker, no law codifier can reduce to a structured pattern all the needs of a society which is almost always in a state of flux. Amendments to a code, and 'amendments upon amendments' will be needed if a code is to maintain links with reality. In a sense, therefore, the code is self-defeating in that changes which are necessary if its content is to be 'realistic' destroy the certainty which is proclaimed as its advantage.

- *'Accessibility' is little more than a fiction.* There is little evidence that the public, even in an advanced and educated democratic community, will consult, or understand, a codified law any more than statutory or case law. There is, it is argued, no 'short cut ' to an adequate comprehension of the law which is based on changes in presentation of its principles and details.

- *The advantages of a case-law system are lost.* Case law, it is suggested, tends to decline in significance with the appearance of a code. The elasticity of case law seems to diminish in importance with the introduction of a 'finite, monolithic, systematised' code. Case law reflects reality and develops from actual controversy, thus reflecting a wide variety of human experience: in Fuller's words, 'it offers an honest reflection of the complexities and perplexities of life itself'. In contrast, codified law, with its 'specious geometry', is based on an oversimplified pattern which is remote from reality; its 'diagrammatically conceived situations' rarely reflect the complexities of actual, 'untidy' events . Because the code is conceived as a totality, it cannot, in the words of Lord Mansfield, 'work itself pure' as can case law, with its inherent process of re-examination and restatement.

- *There would be a heavy price to pay for codification.* Preparation of the code would be an immense and expensive task; re-learning the law would require much time and effort; a new system would require new techniques of advocacy which would require much time for their acquisition and refinement; increased legal uncertainty would surely follow on the introduction of a new code, and would continue to attend subsequent amendments – which would undoubtedly occur. (The first Lord Hailsham referred to 'the normal fate of a code' as 'endless embroidery, commentary and explanation, with resulting obscurity'.)

27.5 Attempts at codification in the UK

The 1866 Cranworth Commission sought to enquire into 'the composition of a digest of the law', but accomplished little save for the recommendation of 'a condensed summary of the law as it exists, arranged into systematic order under proper titles and divided into statements and propositions'. Some digests of conflict of laws and criminal law have been produced, and Halsbury's *Laws of England* provides a digest of statutes. Codes of aspects of commercial law, eg, partnership, have been partially embodied in statute, but an attempt to codify income tax law, in 1927, was unsuccessful.

27.5.1 The 1965 White Paper

The White Paper, *Proposals for English and Scottish Law Commissions* (1965, Cmnd 2573) drew attention to the vast 'size' of English law, arguing that 'English law should be capable of being recast in a form which is accessible, intelligible and in accordance with modern needs...' Consolidation and the pruning of statutes were required urgently. Publication of the White Paper was followed by the Law Commissions Bill, introduced in January 1965.

27.5.2 The Law Commissions Act 1965

The 1965 Act set up Commissions, each of which had the duty 'to take and keep under review all the law with which they are respectively concerned with a view to its systematic development and reform, including in particular the codification of such law, the elimination of anomalies, the repeal of obsolete and unnecessary enactments, the reduction of the number of separate enactments and, generally, the simplification and modernisation of the law...'

The Law Commission published a programme of work soon after appointment: seventeen subject heads were identified, and, in 1967, codification of the criminal law was added.

In 1965, the English and Scottish Law Commissions published plans for the codification of the law of contract: a uniform body of contract law would be drawn up having reference to England and Scotland. The Scottish Law Commission withdrew from the task at a later date and the English Law Commission suspended work on a code, deciding to concentrate on the production of a series of papers concerning the reform of aspects of contract law.

27.5.3 Proposed codification of the criminal law

In its Second Programme (1968), the Law Commission set out its objective of a comprehensive examination of the criminal law *with a view to its codification*. A Code Team was set up in 1981. Its terms of reference were: to consider and make proposals in relation to the aims and objects of a criminal code for England and Wales, its nature and scope, its content, structure, lay-out and inter-relation of its parts and the method and style of its drafting. The team would also formulate in a manner appropriate to such a code, 'the general principles which should govern liability under it, a standard terminology to be used in it, and the rules which should govern its interpretation'.

The Criminal Code Bill was published in 1989, following a draft Code of 1985. The Commission stated:

> 'We believe that codification of the criminal law of England and Wales would be desirable. We respect the views of those who are opposed to it in principle but are unable to accept that their arguments outweigh the strong arguments in favour of codification. Accordingly we recommend that there should be a Criminal Code for England and Wales.'

The Code comprises 220 sections and 10 schedules. It is divided into two parts, General Principles and Specific Offences. A commentary on the Code points out that the existence of a power in the courts to create new offences, 'with the resulting uncertainty as to the scope of the criminal law, is incompatible with the fundamental aims of a criminal code'.

- The Law Commission, in its 1990 Report, suggested that work on the Criminal Code could best be furthered 'by means of a series of reports recommending the reform or restatement of areas of specific crimes ... together with the reformulation of general principles relevant to offences...'
- In 1992, a Consultation Paper was published containing proposals concerning offences against the person. It was stated that enactment of the proposed Bill would be a significant step forward in the process of codification of the whole of the criminal law.

27.6 A Bill of Rights and codification

Chapter 26 noted the continuing jurisprudential and political discussions concerning the desirability of a Bill of Rights for the UK. Advocates of such a Bill have noted that the codification of human rights would be a step along the road to a full codification of English law. Sceptics have questioned the nature of the advantages which might be derived from the existence of a 'rights code': some have asked pointedly how a declaration of the equality of all persons will, in practice, affect the quality of those rights which are currently recognised and protected by the courts.

27.7 A continuing jurisprudential problem

The controversy concerning codification continues, having received fresh impetus from the UK's membership of the European Union, in which a number of partner-States administer their laws on the basis of codes. Some jurists now call for complete codification of English law; others suggest compromises, based, perhaps, on the American Law Institute's

Re-Statement of American Law, which takes the form of a code which is not in statutory form. compromise suggestions have come from jurists who advocate the regular publication of sets of systematically-presented statements of 'the law from all sources' on particular topics, allowing for swiftly-printed amendments. Advances in computer technology and the rapid dissemination of information bring the possibility of easily accessible indexes and commentaries much nearer.

Lord Scarman has noted that many of the problems affecting those who have to deal with statutes and the law reports 'lie more in the system by which law is made and expressed than in the substantive law itself'. His call for codification as a solution to problems of growing complexity remains of importance. Pound's reminder in his *Jurisprudence* (1956) is timely :

> 'Codification ... is part of the quest for government not of men but of laws ... it is a part of the claim that the magistrates shall regulate their conduct and adjust their relations according to pre-established law and not in accordance with their more or less arbitrary will.'

Summary of Chapter 27

Codification of the Law

The call for codification

The demand for a codification of English law is not new : Bentham and Austin argued for an overhaul of the law which would remove the excesses of judicial law-making and would systematise the outlines of law, rendering them more certain and comprehensible.

Codification is viewed as 'the reduction of the whole law of a country, or at least the great bulk of it, to a coherent body of enacted law.' It should not be confused with 'consolidation' which involves the process of enacting in one statute all the law, including case law, relating to one topic.

Examples of Codes

Celebrated codes include the French Code Civil, inspired by Napoleon, the German Civil Code of 1896, and the Swiss Civil Code of 1907. Each set out the general principles of the law and aims to create a schematic, accessible conspectus.

Arguments in favour of codification

The arguments in favour of codification include the following: The law will become more comprehensible, certain and clearer than it is today.

It will be possible to express the law as a unity.

Logical arrangement of the law will become possible.

Accessibility should be improved.

Amendment of the law might become easier.

Law reform might be facilitated.

Flexibility of the law will not be lost and may be intensified.

Arguments against codification

Arguments against codification come in particular from jurists who fear that the traditions of the common law will disappear. These arguments include the following points:

The law will become static.

The law may ossify.

The code is 'all-sufficient' in name only.

'Accessibility' is little more than a fiction.

The advantages of a case-law system are lost.

There would be a heavy price to pay for codification in terms of time, effort, etc.

Work of the Law Commission

The Law Commission was set up in 1965, with the duty to consider the systematic development and reform of the law, including codification. An example of the Commission's work in this area is the Criminal Code Bill, published in 1989: the criminal law is set out in systematised form in 220 sections and 10 schedules.

Problems presented by a Bill of Rights

Recent demands for a Bill of Rights for the UK which would enunciate human rights have given impetus to calls for codification. Advocates of the Bill insist that a clear statement, in systematic form, of fundamental human rights will be, in itself, an important movement along the road to the implementation of rights for all.

Chapter 28

Feminist Jurisprudence

28.1 Background

The feminist jurisprudence movement appears to have originated in the US in the 1970s, possibly as a part of the Critical Legal Studies movement (see Chapter 21). It seems to have taken the form, in its earlier years, of a considered theoretical response by women jurists and lawyers to a widely-held perception of American jurisprudence as the product of an exclusively male ideology which, by its origins and nature, effectively excluded women from significant participation in legal affairs and institutionalised their formal and informal subservience to men. The growth of the movement was recognised by the CLS Conference of 1983 which included in its programme an examination of the basis of feminist jurisprudence.

The literature of the movement is extraordinarily wide and eclectic: useful overviews of its jurisprudential writings appear in *Feminist Legal Theory* (1991), by Bartlett and Kennedy, *Feminist Legal Theory: the Foundations* (1993), by Weisberg, and *Feminist Jurisprudence* (1993), ed P Smith. An interesting anthology of background material (largely by Australian writers) constitutes *A Reader in Feminist Knowledge*, ed Gunew.

28.1.1 The essence of feminist jurisprudence

Feminist jurisprudence is, essentially, a body of legal theory and comment associated with jurists who accept the view that the progress of society *as a whole* requires an intensive, informed struggle against the legal ideologies and practices associated with the *patriarchal form* of society. Within that society has been created and institutionalised, in a variety of forms, discrimination against, and the consequent oppression of, half of humanity – women. The movement's ideologists argue for the analysis and ultimate rejection of a jurisprudential ideology which serves, objectively, the specific interests of men, whose dominance is assumed and asserted, by jurists and legislators alike, to be a 'natural phenomenon'. In the words of Lorenne Clark, the movement is concerned with 'the dominance of those who are naturally stronger and freer from the grinding necessities of biological reality'.

The movement's ideologists call for scholarship which will produce a basic challenge to the fictions and myths propagated largely by male jurists, consciously or unconsciously, and derived solely from a male perspective. In place of a 'gendered jurisprudence', the movement seeks to build the foundations of a legal theory which will neither exclude nor marginalise the historical experience and the contemporary situation of women.

28.1.2 Schools of feminist jurisprudence

The growth of academic research in the areas favoured by feminist jurists – the history of women, the development of the concept of equality in jurisprudence, the struggle for women's rights, contemporary aspects of sex discrimination – has, almost inevitably, produced a variety of approaches to the tasks of the movement's scholars in relation to jurisprudential investigation and interpretation. In her essay, *Feminism and the Limits of Equality* (1990), Professor Patricia Cain notes the existence of separate strands of feminist theory which are at the basis of contemporary schools of feminist jurisprudence.

- *Liberal feminism* appears to concern itself largely with matters such as equal rights and opportunities and the extension and intensification of constitutional rights for American women. It emphasises the concept of women as autonomous members of society; its theorists have expressed much sympathy with the need to liberate women from the private domestic sphere so as to expand opportunities for them in other areas of social endeavour.
- *Radical feminism*, as it relates to jurisprudential thought, stresses the importance of perceiving women *as one class* dominated by another, with a resulting class struggle. Changes in laws which favour the male class are urgently required if inequalities of power are to be brought to an end. Sex equality demands for its attainment a correctly-motivated struggle in which the existing law will be utilised in deliberate fashion so as to provide affirmative action which will result, for example, in the suppression of pornography, which denigrates women.
- *Cultural feminism* recognises the essentially unique nature of women which has contributed to their life experience. Feminist jurisprudence is welcomed as a method of effecting a substantial change in the conditions and overall cultural patterns of women. The movement wishes to utilise in its campaigns the 'different voices' of women which will testify to an understanding of the significance of women's comprehension of relationships and the 'essential connectedness' of the human experience.
- *Post-modern feminism* rejects equality and views it as 'a construct which must be reconstructed'. The very idea of 'a woman's point of view' is cast aside as a fiction which, in practice, merely serves to bind the individual to her identity as a woman. Practical solutions to concrete legal

situations involving women are required rather than elegant abstract notions of the nature of law. In particular, to indulge in arguments with the upholders of a male-dominated jurisprudence on terms of its own choosing can never be to the advantage of women as a group.

28.2 The struggle against patriarchy

The term 'patriarchy' is used in the literature of feminist jurisprudence to refer to a society which rests upon the principles and practices of male domination and which produces jurisprudential ideologies which seek to justify and legitimise this domination. Law in a patriarchy emerges as a powerful symbol and vehicle of male authority and domination. In the name of 'tradition', 'nature', or 'objective reality', the law and legal institutions of a patriarchy seek to induce people to accept specific attitudes to women and to accept the status quo as just and beneficial, with the result that (in the words of Professor Catherine Mackinnon, in *Feminism Unmodified* (1987)) 'the dominance of the male group is made to seem a feature of life, not a one-sided construct imposed by force for the advantage of a dominant group'.

Feminist jurisprudence is characterised by a united rejection of patriarchy; indeed, some jurists view its work as, essentially, 'the analysis and critique of law as a patriarchal institution'.

28.2.1 The pervasive nature of patriarchy

The structures of a patriarchal society affect that society's assumptions, attitudes and practices: this is a point of view which is stressed in the literature of feminist jurisprudence. The law, in particular, is not immune to the pervasive teachings of male-dominated political, social and legal theory. Jurisprudence in a patriarchal society is steeped in age-old views of the place of women in its structures. Professor Janet Rifkin, of Harvard, in *Toward a Theory of Law and Patriarchy* (1980) suggests that patriarchal legal theory pays particular attention to the part females shall and shall not play in the social order, with the result that law in relation to women 'asserts a mythological vision which is believed by many to present an accurate statement of the world'.

All facets of contemporary jurisprudence in the patriarchal society are viewed by feminist jurists as reflecting the distortions of 'gendered thought-patterns'. Property law, the rules concerning damages in the law of torts, the attitudes of the criminal law to assault and battery, are interpreted by feminists as the product of legal thinking which distorts social reality by denying the exploitation and subordination of women.

In particular, family law is seen by many feminist jurists as an outstanding example of the embodiment of an approach to gender-related issues which is false and, therefore, misleading. In *Family Law Matters* (1993), Professor Katherine O'Donovan, of London University, analyses the ideology of the family as reflecting assumptions, often unstated, concerning gender, marriage and children. She concludes that the theory and practice of family law have resulted in the institutionalisation of injustice affecting women, and she emphasises that there is doubt as to whether the tradition in which women were openly subordinated has disappeared. Recent controversy concerning the law in relation to divorce, domestic violence, financial support on the breakdown of marriage, is interpreted within the discourse of feminist jurisprudence (and elsewhere) as illustrating mounting dissatisfaction with the overt discrimination practised against women in our time.

28.2.2 'The weaker vessel': ideology of patriarchy exemplified

Feminist jurists have cited the almost universal prevalence of the myth of women's innate weakness as an example of a sedulously cultivated legend which has been central to 'the long government of male over female' which characterises the patriarchy. The arguments advanced by the jurist, Stephen, in *Liberty, Equality, Fraternity* (1873) against the concept of the equality of women resulted in his advocating that 'if marriage is to be permanent, the government of the family must be put by law and by morals in the hands of the husband'. Dicey's *Law of the Constitution* (1885) inveighs against the claim of votes for women ('which is in reality a claim for the absolute political equality of the two sexes') because it ignores 'the difference of sex ... which can distinguish one body of human beings from another ... It means that Englishwomen should share the jury box and should sit on the judicial bench'.

The much-excoriated judgment of Bradley J in *Bradwell v Illinois* (1872) is often cited in the literature of American feminist jurisprudence as exemplifying the myths which patriarchal society continues to employ so as to give credence to the view that women are 'the weaker vessel'.

> 'Civil law, as well as nature herself, has always recognised a wide difference in the respective spheres and destinies of man and woman. Man is, or should be, woman's protector and defender. The natural and proper timidity and delicacy which belongs to the female sex evidently unfits it for many of the occupations of civil life.'

(It is of interest to note that the *Ladies' Dictionary*, published in London in 1690, refers to women as 'being made of the softest mould'.) Feminist jurisprudential theory seeks to explain the *reasons* for the prevalence of myths of this nature.

28.2.3 'For "him", read "him"'

It is a cardinal concept of feminist jurisprudence that, in the continuing intellectual struggle to rid legal theory of the distortions of patriarchal ideology, there is little to be gained from appeals for support to much of the traditional literature of libertarian philosophy: many of the celebrated texts in this field are written by men concerned with the problems of other men. In Susan Okin's *Women in Western Political Thought* (1979), attention is drawn to the habit of some of the philosophers of political freedom in using generic terms, such as 'man' and 'the allegedly inclusive pronoun "he"' to make clear that they are not referring to women. Rousseau, for example, states in his *Discourse on the Origins and Foundations of Inequality Among Men* (1755), that 'it is of man that I am to speak'. Okin suggests that the Founding Fathers who drafted the American Declaration of Independence, which declares that 'all men are created equal', would have been amused and sceptical on hearing the argument that women, too, should be considered equal.

The Australian feminist, Mary Daly, argues in her essay, *The Spiritual Dimension of Women's Liberation* (1970), that 'the Judaic-Christian tradition has been patriarchal down through the millenia, although sometimes this has been modified or disguised'. Women who strive for emancipation from their 'abject condition' should be aware, Daly claims, that 'brotherhood, even when it attempts to be universal, means a male universalism'.

28.2.4 What is to be done?

The destruction of patriarchal ideology involves the creation of a new jurisprudence *by women who view society, law and legal institutions from their specific, unique perspective.* In pursuance of this task they will find ideological allies, but they themselves must provide the necessary impetus for change. A new perspective demands new tasks and a new methodology of jurisprudential investigation.

In *Feminist Legal Methods* (1990), Professor Kathleen Bartlett outlines a scheme of enquiry appropriate to the aims of feminist jurisprudence, which requires 'the organisation of the apprehension of truth'. The existing formal methods of legal reasoning (deduction, induction, analogy, etc) should be utilised but should be supplemented by the following specific modes of investigation.

- *Asking the 'woman question'*. This technique of investigation is intended to expose the 'gender implications' of legal rules which have the appearance of neutrality and objectivity. What, for example, are the 'gender implications' if any, of the 'improved definition' of rape given in the Criminal Justice and Public Order Act 1994, s 42?

- *Feminist practical reasoning*. Legal decisions ought to be 'more sensitive to the features of a case not already reflected in legal doctrine'. According to Professor Bartlett, women's particular sensitivity to specific situations and general context, and their ability to differentiate the significant and the insignificant, are of particular value in this type of investigation. It might be applied, for example, to a study of the principle of diminished responsibility as it relates to cases involving abused wives: see, eg, *R v Ahluwalia* (1993).
- *Consciousness-raising*. Professor Bartlett argues that this investigatory technique offers to women a means of testing the validity of accepted legal principles 'through the lens of the personal experience' of women who have been involved directly in situations concerning, eg, domestic violence, desertion.

By the use of these techniques, women will fashion the ideological instruments appropriate for viewing the legal problems of a patriarchal society from a new perspective.

28.3 Telling it as it is: the problems of a gendered language

A vital task for feminist jurisprudence is, according to Professor Lucinda Finley, in *The Dilemma of the Gendered Nature of Legal Reasoning* (1989), the production of an appropriate analysis of the discourse typical of patriarchal law. The gendered nature of legal reasoning and expression should be demonstrated as resulting from 'life experiences typical to empowered white males', and deriving from 'the powerful situation of men, relative to women'.

Professor Patricia Smith emphasises that it is possible for a carefully selected terminology to be utilised so as to distort meaning and render terms neutral. Linguistic analysis will expose the distortions of patriarchal terminology, but this must be carried out in the context of an avowedly feminist perspective: formal structural analysis of the Chomsky school is valueless for purposes of feminist jurisprudential enquiry.

28.4 The rejection of the formal ideology of 'equality'

'Equality' is rarely perceived by feminist jurists as a desirable end in itself. In *Reconstructing Sexual Equality* (1987), Professor Christine Littleton states categorically that 'equality', which has been 'the rallying cry of every subordinated group in American society' can no longer be accepted unambivalently by those who have embraced the principles of feminism. A victory for women in a campaign for equal pay is not necessarily to be perceived as a blow against patriarchy; the admission of women to the marine corps does not affect the fundamental pattern of male domination of society; the passing of a Parliamentary bill which seeks to make sexual harassment at the place of work an offence is not necessarily to be interpreted as a successful assault on the commanding heights of masculine domination.

28.5 The rejection of Marxist jurisprudence

Feminist jurisprudence is opposed generally to the political and legal theories of Marxism (see Chapter 14). The thesis forecasting that the disappearance of classes will bring true equality between the sexes is rejected as simplistic and, when judged by the history of the 20th century, unsound. In his tract, *Women and Society* (1912), Lenin outlined the Marxist solution to problems of women's inequality within capitalist society:

> 'As long as women are engaged in housework their position is still a restricted one. In order to achieve the complete emancipation of women and to make them really co-equal with men, we must have social economy, and the participation of women in general productive labour. Then women will occupy the same position as men.'

This is interpreted by feminist jurists as encapsulating the key errors of Marxism in relation to an understanding of the situation of women: it demonstrates a lack of awareness of the exploitation of women *as women*, not merely as workers, and it indicates no comprehension of the unacceptability of male-created norms as a goal for women in a transformed society. Lenin's proposed solution is interpreted as yet another manifestation of the pervasive nature of patriarchal ideology.

In her essay, *Marxism and Feminism* (1980), Elizabeth Grosz, an Australian writer, takes objection to Marxism because it shares with bourgeois thought 'a *universal* representation of humanity that is in fact masculine'. Women are defined by Marxist jurisprudence only in relation to male norms – a reflection of patriarchal thought. Any theoretical alliance of feminism and Marxism should be rejected because it would involve an allegiance to concepts and principles derived from an outlook which negated women's experience *as women*.

It was the perception of the typical Marxist legal system in action in Eastern Europe which was responsible for the total withdrawal of western feminist groups from any lingering support for the jurisprudence associated with the 'people's democracies'. Objections were voiced, in particular, to the persecution of women who campaigned within the Marxist regimes for women's rights, only to be denounced as counter-revolutionaries and punished accordingly.

28.6 Toward the good society

The writings which constitute the core of feminist jurisprudence do not show a general concern with the precise social and legal arrangements which will characterise the fair and just non-patriarchal society. Professor Patricia Smith suggests that the signposts marking the route to that society will take the form of a complete disappearance of discrimination in education and rewards for work, and the total removal of patriarchal bias in law and the processes of adjudication. One of the principal questions to be posed in the evaluation of a rule held to be desirable within the good society will be: 'Does this rule assist in the subordination of women to men, or is it no part of it?'

The good society will not emerge from the patriarchal society without intensive ideological work in which feminist jurisprudence must provide a critique enabling women to interpret, and change law from their own perspective.

28.7 Criticisms of feminist jurisprudence

Early contributors to feminist jurisprudence forecast that the intensity of opposition to the very concept of a legal theory based upon the goal of a non-patriarchal society would grow as the radical nature of its proposals became evident: in the event this has happened. The justification for a jurisprudence which totally rejects 'male-dominated law' has been rejected as lacking any basis in legal history and practice. Male and female jurists and practitioners have cautioned against attempts to present sectional interests in terms of universals, and have urged a rejection of the divisive nature of 'jurisprudence from women's perspective'. A changed society and an appropriate jurisprudence will emerge, it is argued, only from the united activities of men and women.

The presumption that the 'new perspective' advocated by feminist jurists will be free from the type of distortion which is held to characterise the ideology of patriarchy is arguable. There is criticism, too, of the tendency of some prominent theoreticians of the feminist movement to write off the intention and effect of legislation which diminishes discrimination against women. A jurisprudence which is concerned with long-term goals to the exclusion of short-term gains is likely to be ineffectual in providing a guide for action.

It is of interest to note, however, that in the US, the liberal feminist wing of the movement has fought vigorously and effectively against the exclusion of women from the administration of estates, and that Professor Catherine Mackinnon and Andrea Dworkin, attorney and radical feminist, were able to inspire and direct a highly-publicised campaign with the object of making the publication and sale of pornography a violation of women's civil rights: see Dworkin's *Against the Male Flood: Censorship, Pornography and*

Equality (1993). Here, it could be claimed, is a jurisprudential ideology in the service of *society as a whole.*

Summary of Chapter 28

Feminist Jurisprudence

Essential features of feminist jurisprudence

Feminist jurisprudence is concerned with the ideological struggle against the patriarchal society and, in particular, its jurisprudence. The patriarchal society is an expression of male domination and is characterised by the subservient role which is allocated to women. Its jurisprudence assists in the legitimisation of patriarchal social and political structures; in particular it propagates myths relating to the role of women in society. Laws concerning women are often predicated on the legend of woman as 'the weaker vessel'.

Schools of feminist jurisprudence

Four schools of thought seem to have emerged in the feminist jurisprudence movement. Liberal feminism reflects a concern with constitutional rights. Radical feminism utilises the images of the class struggle in calling for urgent changes in legal theory and practice. Cultural feminism calls for women to use to their advantage their unique capacities for comprehending certain types of difficult relationships and situations. The post-modernist school teaches the need for a total rejection of male domination and calls for women to concern themselves with practical situations in legal affairs rather than with a search for elegant legal abstractions.

The struggle against the ideology of patriarchy

Feminist jurisprudence must recognise the pervasive nature of patriarchal ideology; it can be found in all aspects of social activity. The struggle involves an awareness of the power of myths in justifying the historical social role of women which is presented as a 'natural' matter.

Tasks for feminist jurisprudence

New modes of jurisprudential enquiry are called for; these include asking 'the woman question', feminist practical reasoning, consciousness-raising. These activities will allow women to fashion a jurisprudence which will reflect their own perspectives.

Linguistic analysis – but not of the formal type – is needed so as to reveal to women the inherent dangers of a 'gendered language'.

The doctrine of 'equality of women' must be examined carefully where it demands action which does nothing to help to remove patriarchal ideology and practices.

Marxist doctrine, which reflects patriarchal ideology and promises equality for the sexes is to be rejected; its norms are those of male domination.

The good society as viewed by feminist jurisprudence

The fair, just society which represents the goal for feminist jurists characterised by a total absence of discrimination, by full equality of the sexes on the basis of norms reflecting the nature and contribution of men and women, and by law from which patriarchal prejudice has disappeared.

Feminist jurisprudence criticised

The feminist jurisprudence movement has, because of the challenging nature of its pretensions, aroused much criticism. It is claimed that the legal theory associated with feminism is divisive, that it promotes the concept of a 'new perspective' which might turn out to be as skewed as the male perspective, and that it appears to encourage so-called long-term aims while neglecting short-term achievements in favour of the removal of sex discrimination. But there are signs that the movement is prepared to engage in practical political, social and legal activities to better the conditions of women.

Envoi

This text began with a consideration of the essence of definitions of jurisprudence, and ends with a discussion of human rights. The first chapter included a suggestion (see 1.4) that the definitions of jurisprudence given in 1.4 be reconsidered at the end of the course. Is any one of the definitions, ranging from Ulpian to Schumpeter, adequate? Or is the essence of jurisprudence to be found, perhaps, in a much wider type of definition, such as that given by Wortley, in *Jurisprudence* (1967), in a reference to the subject-matter of his text as 'law as prediction, order, rule, expectation, sense of value and justice'?

Recommended Reading List

General texts

C K Allen, *Law in the Making*
(1961), 6th edn (OUP)

H Davies and D Holdcroft, *Jurisprudence: Texts and Commentary*
(1991), 1st edn (Butterworths)

R W Dias, *Jurisprudence*
(1985), 5th edn (Butterworths)

R M Dworkin, *Law's Empire*
(1986), 1st edn (Fontana)

R M Dworkin (ed) *The Philosophy of Law*
(1986), lst edn (OUP)

J Feinberg and H Gross (eds) *Philosophy of Law*
(1991), lst edn (Wadsworth)

MDA Freeman (ed) *Lloyd's Introduction to Jurisprudence*
(1994), 6th edn (Sweet & Maxwell)

J W Harris, *Legal Philosophies*
(1980), lst edn (Butterworths)

H L A Hart, *The Concept of Law*
(1994), 2nd edn (Clarendon)

G W Paton, *A Textbook of Jurisprudence*
(1972), 4th edn (Clarendon)

J G Riddall, *Jurisprudence*
(1991), lst edn (Butterworths)

P Smith (ed), *The Nature and Process of Law*
(1993), 1st edn (OUP)

Specialist texts

J Boyle (ed), *Critical Legal Studies*
(1992), 1st edn (New York University Press)

H Collins, *Marxism and Law*
(1982), 1st edn (Clarendon)

R M Dworkin, *Life's Dominion*
(1993), 1st edn (Harper Collins)

J Finnis, *Natural Law and Natural Rights*
(1992), 1st edn (Clarendon)

J M Kelly, *A Short History of Western Legal Theory*
(1992), 1st edn (OUP)

S Lee, *Law and Morals*
(1986), 1st edn (OUP)

H G Reuschlein, *Jurisprudence - Its American Prophets*
(1971), 1st edn (Greenwood)

P Schuchman (ed), *Readings in Jurisprudence and Legal Philosophy*
(1979), 1st edn (Little, Brown)

J C Smith and D N Weisstub (eds), *The Western Idea of Law*
(1983), 1st edn (Butterworths)

P Smith (ed), *Feminist Jurisprudence*
(1993), 1st edn (OUP)

J Waldron (ed), *Theories of Rights*
(1984), 1st edn (OUP)

Index